Exam Ref 70-412: Configuring Advanced Windows Server 2012 R2 Services

J.C. Mackin
Orin Thomas

PUBLISHED BY
Microsoft Press
A Division of Microsoft Corporation
One Microsoft Way
Redmond, Washington 98052-6399

Library of Congress Control Number: 2014931891
ISBN: 978-0-7356-7361-8

Printed and bound in the United States of America.

4 16

Microsoft Press books are available through booksellers and distributors worldwide. If you need support related to this book, email Microsoft Press Book Support at mspinput@microsoft.com. Please tell us what you think of this book at http://www.microsoft.com/learning/booksurvey.

Microsoft and the trademarks listed at http://www.microsoft.com/en-us/legal/intellectualproperty/Trademarks/EN-US.aspx are trademarks of the Microsoft group of companies. All other marks are property of their respective owners.

The example companies, organizations, products, domain names, email addresses, logos, people, places, and events depicted herein are fictitious. No association with any real company, organization, product, domain name, email address, logo, person, place, or event is intended or should be inferred.

Acquisitions Editor: Anne Hamilton
Developmental Editor: Karen Szall
Editorial Production: Box Twelve Communications
Technical Reviewer: Brian Svidergol
Cover: Twist Creative • Seattle

Contents at a glance

Introduction   *xi*

Preparing for the exam   *xiii*

CHAPTER 1   **Configure and manage high availability**   1

CHAPTER 2   **Configure file and storage solutions**   83

CHAPTER 3   **Implement business continuity and disaster recovery**   151

CHAPTER 4   **Configure network services**   215

CHAPTER 5   **Configure the Active Directory infrastructure**   267

CHAPTER 6   **Configure access and information protection solutions**   309

Index   *349*

Contents

Introduction   **ix**

Microsoft certifications   *ix*

Errata & book support   *x*

We want to hear from you   *x*

Stay in touch   *x*

Preparing for the exam   **xi**

Chapter 1   **Configure and manage high availability**   **1**

Objective 1.1: Configure Network Load Balancing (NLB) 1

Network Load Balancing fundamentals   2

Creating and configuring an NLB cluster   3

Configuring port rules   8

Upgrading an NLB cluster   14

Objective summary   16

Objective review   16

Objective 1.2: Configure failover clustering 17

Understanding failover clustering   18

Creating a failover cluster   20

Configuring cluster networking   23

Using Active Directory Detached Clusters   24

Configuring cluster storage   25

Configuring Quorum   32

Implementing Cluster Aware Updating   34

Migrating a failover cluster   38

Objective summary   40

Objective review   41

What do you think of this book? We want to hear from you!

Microsoft is interested in hearing your feedback so we can continually improve our
books and learning resources for you. To participate in a brief online survey, please visit:

www.microsoft.com/learning/booksurvey/

Objective 1.3: Manage failover clustering roles 42

Configuring roles   42

Assigning role startup priorities   48

Using node drain   49

Monitoring services on clustered virtual machines   50

Objective summary   54

Objective review   55

Objective 1.4: Manage virtual machine (VM) movement 56

Performing a live migration   57

Additional migration considerations   66

Using storage migration   70

Configuring virtual machine network health protection   72

Configuring drain on shutdown   73

Objective summary   74

Objective review   74

Answers. 77

Chapter 2   Configure file and storage solutions   83

Objective 2.1: Configure advanced file services 83

What is BranchCache?   84

Configuring BranchCache   87

Using File Server Resource Manager (FSRM)   92

Implementing file access auditing   95

Installing the Server for NFS component   96

Objective summary   98

Objective review   99

Objective 2.2: Implement Dynamic Access Control (DAC) 100

Introducing DAC   101

Configuring claims-based authentication   103

Configuring file classification   107

Configuring access policies   118

Objective summary   124

Objective review   124

Objective 2.3: Configure and optimize storage. 126

iSCSI storage   126

Using Features on Demand   136

Installing the Data Deduplication component   139

Using storage tiers   142

Objective summary   144

Objective review   144

Answers. 146

Chapter 3 Implement business continuity and disaster recovery 151

Objective 3.1: Configure and manage backups. .151

Using the Windows Server Backup feature   152

Understanding Backup Operators   160

Using the Shadow Copies feature (Previous Versions)   160

Configuring Windows Azure Backup   162

Objective summary   171

Objective review   172

Objective 3.2: Recover servers 174

Using the Advanced Boot Options menu   174

Recovering servers with the Windows installation media   178

Objective summary   184

Objective review   185

Objective 3.3: Configure site-level fault tolerance 186

Configuring Hyper-V physical host servers   186

Configuring VMs   190

Performing Hyper-V Replica failover   197

Using Hyper-V Replica in a failover cluster   201

Configuring Hyper-V Replica Extended Replication   204

Using Global Update Manager   205

Recovering multi-site failover clusters   206

Objective summary   207

Objective review   208

Answers. 210

Chapter 4 Configure network services   215

Objective 4.1: Implement an advanced DHCP solution. 215

Creating and configuring superscopes and multicast scopes   216

Implementing DHCPv6   218

Configuring high availability for DHCP   222

Configuring DNS registration   223

Configuring DHCP Name Protection   224

Objective summary   226

Objective review   227

Objective 4.2: Implement an advanced DNS solution 228

Implementing DNSSEC   229

Configuring DNS Socket Pool   230

Configuring DNS cache locking   230

Configuring DNS logging   231

Configuring delegated administration   232

Configuring recursion   233

Configuring netmask ordering   234

Configuring a GlobalNames zone   235

Analyzing zone-level statistics   235

Objective summary   237

Objective review   238

Objective 4.3: Deploy and manage IPAM. 239

Understanding IPAM   239

Installing and configuring IPAM   240

Managing address space   250

Configuring IPAM database storage   258

Objective summary   260

Objective review   260

Answers. 262

Chapter 5   Configure the Active Directory infrastructure   267

Objective 5.1: Configure a forest or a domain. 267

Implementing multi-domain Active Directory environments   268

Implementing multi-forest Active Directory environments   269

Configuring interoperability with previous versions of
Active Directory   270

Upgrading existing domains and forests   271

Configuring multiple user principal name (UPN) suffixes   272

Objective summary   274

Objective review   275

Objective 5.2: Configure trusts. 276

    Understanding trust concepts   276

    Configuring external trusts and realm trusts   277

    Configuring forest trusts   278

    Configuring shortcut trusts   279

    Configuring trust authentication   280

    Configuring Security IDentifier (SID) filtering   280

    Configuring name suffix routing   281

    Objective summary   282

    Objective review   283

Objective 5.3: Configure sites. 284

    Configuring sites and subnets   284

    Creating and configuring site links   287

    Managing registration of SRV records   290

    Moving domain controllers between sites   291

    Objective summary   293

    Objective review   293

Objective 5.4: Manage Active Directory and SYSVOL replication 294

    Configuring replication to Read-Only Domain Control-
    lers (RODCs)   295

    Monitoring and managing replication   298

    Upgrading SYSVOL replication to Distributed File Sys-
    tem Replication (DFSR)   300

    Objective summary   301

    Objective review   302

Answers. 303

Chapter 6   **Configure access and information protection
solutions**   **309**

Objective 6.1: Implement Active Directory Federation Services (AD FS) . . .309

    Installing AD FS   310

    Implementing claims-based authentication   310

    Configuring authentication policies   312

    Configuring Workplace Join   313

    Configuring multi-factor authentication   315

    Objective summary   316

    Objective review   317

Objective 6.2: Install and configure Active Directory
Certificate Services (AD CS) 318

Installing an Enterprise Certificate Authority (CA)   318

Configuring CRL Distribution Points (CDP)   322

Installing and configuring online responders   323

Implementing administrative role separation   323

Configuring CA backup and recovery   325

Objective summary   327

Objective review   327

Objective 6.3: Manage certificates 328

Managing certificate templates   328

Implementing and managing certificate validation and
revocation   330

Managing certificate enrollment   331

Managing certificate renewal   332

Configuring and managing key archival and recovery   332

Implementing and managing certificate deployment   334

Objective summary   335

Objective review   336

Objective 6.4: Install and configure Active Directory Rights
Management Services (AD RMS) 337

Installing a licensing or certificate AD RMS server   337

Managing AD RMS Service Connection Point (SCP)   338

Managing RMS templates   339

Configuring exclusion policies   340

Backing up and restoring AD RMS   341

Objective summary   342

Objective review   343

Answers. 344

Index   349

What do you think of this book? We want to hear from you!

Microsoft is interested in hearing your feedback so we can continually improve our
books and learning resources for you. To participate in a brief online survey, please visit:

www.microsoft.com/learning/booksurvey/

Introduction

Unlike other exams in the MCSA track, the Microsoft 70-412 certification exam deals with advanced topics such as Active Directory Rights Management Services and Active Directory Federation Services. Much of the exam comprises topics that even experienced systems administrators encounter less frequently than they encounter core infrastructure technologies, like Active Directory Domain Services and Windows Deployment Services.

Candidates for this exam are Information Technology (IT) Professionals who want to validate their advanced Windows Server 2012 R2 operating system configuration skills and knowledge. To pass this exam, candidates require strong understanding of how to configure and manage Windows Server 2012 R2 high availability, file and storage solutions, business and disaster recovery, network services, Active Directory infrastructure, and access and information protection solutions. To pass this exam, candidates require a thorough theoretical understanding as well as meaningful practical experience implementing the technologies involved. If you lack this experience, consider using the Microsoft Press companion title, *Training Guide: Configuring Advanced Windows Server 2012 R2 Services*, which contains extensive practical lab exercises.

This Exam Reference book covers every exam objective, but it does not cover every exam question. Only the Microsoft exam team has access to the exam questions and Microsoft regularly adds new questions to the exam, making it impossible to cover specific questions. You should consider this book a supplement to your relevant real-world experience and other study materials. If you encounter a topic in this book that you do not feel completely comfortable with, use the links you'll find in text to find more information and take the time to research and study the topic. Great Information is available on TechNet as well as in product team blogs and online forums.

Microsoft certifications

Microsoft certifications distinguish you by proving your command of a broad set of skills and experience with current Microsoft products and technologies. The exams and corresponding certifications are developed to validate your mastery of critical competencies as you design and develop, or implement and support, solutions with Microsoft products and technologies both on-premises and in the cloud. Certification brings a variety of benefits to the individual and to employers and organizations.

Errata & book support

We've made every effort to ensure the accuracy of this book and its companion content. Any errors that have been reported since this book was published are listed at:

> *http://aka.ms/ER412R2/errata*

If you find an error that is not already listed, you can report it to us through the same page.

If you need additional support, email Microsoft Press Book Support at *mspinput@microsoft.com.*

Please note that product support for Microsoft software is not offered through the addresses above.

We want to hear from you

At Microsoft Press, your satisfaction is our top priority, and your feedback our most valuable asset. Please tell us what you think of this book at:

> *http://aka.ms/tellpress*

The survey is short, and we read every one of your comments and ideas. Thanks in advance for your input!

Stay in touch

Let's keep the conversation going! We're on Twitter: *http://twitter.com/MicrosoftPress.*

Preparing for the exam

Microsoft certification exams are a great way to build your resume and let the world know about your level of expertise. Certification exams validate your on-the-job experience and product knowledge. While there is no substitution for on-the-job experience, preparation through study and hands-on practice can help you prepare for the exam. We recommend that you round out your exam preparation plan by using a combination of available study materials and courses. For example, you might use the Training Guide and another study guide for your "at home" preparation and take a Microsoft Official Curriculum course for the classroom experience. Choose the combination that you think works best for you.

CHAPTER 1

Configure and manage high availability

This domain relates to multi-server features that help selected services and applications remain online and responsive to clients. These features include Network Load Balancing, failover clustering, and the live migration of virtual machines (VMs). Understanding the topics covered in this domain requires a deep understanding of new technologies that you might not have implemented in your own environment. You should supplement the information in this chapter with some hands-on practice so that you can develop an understanding of how you can use these technologies to address real-world scenarios and solve problems in an advanced server environment.

> **IMPORTANT**
> ### Have you read page xv?
> It contains valuable information regarding the skills you need to pass the exam.

Objectives in this chapter:

- Objective 1.1: Configure Network Load Balancing (NLB)
- Objective 1.2: Configure failover clustering
- Objective 1.3: Manage failover clustering roles
- Objective 1.4: Manage virtual machine (VM) movement

Objective 1.1: Configure Network Load Balancing (NLB)

Network Load Balancing (NLB) is a Windows Server feature that lets you make a group of servers appear as one server to external clients. This group of servers joined through NLB is called an *NLB cluster* or a *server farm*, and each member server in the farm is usually called a *host* or *node*. The purpose of NLB is to improve both the availability and scalability of a service hosted on all the individual nodes.

NLB is surprisingly easy to get up and running in a default configuration. However, for the purposes of the 70-412 exam, you need to understand more than the basics about NLB. Make sure you also learn about the advanced configuration choices for the feature, such as priority settings and all port rule settings.

Network Load Balancing fundamentals

NLB improves both the availability and scalability of a service by receiving all client requests and distributing them among two or more servers. To each client, an NLB cluster just looks like a single server assigned one name and one address.

In the most typical scenario, NLB is used to create a *web farm*—a group of computers running Windows Server and working to support a website or a web application. But you can also use NLB to create other types of server farms: Remote Desktop Server farms, VPN server farms, or proxy server/firewall farms. Figure 1-1 shows a deployment of an NLB cluster of servers running Internet Information Services (IIS) behind an NLB cluster of servers running Forefront Threat Management Gateway (TMG).

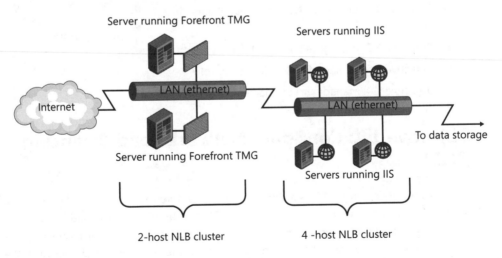

FIGURE 1-1 Basic diagram for two connected NLB clusters

First, NLB improves the availability of a service by absorbing individual server failures and hiding these failures from clients. NLB automatically detects servers that are unresponsive or disconnected from the farm and then redistributes new client requests among the remaining live hosts. Second, NLB supports scalability because a group of servers can handle more client requests than a single server can. And as the demand for a service such as a website grows, you can keep adding more servers to the farm so that it can handle an even greater workload.

An important point to understand about NLB is that each individual client is directed to exactly one server in the NLB cluster. The client therefore gets just the processing, memory, and storage resources of that one host only. Each node in the NLB cluster works independently without access to the resources in the other servers, and changes made on one server are not copied to other nodes in the farm. You use NLB to support what are termed *stateless applications*. You shouldn't use NLB with *stateful applications* such as database servers that allow individual clients to update data because such an arrangement would result in an inconsistent experience from client to client.

Creating and configuring an NLB cluster

Next, install the Network Load Balancing feature on the servers. You can install the NLB feature by using the Add Roles and Features Wizard available in Server Manager. On the 70-412 exam, you're more likely to need to know how to install this feature by using Windows PowerShell. To do that, type the following at an elevated Windows PowerShell prompt:

```
Install-WindowsFeature NLB -IncludeManagementTools
```

> **NOTE** **ALIASES**
>
> Add-WindowsFeature is an alias of Install-WindowsFeature, and Remove-WindowsFeature is an alias of Uninstall-WindowsFeature.

After you install the NLB feature with the management tools, you need to configure the NLB cluster by using either the Network Load Balancing Manager graphical tool or Windows PowerShell. You can access Network Load Balancing Manager from the Tools menu of Server Manager. You can also open Network Load Balancing Manager by typing Nlbmgr at a command prompt.

> **EXAM TIP**
>
> In Windows Server 2012 R2, management tools are *not* always installed alongside the associated roles or features as they were in previous versions of Windows Server. A management tool is installed by default only when you install the associated role or feature by using the Add Roles and Features Wizard. If you use the Install-WindowsFeature cmdlet to install a role or feature, the associated management tool is not automatically installed. To install the tool with the role or feature, use the -IncludeManagementTools option. When managing multiple servers from a single server, also known as fan-out administration, you're likely to install management tools for remote roles and features on the local server or even on the desktop computer running Windows 8.1 that you are using on a day-to-day basis as a systems administrator.

To start the New Cluster Wizard, in the Network Load Balancing Manager console tree, right-click Network Load Balancing Clusters and then click New Cluster as shown in Figure 1-2. Note that even though the user interface refers an NLB cluster as simply a "cluster," on the 70-412 exam, you are much more likely to see such a cluster called specifically an "NLB cluster" or a "farm."

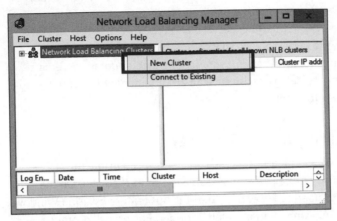

FIGURE 1-2 Creating a new NLB cluster

The first page of the New Cluster Wizard is the New Cluster: Connect page, shown in Figure 1-3. This page first requires you to connect to a server on which you have installed the NLB feature. After connecting to a server, you choose an interface on that server to use for NLB traffic. It's fine for testing purposes if the server you want to add to the NLB cluster has only one network interface—you can technically share one interface for NLB and normal network communication. But in a production environment, you normally want to reserve for NLB a dedicated network adapter on every node and then assign these interfaces to one separate network segment that has its own connection to the local router. Whether you reserve a dedicated interface to NLB or not, the interface you do assign to NLB must be given a static address. You will later assign this interface a second IP address that will be shared by every node in the NLB cluster.

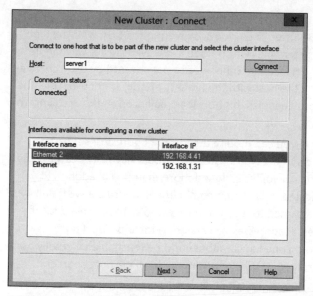

FIGURE 1-3 Specifying an interface reserved for NLB cluster traffic

The second page of the wizard is the New Cluster: Host Parameters page, shown in Figure 1-4. The settings on this page apply only to the local host (node), not to the entire NLB cluster.

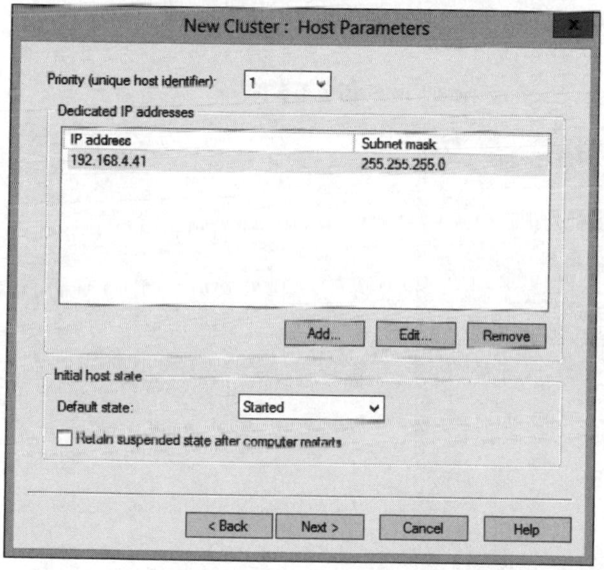

FIGURE 1-4 The second page of the New Cluster Wizard

There are essentially three configuration areas on this page: Priority (Unique Host Identifier), Dedicated IP Addresses, and Initial Host State.

- **Priority (Unique Host Identifier)** The Priority setting is a value from 1 to 32 that is unique to each host in the NLB cluster. The value 1 is given to the host with the highest priority. This priority value determines which node in the NLB cluster will handle network traffic that is *not* load balanced (in other words, *not* covered by the port rules you create later in the wizard). If the host with the highest priority is not available, the host with the next highest priority handles this non-load-balanced traffic. Also known as the *Host Priority* setting.

- **Dedicated IP Addresses** Here you can modify the local IP address or set of addresses that the host connects to the NLB cluster. You would normally need to adjust the default IP addresses here only if you've assigned more than one IP address to the interface you already dedicated to NLB. Remember, the IP addresses we're talking about on this page aren't assigned to the cluster as a whole. They're used for the local host only. These dedicated IP addresses you assign to the individual hosts in an NLB cluster must all be located on one logical subnet and be reachable externally as necessary through a working routed pathway or from the local network segment.

- **Initial Host State** Here you can set the default state of the local node within the NLB cluster. The options are Started (the default), Suspended, or Stopped. As you can see in Figure 1-4, you can also enable the option to retain the suspended state after the computer restarts.

Now you get to choose the virtual IP address or addresses that will be assigned to the entire server farm as a whole. The "virtual" cluster address or addresses you choose here must be on the same logical subnet as the "dedicated" host IP address or addresses you just chose on the previous page.

The New Cluster: Cluster IP Addresses page is shown in Figure 1-5.

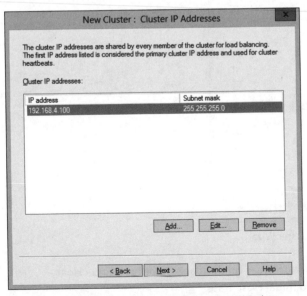

FIGURE 1-5 Assigning a virtual IP address to an NLB cluster

During setup, you use the New Cluster: Cluster Parameters page, shown in Figure 1-6, to configure the cluster's IP address, subnet mask, fully qualified domain name, network address, and cluster operation mode. These settings can be modified after the cluster is created.

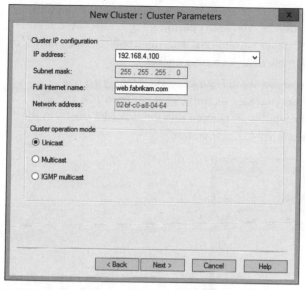

FIGURE 1-6 The fourth page of the New Cluster Wizard

This page includes a Cluster IP Configuration area at the top and a Cluster Operation Mode at the bottom.

- **Cluster IP Configuration** These settings are easy to understand. Here you just verify the virtual IP address and add a Fully Qualified Domain Name (FQDN) for the entire NLB cluster in the Full Internet Name text box. But you should also note the Network Address value: It's a virtual MAC address assigned to all network adapters that you have dedicated to the NLB cluster.

- **Cluster Operation Mode** The meaning of this setting is a bit less obvious. In it you set the new NLB cluster's operation mode to Unicast, Multicast, or IGMP Multicast. Let's go over what these mean in this context.

  - Unicast: Unicast mode (the default) allows the NLB cluster's MAC address to completely replace each host adapter's MAC address. This setting is technically efficient, but it's incompatible with some network adapters and in some virtual environments.

  - Multicast: In this setting, each host can keep its original MAC address. The cluster MAC address is used as a multicast address, which each host eventually translates into its own original MAC address.

  - IGMP Multicast: This option configures multicast at the IP address level. The advantage of this option is that it prevents switch flooding by limiting NLB traffic to NLB ports only. The disadvantage of this option is that not all switches can handle IGMP Multicast.

Configuring port rules

Port rules are the most important part of an NLB cluster's configuration. These port rules define which traffic will be load balanced in the NLB cluster and how it will be load-balanced. Each port rule matches incoming traffic as defined by a range of destination TCP or UDP ports and (optionally) a destination IP address. You aren't permitted to create two rules that match the same incoming traffic, so you never have to deal with rule conflicts, rule priority, or rule order. Only one port rule can ever apply to an incoming packet.

One port rule is predefined, which you can see in Figure 1-7. The predefined rule essentially matches all TCP/IP traffic (more precisely, all traffic sent between TCP and UDP ports 0 and 65535). You might want to keep this predefined rule for your NLB cluster in the real world, but it's not very useful for exam 70-412 preparation.

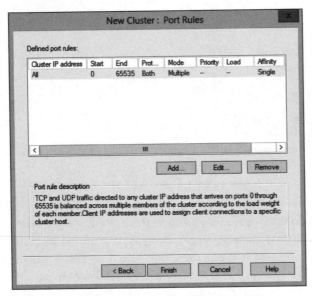

FIGURE 1-7 The fifth page of the New Cluster Wizard

For the 70-412 exam, assume that in any NLB scenario you see, the predefined port rule will be removed and all port rules will be custom-configured. So, to prepare for the exam, you need to understand all of the customizable configuration options on the Add/Edit Port Rule dialog box, shown in Figure 1-8. You also need to understand the two additional options that appear in this dialog box when you later edit an existing port rule within a particular *host's* properties (not the cluster's properties) in Network Load Balancing Manager.

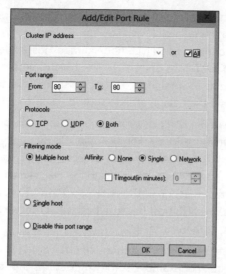

FIGURE 1-8 Adding or editing an NLB port rule

On the Add/Edit Port Rule page, you can edit the following options:

- **Cluster IP Address**   This area lets you define the matching criteria for a new port rule so that it matches incoming traffic directed at just one of the cluster's addresses. By default, a new port rule matches all of an NLB cluster's addresses.

- **Port Range and Protocols**   These sections let you define the matching criteria for a new port rule so that it matches incoming traffic directed at a contiguous range of one or more TCP ports, UDP ports, or both. The range you define cannot overlap a range defined in another port rule.

- **Filtering Mode**   This section allows you to specify how requests are distributed. You can choose between Multiple Host, Single Host, and Disable This Port Range.

The Multiple Host filtering mode is the default setting. *Multiple Host filtering mode* provides both load balancing and fault tolerance for all incoming requests matching the port rule. Client requests matching the port rule are distributed among active nodes in the farm. When you choose the Multiple Host filtering mode, you need to choose an affinity setting, which determines how a client that is interacting with the cluster during a session will respond. The options are None, Single and Network and work in the following manner:

- **None**   With this setting, each client traffic is directed to any node in the cluster, dependent on existing load. Subsequent traffic from the client will be directed to any node in the cluster dependent on existing load.

- **Single** With this setting, if a client named Client1 connects to a node named Host1 on the first connection to an NLB cluster, then Client1 will keep connecting to Host1 in the future. If a client named Client2 connects to an NLB node named Host2, then Client2 will keep connecting to Host2 in the future, and so on. The advantage of this setting is that it allows user state data to be maintained from one session to the next if this data is saved on the local node. This is the default affinity setting.

- **Network** With this option, each node in the NLB cluster is responsible for all connections that match a given /24 IPv4 network address. For example, if a client named Client1 first connects to the NLB cluster through a proxy server named Proxy1 that is assigned the address 207.46.130.101 and then later connects to the NLB cluster through a proxy server named Proxy 2 that is assigned the address 207.46.130.102, the connection will be returned to the same NLB host because both proxy servers are assigned the same /24 network address. (207.46.130.z).

Be aware that your choice here among these three Affinity settings can be restricted by the application you are hosting in the NLB cluster. For example, some applications support the Affinity-None setting, but others don't.

The *Single Host filtering mode* directs all matching traffic toward the host with the highest priority value. If that host fails, then the traffic is directed to the host with the next highest priority. You might remember that this same service is provided for traffic that does not match any port rule at all. So why bother creating a port rule in Single Host mode? The advantage of configuring a port rule in Single Host mode is that with a port rule you can later define a custom server priority for this particular traffic with the *Handling Priority* setting in Network Load Balancing Manager.

EXAM TIP

You need to understand the Affinity-None, Affinity-Single, and Affinity-Network settings for the 70-412 exam.

The Timeout setting extends affinity through configuration changes in the NLB cluster up to the number of minutes specified. If, for example, the NLB cluster is used to support a web storefront, a customer might experience the benefit of the Timeout setting by always being able to retain items in a shopping cart for the number of minutes specified. Without extending affinity with the Timeout setting, the items in the shopping cart could theoretically disappear if the customer's connection is redirected to another host after a configuration change to the server farm. The Disable This Port Range setting allows you to have the NLB cluster drop all traffic on the specified ports.

The Load Weight and Handling Priority settings are available for you to configure only when editing an existing port rule through a host's properties in Network Load Balancing Manager. When you edit an existing port rule, a special version of the Add/Edit Port Rule dialog box opens, which is shown in Figure 1-9.

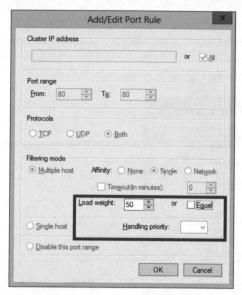

FIGURE 1-9 The host-specific Add/Edit Port Rule dialog box

When editing an existing port rule, you can configure the following settings:

- **Load Weight**   This setting allows you to assign a disproportionate weight of the workload to the host whose properties you are editing. By default, Equal is selected, which gives the node an average-weighted or proportional distribution of the network load. If you clear the Equal setting (as shown in Figure 1-9), you can assign the host a greater or smaller share of the network traffic directed at the farm. In this case, the proportion handled is determined by the local load weight divided by the total of all the load weights across the NLB cluster. The default weight is 50.

- **Handling Priority**   This setting is configurable only if you have enabled Single Host filtering mode for the rule. With Single Host filtering mode, the server available with the highest priority always receives the traffic specified in the port rule. The advantage of creating for specific traffic a port rule with Single Host filtering mode enabled, as opposed to creating no port rule at all, is that with a defined port rule you can set custom server priority for that traffic. The Handling Priority is where you set that custom server priority. If this value is not set here, the priority value assigned to the local host is the one set in Host Parameters for the entire cluster.

EXAM TIP

Remember the difference between Host Priority and Handling Priority. *Host Priority* determines which server in an NLB cluster receives traffic that is not covered by a port rule. *Handling Priority* is a custom server priority value used for traffic covered by a port rule but assigned Single Host filtering mode.

Adding hosts in the NLB cluster

To add hosts to an existing NLB cluster, in the Network Load Balancing Manager console tree, right-click the cluster and then select Add Host To Cluster, as shown in Figure 1-10. This step opens the Add Host To Cluster Wizard. You can add up to 16 hosts to an NLB cluster.

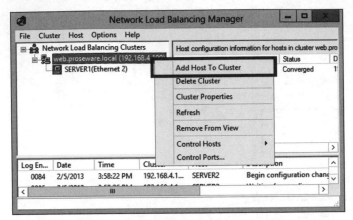

FIGURE 1-10 Installing hosts in an NLB cluster after it is created

Understanding NLB cmdlets for Windows PowerShell

To show all available cmdlets for NLB, type Get-Command *nlb* or Get-Command -Module NetworkLoadBalancingClusters at a Windows PowerShell prompt.

TABLE 1-1 Network Load Balancing cmdlets in Windows Server 2012 and Windows Server 2012 R2

cmdlet	Description
Add-NlbClusterNode	Adds a new node to an NLB cluster
Add-NlbClusterNodeDip	Adds a dedicated IP address to an NLB cluster
Add-NlbClusterPortRule	Adds a new port rule to an NLB cluster
Add-NlbClusterVip	Adds a virtual (cluster-wide) IP address to an NLB cluster
Disable-NlbClusterPortRule	Disables a port rule on an NLB cluster or on a specific host in the cluster
Enable-NlbClusterPortRule	Enables a port rule on an NLB cluster or on a specific node in the cluster
Get-NlbCluster	Retrieves information about an NLB cluster

cmdlet	Description
Get-NlbClusterNode	Retrieves information about an NLB cluster node
Get-NlbClusterNodeDip	Retrieves the dedicated IP address
Get-NlbClusterNodeNetworkInterface	Retrieves information about interfaces on an NLB host
Get-NlbClusterPortRule	Retrieves port rule objects
Get-NlbClusterVip	Retrieves virtual IP addresses
New-NlbCluster	Creates an NLB cluster on the specified interface that is defined by the node and network adapter name
Remove-NlbCluster	Deletes an NLB cluster
Remove-NlbClusterNode	Removes a node from an NLB cluster
Remove-NlbClusterNodeDip	Removes a dedicated IP address from an NLB cluster
Remove-NlbClusterPortRule	Removes a port rule from an NLB cluster
Remove-NlbClusterVip	Removes a virtual IP address from an NLB cluster
Resume-NlbCluster	Resumes all nodes in an NLB cluster
Resume-NlbClusterNode	Resumes the node in an NLB cluster that was suspended
Set-NlbCluster	Edits the configuration of an NLB cluster
Set-NlbClusterNode	Edits an NLB cluster's node settings
Set-NlbClusterNodeDip	Edits the dedicated IP address of an NLB cluster
Set-NlbClusterPortRule	Edits the port rules for an NLB cluster
Set-NlbClusterPortRuleNodeHandlingPriority	Sets the host priority of a port rule for a specific NLB node
Set-NlbClusterPortRuleNodeWeight	Sets the load weight of a port rule for a specific NLB node
Set-NlbClusterVip	Edits the virtual IP address of an NLB cluster
Start-NlbCluster	Starts all nodes in an NLB cluster
Start-NlbClusterNode	Starts an NLB cluster
Stop-NlbCluster	Stops all nodes of an NLB cluster
Stop-NlbClusterNode	Stops a node in an NLB cluster
Suspend-NlbCluster	Suspends all nodes of an NLB cluster
Suspend-NlbClusterNode	Suspends a specific node in an NLB cluster

Upgrading an NLB cluster

To upgrade an existing NLB cluster to Windows Server 2012 or Windows Server 2012 R2, you always have the option of taking the entire cluster offline, upgrading all the hosts, and then bringing the cluster back online. However, the disadvantage of this procedure is that the cluster naturally cannot service client requests during the period that it is offline.

Fortunately, many applications and services hosted in NLB support a better option, called a *rolling upgrade*, for upgrading NLB clusters. A rolling upgrade lets you leave the NLB cluster online during the upgrade process. In a rolling upgrade, you take each individual node offline, upgrade it, and then bring the node back online, one at a time. You use the Drainstop function to take each node offline to ensure that existing connections to that host are terminated gracefully. (In Network Load Balancing Manager, you can find the Drainstop function on the Control Host submenu of the shortcut menu that appears when you right-click a host in the console tree.) With Drainstop, the node refuses new connections and new client requests are simply directed to the nodes that remain online. To bring each host back online after you upgrade it, use the Start function for the same host (and available on the same submenu). You complete the process by continuing to upgrade each individual cluster host one at a time until the entire cluster is upgraded.

Thought experiment

Configuring Network Load Balancing at Tailspin Toys

In the following thought experiment, apply what you've learned about this objective to predict what steps you need to take. You can find answers to these questions in the "Answers" section at the end of this chapter.

You are the systems administrator at Tailspin Toys and you are responsible for managing the server infrastructure that hosts the Tailspin Toys website. The traffic to Tailspin Toys website has been gradually increasing. At present the website design has a single Windows Server 2012 R2 server running IIS as the front end, hosting the site and a single Windows Server 2012 R2 server hosting a SQL Server 2012 instance hosting customer data. Increased traffic to the website has decreased the speed at which it responds. Additionally, in the last month, the website has been offline when software updates are applied. In the past, this was considered acceptable by management, but now they want the website to be available to customers even when software updates are being applied.

You have the following objectives:

- Make the IIS and SQL Servers highly available.
- Ensure that the website remains online when any single server is restarted to apply software updates.
- Clients that are browsing the Tailspin Toys website should interact with the same IIS server for the duration of their session and should connect to a different server running IIS only in the event that the one they were initially connected to fails.
- Ensure that clients who are connected to a server running IIS are disconnected gracefully prior to software updates being applied to the server.

With the preceding information in mind, answer the following questions.

1. Which of the Tailspin Toys servers can you make highly available by deploying Network Load Balancing?

2. After implementing Network Load Balancing, what function should you use to ensure that any connections to the highly available servers are terminated gracefully?

3. Which filtering and affinity mode and option would you select to ensure that clients interact with the same IIS server during a session?

Objective summary

- Network Load Balancing (NLB) lets you configure a group of servers so that they appear as one server to external clients. Client requests received by the NLB cluster are distributed among all the hosts (also called nodes) when these requests match configured port rules.

- To best learn what you need to know about NLB for the 70-412 exam, you should learn all of the configuration settings available in the five pages of the New Cluster Wizard and all port rule settings.

- When no port rule matches a client request, the request is directed to the node with the highest host priority.

- The Affinity setting determines whether a particular client will continue to be directed back to the same host in the NLB cluster on successive visits. Single Affinity provides client-host affinity on a per-client basis. Network Affinity assigns to one host all clients assigned the same /24 network address.

- You can override the default host priority for any traffic that you don't want to be load-balanced among all nodes in the NLB cluster. To set a custom host priority, first create a port rule matching the desired traffic with Single Host filtering mode enabled. Then modify the Handling Priority parameter by editing the port rule in the properties of the node you want to assign the custom priority.

- You can use the Load Weight setting to modify the relative weight of the client work-load assigned to a particular node in the cluster.

Objective review

Answer the following questions to test your knowledge of the information in this objective. You can find the answers to these questions and explanations of why each answer choice is correct or incorrect in the "Answers" section at the end of the chapter.

1. You have configured an NLB cluster of 10 web servers running Windows Server 2012 R2 and IIS. You discover that web traffic destined for the NLB cluster is distributed very unevenly among the individual NLB cluster members. Port rule settings for each node have not been modified from the defaults.

   You want to ensure that client web requests are distributed as evenly as possible among all 10 nodes in the NLB cluster. Which setting should you enable?

   A. Affinity-None

   B. Affinity-Single

   C. Affinity-Network

   D. Load Weight

2. Your network includes an NLB cluster that is used to support an e-commerce site. Use of the site is growing. Whenever you add a new node to the NLB cluster, you receive complaints from customers that items in their shopping carts disappear. You want to reduce the likelihood that users will experience this problem in the future.

   What should you do?

   A. Modify the Load Weight settings

   B. Enable the Single Host filtering mode

   C. Enable the Multiple Host filtering mode

   D. Modify the Timeout settings

3. You have configured an NLB cluster. You want to designate a particular server within the NLB cluster to handle all the traffic that is not caught by any port rule. What should you do?

   A. Modify the Load Weight setting

   B. Enable the Single Host filtering mode

   C. Configure the Host Priority settings

   D. Configure a Handling Priority

Objective 1.2: Configure failover clustering

Failover clustering is a feature that helps ensure that selected services or applications remain available even if a server hosting them fails. Unlike NLB, failover clustering is normally used to provide high availability for data that can be frequently updated by clients. Typical services hosted in failover clusters include database servers, mail servers, print servers, virtual machines hosted in Hyper-V (often hosting a critical application), and file servers.

Failover clusters are one of the most advanced topics you need to learn for the 70-412 exam. To prepare for this objective, you first need to understand basic concepts about failover clusters, such as what they're for, how they work, and which components they require. Then you'll need to learn the concepts needed to properly configure components of a failover cluster, including cluster Quorum settings, cluster networking, and cluster storage.

This objective covers how to:

- Configure Quorum
- Configure cluster networking
- Restore single node or cluster configuration
- Configure cluster storage
- Implement Cluster Aware Updating
- Upgrade a cluster
- Configure and optimize clustered shared volumes
- Configure clusters without network names
- Configure storage spaces

Understanding failover clustering

A failover cluster is a group of servers configured in a way that protects chosen services or applications from failure. The services or applications configured for protection in a failover cluster are known alternately as *roles,* as *clustered roles,* as *clustered services and applications,* as *highly available services and applications,* or as *services and applications configured for high availability.* The individual servers in a failover cluster are called nodes. In a failover cluster, if a node fails, each role hosted on that failed node will immediately "fail over to" (start on) another node specified for that particular role. If just a role fails but the entire node doesn't fail, that role is attempted to be restarted and eventually failed over to another node, if necessary. Users experience only minimal disruption, if any, as a result of this failover process.

There are important differences between NLB clusters and failover clusters. First of all, in a failover cluster, only one server normally hosts a clustered service at a time. And instead of each node reading from and writing to its own local disk, in a failover cluster the nodes store role data only in volumes that are located on *shared storage* such as on logical unit numbers (LUNs) located on an iSCSI or Fibre Channel SAN or on a shared Serial SCSI (SAS) disk array. This fact that there is only one source of data for roles in a failover cluster prevents the possibility of data inconsistency for these clustered services from client to client. Consequently, failover clusters are especially useful to help ensure the availability of services for which clients can update data. Typical services you see hosted as roles in a failover cluster include a file server, a database server, a print server, a mail server, and even a virtual machine.

Figure 1-11 illustrates the process of failover in a basic, two-node failover cluster.

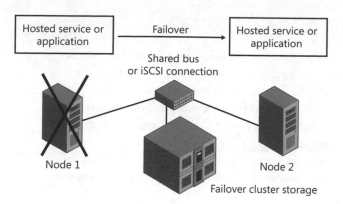

FIGURE 1-11 In a failover cluster, when one server fails, another takes over and uses the same storage

Understanding the hardware components of a failover cluster

The hardware requirements for failover clusters extend to servers and storage. All components must meet the qualifications for the Certified for Windows Server 2012 or Windows Server 2012 R2 logo.

- **Server requirements** A failover cluster requires at least two networked physical servers, or one physical server for each node you want in the cluster (up to a maximum of 64).

> **NOTE CONFIGURING VIRTUAL MACHINES FOR TESTING**
>
> You can configure a single-node cluster for testing purposes. An even better option for testing and learning about the feature, if you have only one physical server, is to configure two or more virtual machines as your nodes. Naturally, this option doesn't provide protection from physical server failure or allow you to host virtual machines as a clustered role on these already-virtual nodes.

- **Storage requirements** Failover clusters rely on shared storage through a SAN (iSCSI or Fibre Channel) or a shared Serial-attached SCSI (SAS) disk array. If the role you are clustering is a virtual machine hosted in Hyper-V, you have an additional convenient option: You can store the VM files on a Windows Server 2012 or Windows Server 2012 R2 network share.

- **Hardware recommendations** Recommendations are less likely to appear in a Microsoft exam than requirements are. Still, to help you understand how Windows Server 2012 or Windows Server 2012 R2 failover clusters are deployed in a production environment, you should know to follow these guidelines:
  - Use identical or nearly identical servers for each node.
  - If you use iSCSI or Fibre Channel over Ethernet (FCoE), each network adapter should be dedicated either to the LAN or the SAN, not both.
  - For fault tolerance, ensure that you assigned teamed network adapters for all connections. Ideally, you should also configure redundant switches, routers, and network paths to the cluster.

Understanding the software requirements of a failover cluster

Windows Server 2012 or Windows Server 2012 R2 failover clusters require either the Standard or Datacenter version of Windows Server 2012 or Windows Server 2012 R2. Failover clusters also require that all nodes be joined to the same Active Directory Domain Services (AD DS) domain. Finally, all nodes must have installed the Failover Clustering feature.

Creating a failover cluster

The questions you'll see within Objective 1.2 on the 70-412 exam will most likely relate to the settings you can configure within an existing failover cluster. The steps required to create a new failover cluster are less likely to appear. Still, to prepare for the 70-412 exam, you really need to create your own failover cluster in a test network. Failover clusters are best understood when you see them in action. You can begin by creating a bare-bones failover cluster with an empty role and then configure all the required components later.

To create a failover cluster, join the servers to the appropriate AD DS domain and connect these servers to shared storage. You also need to install the Failover Clustering feature on all nodes in the cluster. You can use Server Manager or the following Windows PowerShell command:

```
Install-WindowsFeature Failover-Clustering –IncludeManagementTools
```

You also run checks to validate that your nodes meet the hardware and software pre-requisites for a failover cluster before you create a cluster. You can run the validation tests by using the Validate A Configuration Wizard (by clicking Validate Configuration in the Actions pane of Failover Cluster Manager, as shown in Figure 1-12) or by using the Test-Cluster cmdlet in Windows PowerShell. If you don't choose to run the validation tests manually, they will be performed automatically when you run the Create Cluster Wizard.

When you run the tests, you simply specify the nodes you will add to the cluster. You can also run the tests later again after you create the cluster by specifying the cluster by name, instead of specifying them according to node.

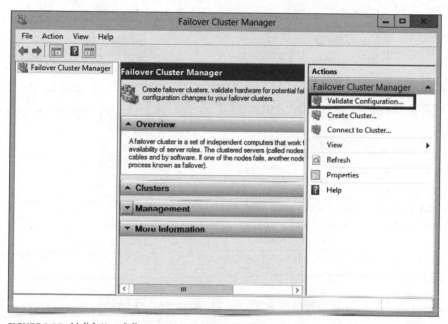

FIGURE 1-12 Validating failover server prerequisites

After the wizard completes, make any necessary configuration changes and then rerun the test until the configuration is successfully validated. Once the configuration is validated, create the cluster by using the Create Cluster Wizard or the New-Cluster cmdlet in Windows PowerShell. This step installs the software foundation for the cluster, converts the attached storage into cluster disks, and creates a computer account in Active Directory for the cluster.

To launch the Create Cluster Wizard, in Failover Cluster Manager, click Create Cluster in the Actions pane. The procedure is simple. You need to make only the following decisions:

- The nodes you want to add to the cluster.
- The name of the new cluster.
- The IP address you want to assign for each network to which the nodes are connected. (You can also de-select a particular network if you don't want clients to connect to the cluster through that network.)

- Whether to keep the default option of adding all eligible storage to the cluster. To override this default behavior in the wizard, you can clear Add All Eligible Storage To The Cluster. With the New-Cluster cmdlet, use the -NoStorage option.

You can use an empty role to test the basic functionality of the failover cluster before you configure any components such as networking, storage, Quorum, or roles. To create an empty role in a failover cluster, select the Roles node in the console tree in Failover Cluster Manager and then click Create Empty Role in the Actions pane, as shown in Figure 1-13.

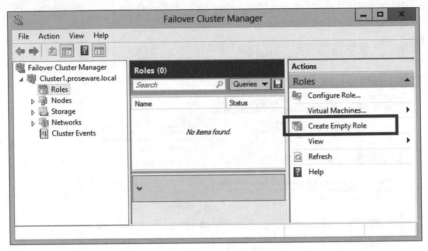

FIGURE 1-13 Creating an empty role

After you click Create Empty Role, a new role appears in the center pane when the Roles node is selected, as shown in Figure 1-14.

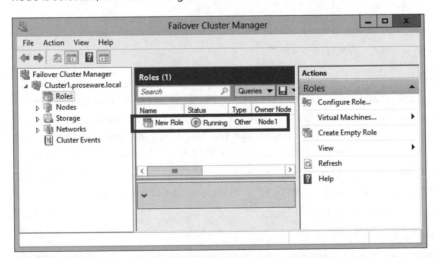

FIGURE 1-14 An empty role as it appears in Failover Cluster Manager

After you create the basic failover cluster and create an empty role, you can test the failover functionality of the cluster in Failover Cluster Management. To do this, in the center pane of the console, select the role. Then, in the Actions pane, click Move, and then click Best Possible Node, as shown in Figure 1-15. You can observe the status changes in the center pane of the snap-in as the clustered service instance is moved. If the Owner Node value changes successfully from the name of one node to another, the failover is functional in the cluster.

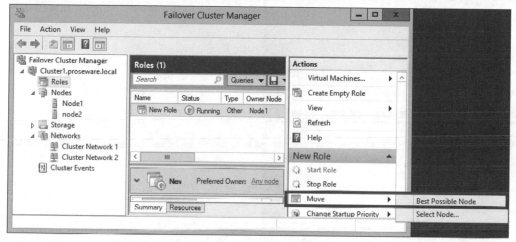

FIGURE 1-15   Testing a failover cluster by moving a role to another node

To really make the failover cluster fully functional, you need to configure other components after the cluster is created. The following sections provide a brief overview of what you need to need to understand for the exam about configuring cluster networking, storage, and Quorum.

Configuring cluster networking

The cluster networking settings you need to know for the 70-412 exam can be found in the cluster network properties dialog box shown in Figure 1-20. You access these settings by right-clicking a particular network in the console tree of Failover Cluster Manager and then clicking properties.

As shown in Figure 1-16, networks that are detected in Failover Cluster Manager can be assigned to one of three categories:

- Allow Cluster Network Communication On This Network
- Allow Cluster Network Communication On This Network *and* Allow Clients To Connect Through This Network
- Do Not Allow Cluster Communication On This Network

If you want to reserve a network for intra-cluster or "heartbeat" communication and prevent clients from communicating through the network, clear Allow Clients To Connect Through This Network. (The heartbeat determines whether a service is still available on a given node.) If you are reserving the network for the nodes' connection to iSCSI storage or some other function, select Do Not Allow Cluster Network Communication On This Network.

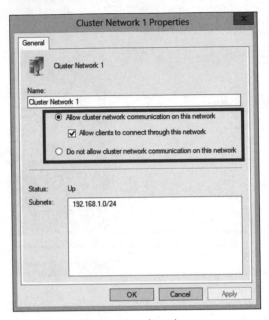

FIGURE 1-16 Cluster network settings

Using Active Directory Detached Clusters

Windows Server 2012 R2 allows you to deploy a failover cluster without the dependency on Active Directory Domain Services to provide network name information. When you deploy a cluster in this manner, the cluster network name or administrative access point and the network names of any clustered roles are stored within DNS but objects aren't created in the AD DS database. Active Directory Detached Clusters do not require computer objects representing the cluster to be present within Active Directory. The key to understanding Active Directory Detached Clusters is that while AD DS is not required for the cluster network name, the nodes that comprise the cluster must still be members of an Active Directory domain. The benefit of this new feature is that it is possible to create failover clusters without requiring the permission to create computer objects within AD DS. Microsoft recommends not using Active Directory-detached clusters in scenarios that require Kerberos authentication. This cluster type can also only be deployed using Windows PowerShell.

Configuring cluster storage

In the real world, configuring cluster storage is a fairly complicated topic. On the 70-412 exam, however, there are only a few concepts you need to focus on: Adding disks to the cluster, understanding and configuring cluster storage pools, and understanding and configuring cluster-shared volumes.

Adding new disks to a cluster

If you want to add disks to an existing failover cluster, begin by provisioning the logical disks from shared storage, such as from an iSCSI target. Once the shared disk appears in Server Manager, initialize the disk and bring it online.

Next, create a volume from this disk, as shown in Figure 1-17.

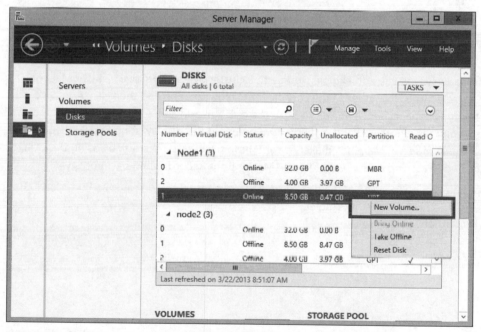

FIGURE 1-17 Creating a new volume in Server Manager

Assign the new volume to the desired failover cluster, as shown in Figure 1-18. (The name of the cluster appears as a server name.)

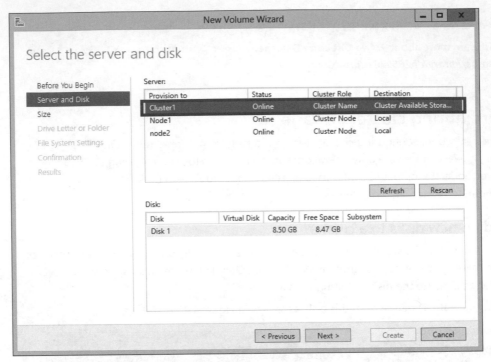

FIGURE 1-18 Assigning a new volume to a cluster

Alternatively, you can add eligible storage to a cluster by using Failover Cluster Manager. To do so, select the Disks node in the console tree below Storage and then click Add Disk in the Actions pane, as shown in Figure 1-19. The disk you add should already include one or more volumes before you add it. If you have prepared the disk by using Disk Management instead of Server Manager, make sure you have partitioned the disk by using the GUID Partition Table (GPT) partition style, not the Master Boot Record (MBR) partition style.

As a final option, you can add a disk to a failover cluster by using Windows PowerShell. To do so, use the Add-ClusterDisk cmdlet.

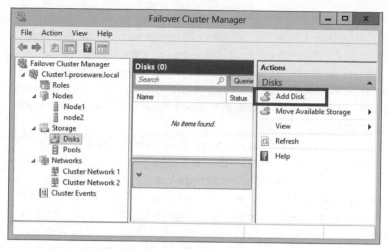

FIGURE 1-19   Adding a new disk to a failover cluster

After you add the disk to the cluster, the new disk along with its volumes appears in Failover Cluster Manager, as shown in Figure 1-20.

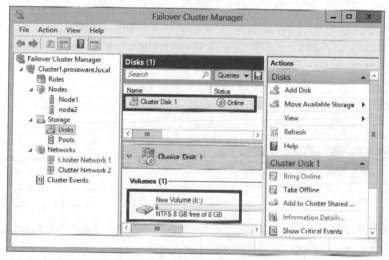

FIGURE 1-20   Disk added to a failover cluster

Creating cluster storage pools

In Windows Server 2012 or Windows Server 2012 R2, you can now draw upon data storage provided by a Serial Attached SCSI (SAS) disk array to create one or more storage pools for a failover cluster. These storage pools are similar to the ones you can create for an individual server by using Storage Spaces (covered in Exam 70-410). As with the Storage Spaces feature, you can use these storage pools in a failover cluster as source from which you can then create virtual disks and finally volumes.

To create a new storage pool, in Failover Cluster Manager, navigate to Failover Cluster Manager\[Cluster Name]\Storage\Pools, right-click Pools, and then select New Storage Pool from the shortcut menu, as shown in Figure 1-21. This step starts the same New Storage Pool Wizard used with Storage Spaces. (In fact, if you have a shared SAS disk array, you can use Server Manager to create the pool and use the Add Storage Pool option to add it to the machine.) After you create the pool, you need to create virtual disks from the new pool and virtual volumes from the new disks before you can use the clustered storage space for hosting your clustered workloads.

> **MORE INFO   CONFIGURING CLUSTER STORAGE POOLS**
>
> For more information about configuring cluster storage pools, visit "How to Configure a Clustered Storage Space in Windows Server 2012" at *http://blogs.msdn.com/b/clustering/archive/2012/06/02/10314262.aspx* and "Deploy Clustered Storage Spaces" at *http://technet.microsoft.com/en-us/library/jj822937.aspx*.

FIGURE 1-21 Creating a new storage pool for a cluster

The availability of storage pools for failover clusters has implications for the 70-412 exam, especially because these storage pools have a number of requirements and restrictions that could easily serve as the basis for a test question. Note the following requirements for failover cluster storage pools:

- A minimum of three physical drives, with at least 4 gigabytes (GB) capacity each.
- Only SAS connected physical disks are allowed. No additional layer of RAID (or any disk subsystem) is supported, whether internal or external.
- Fixed provisioning only for virtual disks. No thin provisioning.
- When creating virtual disks from a clustered storage pool, only simple and mirror storage layouts are supported. Parity layouts are not supported.
- The physical disks used for a clustered pool must be dedicated to that one pool. Boot disks should not be added to a clustered pool.

Using cluster-shared volumes (CSVs)

Cluster-shared volumes (CSVs) are a type of volume that first appeared in Windows Server 2008 R2 and that is used only in failover clusters. The biggest advantage of CSVs is that they can be shared by multiple active cluster nodes at a time. This is not normally possible with shared storage. In fact, two cluster nodes cannot normally use even two separate volumes residing on the same logical disk or LUN.

CSVs achieve this shared access of volumes by separating the data from different nodes into VHD files. Within each shared volume, multiple VHDs are stored, each used as the storage for a particular role for which high availability has been configured. The CSVs containing these VHDs are then mapped to a common namespace on all nodes in the cluster. On every failover cluster configured with CSVs, the CSVs appear on every node as subfolders in the \ClusterStorage folder on the system drive. Example pathnames are C:\ClusterStorage\ Volume1, C:\ClusterStorage\Volume2, and so on.

CSVs are formatted with NTFS, but to distinguish them from normal NTFS volumes, the Windows Server 2012 or Windows Server 2012 R2 interface displays them as formatted with "CSVFS", or the Cluster Shared Volume File System. An example of a CSV is shown in Figure 1-22.

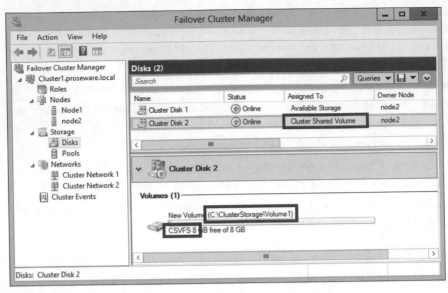

FIGURE 1-22 A Cluster shared volume

To create a CSV in Failover Cluster Manager, select the disk and click Add To Cluster Shared Volumes in the Actions pane, as shown in Figure 1-23. In Windows PowerShell, use the Add-ClusterSharedVolume cmdlet.

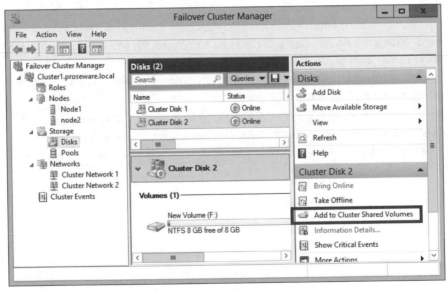

FIGURE 1-23 Adding a volume to cluster-shared volumes

In Windows Server 2008 R2, CSVs were used as storage for only one type of workload hosted in a failover cluster: a highly available virtual machine. In Windows Server 2012 and Windows Server 2012 R2, CSVs are now also used as the only storage type for a new role, the

Scale-Out File Server, which is described later in the "Configuring File Server role types" section of this chapter. Another important use for CSVs is with live migration in failover clusters (a feature also described later in this chapter). Though CSVs are not required for live migration, they are highly recommended because they optimize the performance of the migration and reduce downtime to almost zero.

How might CSVs appear on the 70-412 exam? If there's a question about CSVs directly, it could come in the form of a requirement that states you want to "minimize administrative overhead" when designing storage for a highly available virtual machine. More likely, you will simply see CSV mentioned in the setup to a question that isn't just about CSVs.

REAL WORLD   WHY ARE CLUSTER-SHARED VOLUMES USEFUL?

Here is the original problem CSVs were designed to solve: In Windows Server 2008 and earlier versions of Windows Server, only one cluster node could access a LUN at any given time. If an application, service, or virtual machine connected to the same LUN failed and needed to be moved to another node in the failover cluster, every other clustered application or virtual machine on that physical node would also need to be failed over to a new node and potentially experience some downtime. To avoid this problem, each clustered role was typically connected to its own unique LUN as a way to isolate failures. This strategy created another problem, however: a large number of LUNs that complicated setup and administration.

With CSVs, a single LUN can thus be accessed by different nodes at a time, as long as the different nodes are accessing distinct VHDs on the LUN. You can run these roles on any node in the failover cluster, and when the role fails, it can fail over to any other physical node in the cluster without affecting other roles (services or applications) hosted on the original node. CSVs thus add flexibility and simplify management.

Using shared virtual hard disk

Shared virtual hard disk allows you to share a virtual hard disk file in .vhdx format between two or more virtual machines. You can use these special shared virtual hard disks as shared storage for virtual machine failover clusters. For example, one shared virtual hard disk might host the disk witness and other shared virtual hard disks might host data for the highly available application. Shared virtual hard disks substantially simplify the process of deploying guest clusters because you can use a special .vhdx file rather than having to configure iSCSI or Fibre Channel. Shared virtual hard disk is a feature new to Windows Server 2012 R2 and is not available to guest failover clusters running on Windows Server 2012 Hyper-V hosts. Guest clusters running the Windows Server 2012 operating system can access shared virtual hard disks as shared storage as long as you have installed Windows Server 2012 R2 Integration Services. You can deploy a shared virtual hard disk for a Hyper-V guest failover cluster either by using cluster-shared volumes on block storage or by deploying them on a scale-out file server with SMB 3.0 on file-based storage.

Configuring Quorum

The Quorum configuration in a failover cluster determines the number of active, communicative nodes that are required for the cluster to run. In a failover cluster, every node that remains functional and communicative with other nodes submits one vote in favor of the cluster remaining online. If a majority of the nodes added to the cluster are functional and communicative, the cluster is said to "reach Quorum" and is allowed to run.

In the most basic Quorum configuration, called *Node Majority*, all votes are cast by the nodes. If the cluster is made up of an even number of nodes, however, it's recommended you choose a Quorum configuration with a tiebreaker element called a witness. A *witness* is a shared disk or file share accessible by all nodes in the cluster and that contains a copy of the failover cluster database. When you configure Node and File Share Majority or Node and Disk Majority as your Quorum configuration, the failover cluster can reach Quorum when only half of the nodes remain online (as opposed to a clear majority), as long as they can also communicate with the disk witness or file share witness.

To configure a Quorum witness or to modify the default Quorum settings in a failover cluster in Failover Cluster Manager, right-click the cluster node in the console tree, click More Actions, and then click Configure Cluster Quorum Settings, as shown in Figure 1-24.

NOTE **MANAGE QUORUM DYNAMICALLY**

In Windows Server 2012 or Windows Server 2012 R2, you can choose an option to manage Quorum dynamically. With this recommended setting, the number of nodes required to reach Quorum adjusts if nodes are removed from the cluster.

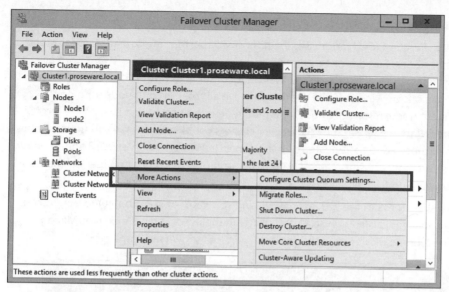

FIGURE 1-24   Selecting a Quorum configuration

EXAM TIP

On the 70-412 exam, remember above all that the Quorum configuration determines how many nodes in a cluster can fail before the cluster stops running.

MORE INFO   QUORUM SETTINGS

For more information about Quorum settings, see "Configure and Manage the Quorum in a Windows Server 2012 Failover Cluster" at *http://technet.microsoft.com/en-us/library/jj612870.aspx*.

Implementing Cluster Aware Updating

Cluster Aware Updating (CAU) addresses the difficulty of performing software updates on failover cluster nodes. This difficulty stems from the fact that updating software normally requires a system restart. To maintain the availability of services hosted on failover clusters in previous versions of Windows, you needed to move all roles off one node, update the software on that node, restart the node, and then repeat the process on every other node, one at a time. Windows Server 2008 R2 failover clusters could include up to 16 nodes, so this process sometimes had to be repeated as many times. In Windows Server 2012 and Windows Server 2012 R2, failover clusters can scale up to 64 nodes. At this point, the manual method of updating software on failover clusters is simply no longer a practical option.

Instead, CAU automates the process of updating software for you. To initiate the process of updating a failover cluster, right-click the cluster in the list of servers in Server Manager and then click Update Cluster from the shortcut menu, as shown in Figure 1-25.

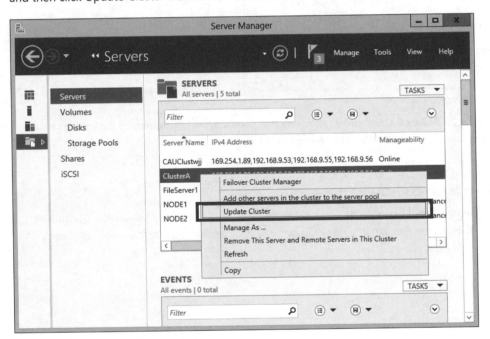

FIGURE 1-25 Manually updating a cluster

By default, only updates configured through Windows Update are performed. Updates are received as they normally would be, either directly from the Microsoft Update servers or through Windows Software Update Services (WSUS), depending on how Windows Update is configured. Beyond this default functionality, CAU can be extended through third-party plugins so that other software updates can also be performed.

The step just described shows how to trigger an update to a cluster manually, which might
be too straightforward a task to appear on the 70-412 exam. More likely, you could see a
question about configuring self-updates. You can access these self-update configuration
settings in Failover Cluster Manager by right-clicking the cluster name in the console
tree, pointing to More Actions, and then selecting Cluster-Aware Updating, as shown in
Figure 1-26.

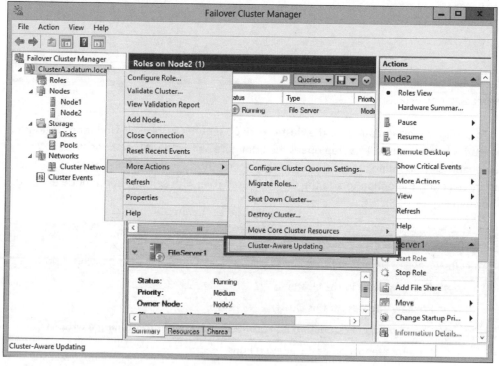

FIGURE 1-26 Opening CAU actions

This step opens the Cluster-Aware Updating dialog box, shown in Figure 1-27.

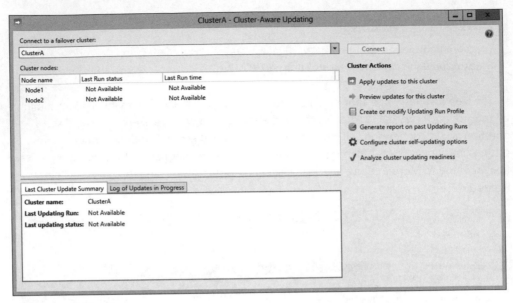

FIGURE 1-27 CAU actions

To configure self-updating for the cluster, click Configure Cluster Self-Updating Options beneath Cluster Actions. This step opens the Configure Self-Updating Options Wizard. You can enable self-updating on the cluster on the second (Add Clustered Role) page of the wizard by selecting the option to add the CAU clustered role, with self-updating mode enabled (shown in Figure 1-28).

IMPORTANT **ADMINISTRATIVE TASKS**

The Cluster-Aware Updating dialog box also allows you to perform the following actions:

- Apply updates to the cluster
- Preview updates for this cluster
- Create or modify Updating Run Profile directly (without running a wizard)
- Generate report on past Updating Runs
- Analyze cluster updating readiness

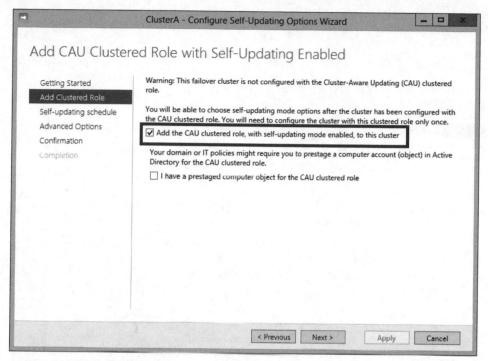

FIGURE 1-28 Enabling self-updating mode for Cluster-Aware Updating

The third (Self-Updating Schedule) page of the wizard lets you specify a schedule for updating. The fourth (Advanced Options) page lets you change profile options, as shown in Figure 1-29. These profile options let you set time boundaries for the update process and other advanced parameters.

> *MORE INFO* **PROFILE SETTINGS**
>
> For more information about profile settings for CAU, visit *http://technet.mlcrosoft.com/en-us/library/jj134224.aspx.*

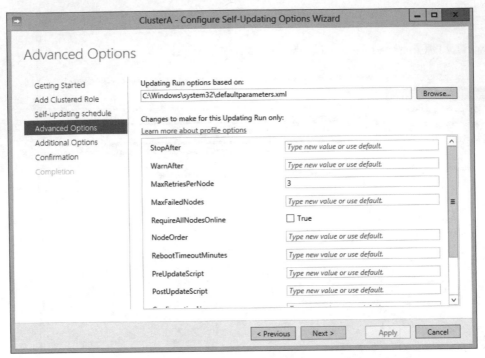

FIGURE 1-29 Configuring advanced options for Cluster-Aware Self-Updating

Migrating a failover cluster

Unlike with NLB, you can't perform a rolling upgrade to a failover cluster. The only way you can upgrade a failover cluster to Windows Server 2012 or Windows Server 2012 R2 is to create a new cluster with the new operating system and migrate the roles on the old cluster to it.

Fortunately, Windows Server 2012 and Windows Server 2012 R2 include a wizard to help you do that. By using the wizard, you create the new cluster, shut down the roles on the old cluster, and then use the wizard to pull the roles to the new cluster. To start the Migrate a Cluster Wizard, in Failover Cluster Manager, right-click the cluster icon in the console tree, click More Actions, and then click Migrate Roles as shown in Figure 1-30.

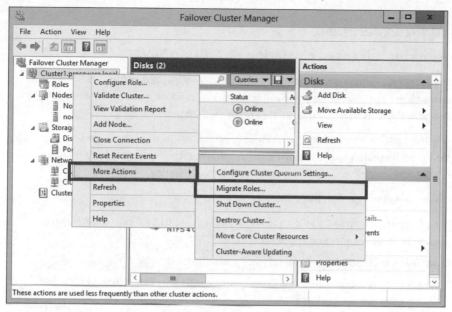

FIGURE 1-30 Configuring advanced options for Cluster-Aware Self-Updating

> **MORE INFO** **MIGRATING A CLUSTER**
>
> For more information about using the Migrate a Cluster Wizard to migrate a cluster to Windows Server 2012, see "How to Move Highly Available (Clustered) VMs to Windows Server 2012 with the Cluster Migration Wizard" at *http://blogs.msdn.com/b/clustering/archive/2012/06/25/10323434.aspx*.

Thought experiment

Configuring advanced clustering at Tailspin Toys

In the following thought experiment, apply what you've learned about this objective to predict what steps you need to take. You can find answers to these questions in the "Answers" section at the end of this chapter.

You are the systems administrator at tailspin toys. You are in the process of preparing a submission to the procurement committee for a seven-node Windows Server 2012 R2 cluster that will have the Hyper-V role installed.

You have the following objectives:

- Provide guest clusters hosted on the Windows Server 2012 R2 cluster with shared storage to store witness and application data.
- Avoid using iSCSI and Fibre Channel with guest clusters.
- Ensure that cluster updating occurs sequentially with only one cluster node applying software updates at a time.

With the preceding information in mind, answer the following questions.

1. Which Quorum model is appropriate for the cluster?
2. Which technology can you implement to ensure that software updates are applied to cluster host nodes sequentially?
3. What technology could you use to provide shared storage to guest clusters?

Objective summary

- A failover cluster is a group of servers configured in a special way that protects a selected service or application from failure. In the failover cluster, servers (called nodes) are connected to each other and to shared storage such as a SAN or a shared SAS disk array. When a service or application configured for high availability fails on one server, the service or application immediately starts up on another.
- You can create a basic failover cluster and test its functionality by using an empty role.
- In Windows Server 2012 and Windows Server 2012 R2, you can create storage pools for failover clusters. Cluster storage pools can be configured only from a shared SAS disk array.
- Cluster shared volumes (CSVs) are a new type of storage used only in some failover clusters. With CSVs, each node on a failover cluster creates its own virtual disk on the volume. The storage is then accessed through pathnames that are common to every node on the cluster.

- The Quorum configuration in a failover cluster determines how many nodes in a cluster can fail before the cluster stops running. In a basic configuration, a majority (more than 50 percent) of the nodes need to be active for the failover cluster to run. In a configuration with a witness disk or witness file share, only half of the nodes need to be active.

- Cluster Aware Updating (CAU) allows you to automate the process of updating Windows in a failover cluster.

- Shared virtual hard disk is a Windows Server 2012 R2 feature that allows a virtual hard disk file in .vhdx format to function as shared storage.

- Active Directory Detached Clusters are a Windows Server 2012 R2 feature that allows for cluster names to be stored in DNS and which do not require a computer object stored in Active Directory.

Objective review

Answer the following questions to test your knowledge of the information in this objective. You can find the answers to these questions and explanations of why each answer choice is correct or incorrect in the "Answers" section at the end of the chapter.

1. You are designing storage for a failover cluster on two servers running Windows Server 2012 R2. You want to provision disks for the cluster that will enable you to create a storage pool for it. Which of the following sets of physical disks could you use to create a storage pools for the failover cluster?

   A. Three individual disks in an iSCSI storage array without any RAID configuration

   B. Four disks in an iSCSI storage array configured as a RAID 5

   C. Three individual disks in a SAS storage array without any RAID configuration

   D. Four disks in a SAS storage array configured as a RAID 5

2. You are an IT administrator for Adatum.com. The Adatum.com network includes 50 servers and 750 clients. Forty of the servers are virtualized. To provide storage for all servers, the Adatum.com network uses an iSCSI-based SAN.

   You are designing storage for a new virtual machine hosted in a failover cluster. Your priorities for the storage are to simplify management of SAN storage and to minimize downtime in case of node failure.

   What should you do?

   A. Use Server Manager to create a storage pool

   B. Keep VM storage on a cluster shared volume

   C. Provision volumes from an external Serial Attached SCSI (SAS) disk array instead of the iSCSI SAN

   D. Assign a mirrored volume to the cluster

3. Your network includes an Active Directory domain named Contoso.com. You have purchased four servers that you plan to configure in a failover cluster. You want the failover cluster to run even if two of the nodes fail. What should you do?

   A. Adjust the Quorum configuration

   B. Configure the cluster storage from a storage pool

   C. Configure Cluster Aware Updating

   D. Add the cluster disks to cluster-shared volumes

Objective 1.3: Manage failover clustering roles

This objective covers the configuration of roles in failover clusters. To prepare for questions that fall within this objective, you need to understand how to add a role and configure role properties such as preferred owners, failover settings, and role startup priority. You also need to know how to manage a role through features such as node drain and VM monitoring.

> **This objective covers how to:**
> - Configure role-specific settings including continuously available shares
> - Configure VM monitoring
> - Configure failover and preference settings
> - Configure guest clustering

Configuring roles

To prepare a service or application for high availability in a failover cluster, you first have to install that service or application on all the failover cluster nodes. Then you can cluster the role by running the High Availability Wizard on one of the nodes. You can start this wizard by clicking Configure Role in the Actions pane of Failover Cluster Manager, as shown in Figure 1-31.

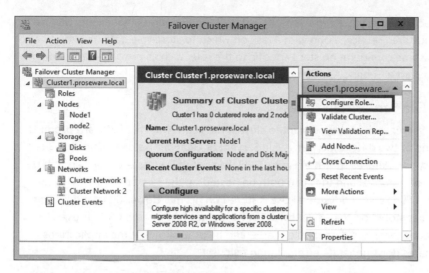

FIGURE 1-31 Configuring a service for failover

In the High Availability Wizard, you select the role that you want to configure for high availability, as shown in Figure 1-32.

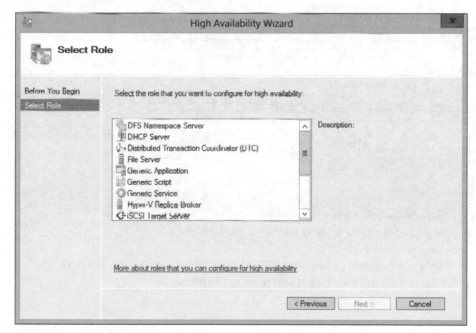

FIGURE 1-32 Selecting a role to be clustered

Other roles you can choose that are not shown in Figure 1-36 include Virtual Machine and WINS Server.

After you select the role, you need to specify a name and IP address that clients will use to connect to the clustered service, along with a disk on which to store role data. You might also have to perform some configuration steps specific to the role, such as providing a command-line command to start a Generic Application role.

Configuring File Server role types

If you select File Server as the role you want to cluster, the High Availability Wizard prompts you to choose one of two different types: A File Server For General Use or a Scale-Out File Server For Application Data, as shown in Figure 1-33. Each of these clustered file server types is used for different purposes and they can both be hosted on the same node at the same time. In general, a File Server For General Use is stored on normal cluster disks and is used to support user files stored on shares. A Scale-Out File Server is stored on CSVs, is used to support applications that store data on file shares, and helps ensure that the applications connecting to shares don't generate errors during failover.

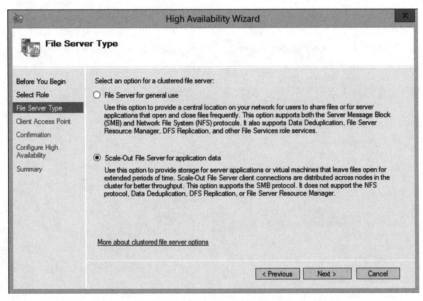

FIGURE 1-33 Selecting a Scale-Out File Server for the File Server role type

You will likely see a question or two on the 70-412 exam that tests basic knowledge about Scale-Out File Servers (SoFS). Here's what you need to remember:

- SoFS clusters are not designed for everyday user storage; they are designed for applications, such as SQL database applications, that store data on file shares and keep files open for extended periods of time.

- SoFS is highly unusual as a clustered role in that all nodes remain active at once. Client requests to connect to an SoFS cluster are distributed among all nodes in the cluster. For this reason, SoFS clusters can handle heavy workloads that increase proportionally to the number of nodes in the cluster.

- SoFS clusters use *only CSVs* for storage.

- SoFS clusters are not compatible with BranchCache, Data Deduplication, DFS Namespace servers, DFS Replication, or File Server Resource Manager.

EXAM TIP

Learn the limitations of SoFS well. Don't be tricked into selecting SoFS as the file server type for a new clustered file server just because the question states it will host application data. If the file server is also used with incompatible features (such as BranchCache, DFS, or File Server Resource Manager), or if no CSVs are available, you must choose File Server For General Use as the file server type.

MORE INFO SCALE-OUT FILE SERVERS

For more information about Scale-Out File Servers, visit *http://technet.microsoft.com/ en-us/library/hh831349.*

Configuring role properties

After you run the High Availability Wizard, the role you have clustered appears in the center pane of Failover Cluster Manager when the Roles icon is selected in the console tree. At this point, you can configure preferred owner and failback behavior by right-clicking the role and then selecting Properties. The General tab of the role properties, shown in Figure 1-34, enables you to designate one or more preferred owners of the service, in a specified order.

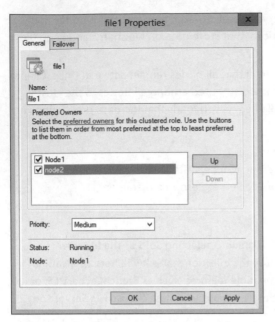

FIGURE 1-34 Configuring preferred owners for a role

Selecting the Failover tab reveals the configuration options shown in Figure 1-35. In the Failover (top) area of this tab, you can specify the maximum number of failures that you want to allow the failover cluster to sustain within a given time period. When the maximum number is exceeded, the service is left in the failed state. By default, a service is allowed to fail over only once every 6 hours.

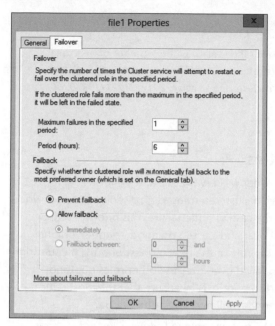

FIGURE 1-35 Configuring failover and failback settings for a role

In the Failover (top) area of this tab, you can specify the maximum number of failures that you want to allow the failover cluster to sustain within a given time period. When the maximum number is exceeded, the service is left in the failed state. By default, a service is allowed to fail over only once every 6 hours.

In the Failback (lower) area of this tab, you can choose whether you want a failed service to automatically be moved (fail back) to the most preferred owner or node available, the order of which you configure on the General tab of the service properties. If you choose to allow failback, you must specify the hours that failback is allowed according to a 24-hour clock. For example, if you want to allow failback only during business hours of 9 A.M. to 5 P.M., you should choose the Allow Failback option and then specify failback between 9 and 17 hours.

EXAM TIP

You need to understand the preferred owner, failover, and failback settings for the 70-412 exam. Note also that you can further tweak failover settings by specifying how many "heartbeat" (intra-cluster alive status) messages can be missed by a node before a role is failed over to another node. These failover settings are configured in Windows PowerShell, not in the GUI.

Assigning role startup priorities

Unlike previous versions of Windows Server, Windows Server 2012 and Windows Server 2012 R2 let you assign one of four startup priorities to clustered roles: High, Medium, Low, or No Auto Start. Medium is the default priority. In the case of node failure, this priority setting determines the order in which roles are failed over and started on another node. A higher priority role both fails over and starts before the role of the next highest priority. If you assign the No Auto Start priority to a role, the role is failed over after the other roles but is not started on the new node. The purpose of startup priority is to ensure that the most critical roles have prioritized access to resources when they fail over to another node.

To change the startup priority of a role, right-click the role in Failover Cluster Manager, point to Change Startup Priority, and select the desired priority, as shown in Figure 1-36.

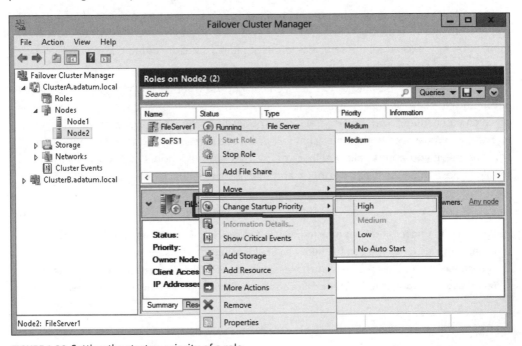

FIGURE 1-36 Setting the startup priority of a role

Role startup priority is a fairly easy feature to understand and is also likely to appear on the 70-412 exam. Be sure you remember the No Auto Start priority, especially because that's the only priority setting with a meaning that isn't made obvious by its name.

EXAM TIP

Make sure you understand the difference between startup priority settings and preferred owner settings. Startup priority settings determine which roles should be failed over and started after node failure. Preferred owner settings determine *which node*, if available, should handle the client requests for a role both before and after a node failure.

Using node drain

Node drain is a feature that simplifies the process of shutting a node down for maintenance. In previous versions of Windows, if you wanted to bring a node down for maintenance, you first needed to pause the node and then move all the clustered roles over to other nodes. With node drain, these two steps are combined into one.

To prepare a node to be shut down for maintenance in this way, first navigate to the Nodes container in the Failover Cluster Manager console tree. Then right-click the node you want to shut down in the details pane, point to Pause, and then select Drain Roles, as shown in Figure 1-37.

To achieve this same result by using Windows PowerShell, use the Suspend-ClusterNode cmdlet.

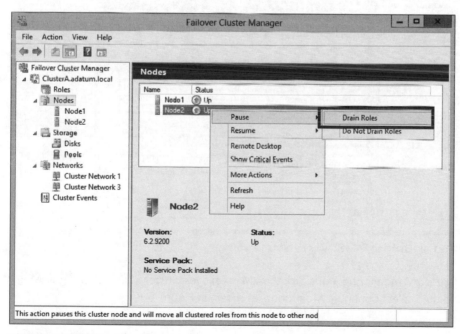

FIGURE 1-37 Draining roles from a node

Monitoring services on clustered virtual machines

Windows Server 2012 introduces the ability for a Hyper-V host to monitor the health of chosen services running on a clustered virtual machine (VM). If the Hyper-V host determines that a monitored service in a guest VM is in a critical state, the host is able to trigger a recovery. The Cluster Service first attempts to recover the VM by restarting it gracefully. Then, if the monitored service is still in a critical state after the VM has restarted, the Cluster Service fails the VM over to another node.

To monitor VM services with the VM Monitoring feature in Windows Server 2012 or Windows Server 2012 R2, the following requirements must be met:

- Both the Hyper-V host and its guest VM must be running Windows Server 2012 or Windows Server 2012 R2.

- The guest VM must belong to a domain that trusts the host's domain.

- The Failover Clustering feature must be installed on the Hyper-V host. The guest VM must also be configured as a role in a failover cluster on the Hyper-V host.

- The administrator connecting to the guest through Failover Cluster Manager must be a member of the local administrators group on that guest.

- All firewall rules in the Virtual Machine Monitoring group must be enabled on the guest, as shown in Figure 1-38.

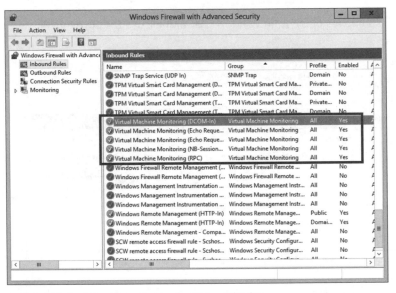

FIGURE 1-38 Enabling firewall rules for VM monitoring

To configure VM monitoring, right-click the VM in Failover Cluster Manager, point to More Actions, and then select Configure Monitoring, as shown in Figure 1-39.

FIGURE 1-39 Configuring monitoring of a VM application

In the Select Services dialog box that opens, select the services that you want to monitor, as shown in Figure 1-40.

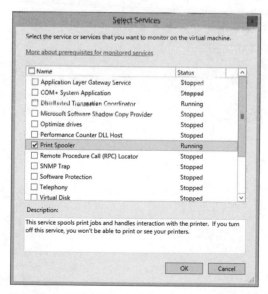

FIGURE 1-40 Selecting services to be monitored in a VM

By default, the recovery properties for a service are configured so that it will automatically attempt to restart the first and second time after it fails. After the third failure, however, the Cluster Service running in the Hyper-V host takes over recovery of the service if you have configured it to do so by selecting the service in the dialog box shown in Figure 1-41.

In some circumstances, you might want to redirect the Cluster Service recovery to a third-party application that allows you more control over the recovery process. In this case, you can disable the default behavior to restart and fail over the virtual machine.

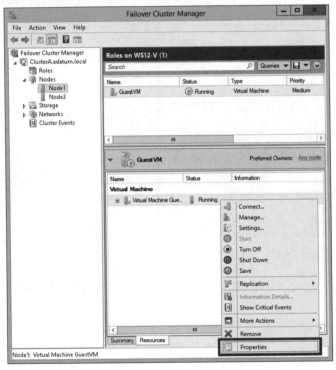

FIGURE 1-41 Modifying properties of a clustered VM

Then on the Settings tab of the properties dialog box shown in Figure 1-42, clear the Enable Automatic Recovery For Application Health Monitoring option. The Cluster Service will still log an error when a monitored service is in a critical state, but it will no longer attempt to restart or fail over the virtual machine.

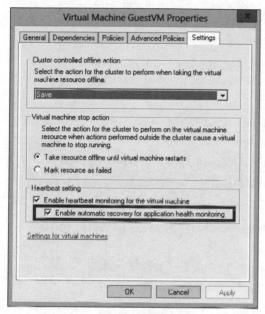

FIGURE 1-42 The setting to enable automatic recovery for a monitored VM application

Objective summary

- You use the High Availability Wizard to configure a clustered role.
- When you choose to configure a File Server role for clustering, you must choose a File Server For General Use or a Scale-Out File Server For Application Data. A File Server For General Use is typically used to support users who want to store files on file shares. A Scale-Out File Server can be used to ensure that an application that connects to a file share doesn't generate errors during failover. In addition, a Scale-Out File Server works on many live nodes at a time, so every additional node you add enables the cluster to handle more requests.
- Role properties you can configure include the preferred owners, which are the nodes listed in order of preference to which a role should be failed over, and failover settings, in which you can specify the maximum number of failures you want to allow the failover cluster to sustain within a given time period.

- With role startup priority, you can determine the order in which roles should be failed over from one node to the next in case of node failure.

- Windows Server 2012 and Windows Server 2012 R2 let you monitor the health of an application running in a VM configured as a clustered role. When a monitored application reaches a critical state, the host computer can trigger the VM to restart. If the application remains in a critical state after the system restart, the host computer will trigger failover to another node.

Objective review

Answer the following questions to test your knowledge of the information in this objective. You can find the answers to these questions and explanations of why each answer choice is correct or incorrect in the "Answers" section at the end of the chapter.

1. You work as a network administrator for Adatum.com. The Adatum.com network includes 25 servers running Windows Server 2012 R2 and 400 clients running Windows 8.1.

    You want to create a failover cluster to support a file share used by a resource-intensive application. Your priorities for the failover cluster are to prevent file-handling errors in the event of failover and to maintain high performance as the usage of the application grows. Which role and storage type should you configure for the failover cluster? (Choose two. Each answer represents part of the solution.)

    A. Configure as the role for the failover cluster a File Server for general use.

    B. Configure as the role for the failover cluster a Scale-Out File Server.

    C. Store the share on an NTFS volume provisioned from shared storage. Do not add the volume to Cluster-shared volumes.

    D. Store the share on a Cluster Shared Volume.

2. You work as a network administrator for Fourth Coffee, Inc. The Fourthcoffee.com network spans offices in five cities in Australia. All servers in the network are running Windows Server 2012 R2 and all clients are running Windows 8.1.

    You want to create a failover cluster to support a new file share that will be used by members of the marketing team in all branch offices. Your requirements for the failover cluster and the file share in general are to minimize downtime if a node fails, to minimize storage space needed for the share, to reduce or eliminate the possibility of file conflicts, and to minimize the amount of data transferred over WAN links.

    How should you configure the failover cluster and file server? (Choose all that apply.)

    A. Configure as the role for the failover cluster a File Server for general use.

    B. Configure as the role for the failover cluster a Scale-Out File Server.

    C. Enable Data Deduplication on the file share.

    D. Enable BranchCache on the file share.

3. You want to create a two-node failover cluster to provide high availability for a virtual machine. The virtual machine will host an important line-of-business (LOB) application used often by members of your organization throughout the day. You want to configure VM monitoring of the application so that the virtual machine will restart if the application is found to be in a critical state and will fail over to the other node if the application still is in a critical state after the system restart.

   Which of the following is *not* a requirement of meeting this goal?

   A. The host Hyper-V server needs to be running Windows Server 2012 or Windows Server 2012 R2.

   B. The guest VM needs to be running Windows Server 2012 or Windows Server 2012 R2.

   C. The host and the guest need to be members of the same domain.

   D. The guest VM needs to have enabled the firewall rules in the Virtual Machine Monitoring group.

4. You have configured high availability for a cluster-aware application named Prose-WareApp in a 2-node failover cluster named Cluster1. The physical nodes in Cluster1 are named Node1 and Node2; they are both running Hyper-V in Windows Server 2012 R2. Node1 is currently the active node for ProseWareApp.

   You want to configure Cluster1 to perform critical Windows Updates with a minimum of administrative effort and a minimum of downtime for ProseWareApp users. What should you do?

   A. Drain the roles on Node1 and then start Windows Update on Node1.

   B. In Server Manager on Node1, right-click Cluster1 and select Update Cluster.

   C. Configure Cluster-Aware Updating to add the CAU clustered role to Cluster1 with self-updating mode enabled.

   D. Configure Task Scheduler to run Windows Update daily on Node1 outside of business hours.

Objective 1.4: Manage virtual machine (VM) movement

Windows Server 2012 and Windows Server 2012 R2 allow you to move virtual machines from one Hyper-V host to another, both inside and outside of clustered environments. To prepare for the questions you will see in this objective on the 70-412 exam, you need to understand the differences among the various VM migration types, how to configure Hyper-V hosts for these different types of VM migration, and how to perform these different migrations.

This objective covers how to:

- Perform live migration
- Perform quick migration
- Perform storage migration
- Import, export, and copy VMs
- Configure virtual machine network health protection
- Configure drain on shutdown

Performing a live migration

Live migration is a feature that first appeared in Windows Server 2008 R2. Live migration lets you move a running VM from one Hyper-V host to another without any downtime. Originally, this feature was available only for VMs hosted in failover clusters, but in Windows Server 2012, you can now perform live migration of a VM outside of a clustered environment. However, the process of performing live migration is different inside and outside of clusters, and each of these live migration types has slightly different requirements.

Live migration requires a few configuration steps that you need to understand for the exam. To start configuring this feature, open Hyper-V Settings for each Hyper-V host, as shown in Figure 1-43.

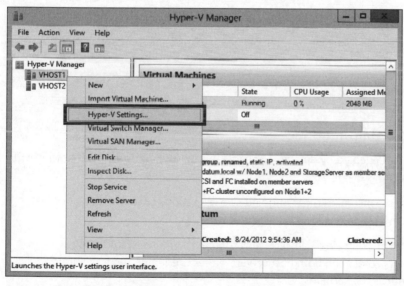

FIGURE 1-43 Configuring Hyper-V settings

In the Hyper-V Settings dialog box that opens, click Live Migrations on the menu on the left. The associated live migration settings are shown in Figure 1-44.

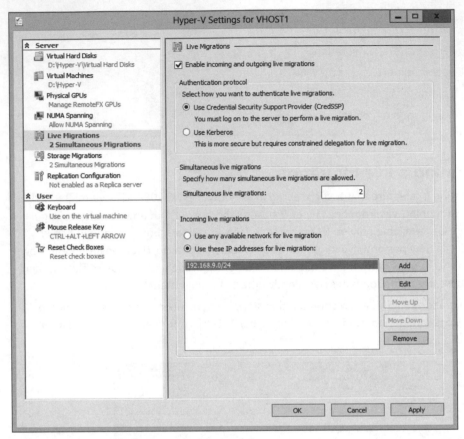

FIGURE 1-44 Live migration settings

Preparing for live migration

Live migrations are not enabled by default. To enable this feature, perform the following four configuration steps in this dialog box:

1. Select the Enable Incoming And Outgoing Live Migrations check box for both the source and destination hosts.

2. For live migrations outside of clustered environments, you need to choose an authentication protocol on both host servers: either Credential Security Support Provider (CredSSP) or Kerberos.

   - **CredSSP** The advantage of this choice is that it requires no configuration. The limitation of choosing CredSSP as the authentication protocol, however, is that you need to be logged on to the source computer when you perform a live migration. You can't perform live migrations through Hyper-V Manager on a remote computer.

- **Kerberos** The advantage of choosing Kerberos as the authentication protocol is that you don't need to be logged on to a source computer to perform the live migration. The disadvantage of using Kerberos as the authentication protocol for live migrations is that it requires configuration. Specifically, aside from selecting Kerberos in Hyper-V Settings, you need to adjust the properties of the source and destination computer accounts in Active Directory Users and Computers, on the Delegation tab. On each computer account, select the option to trust this computer for delegation, specify the opposite server, and then specify two service types: CIFS and Microsoft Virtual System Migration Service. The actual configuration required is shown in Figure 1-45. Note that this configuration step is also known as configuring *constrained delegation*. Expect to see a question about configuring constrained delegation on the 70-412 exam.

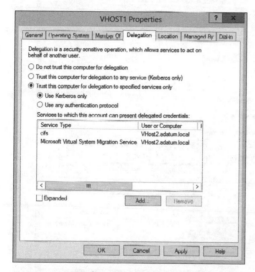

FIGURE 1-45 Configuring constrained delegation

3. Set a value for the maximum number of simultaneous live migrations you want to allow on the network. This is a new feature of Windows Server 2012. In Windows Server 2008 R2, you were limited to one live migration at a time. (In the real world, you can estimate 500 Mbps of network bandwidth required per individual live migration. In a Gigabit Ethernet network, you can safely leave the default value of 2.)

4. Add a list of subnets or individual IP addresses from which you want to allow live migrations. Live migration does not provide data encryption of VMs and storage as they are moved across the network, so security is an important consideration. Do not leave the default selection to use any available network for live migration unless you are in a testing environment.

Although CSVs are not required for VM storage when you perform live migration in a failover cluster, CSVs are nonetheless highly recommended. If the VM is not already stored in a CSV, you should move it there to prepare for clustered live migration.

Moving VM storage to a CSV

To move VM storage to a CSV, right-click the VM in Failover Cluster Manager, point to Move, and then click Virtual Machine Storage, as shown in Figure 1-46.

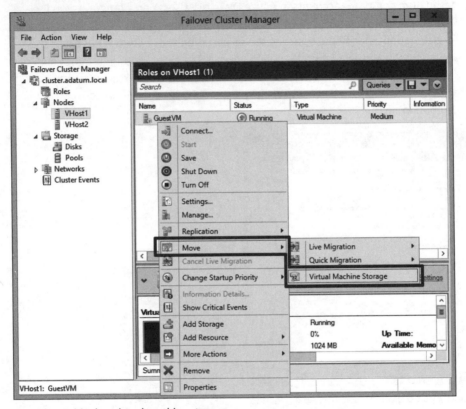

FIGURE 1-46 Moving virtual machine storage

Then, in the Move Virtual Machine Storage dialog box that opens, shown in Figure 1-47, select the VM in the top pane and drag it to a CSV folder in the bottom-left pane. Click Start to begin the copy operation.

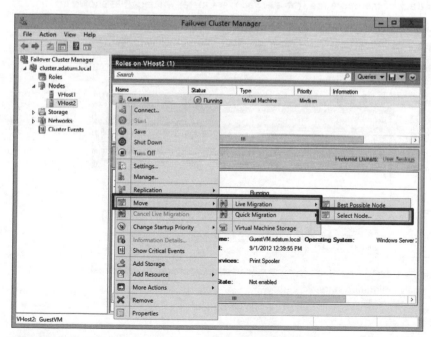

Move Virtual Machine Storage

In the upper pane, select a virtual machine or specific files on a virtual machine, then drag and drop them into a folder in the lower pane. Review the upper pane to confirm that the Destination Folder Path is correct. Then click Start.

Copy

File Type	Source Folder Path	Destination Folder Path
⊟ Virtual Machine GuestVM		
SERVER13.VHDX	D:\Hyper-V\GuestVM\Virtual Hard Disks	
Snapshots	D:\Hyper-V\GuestVM	
Second level paging	D:\Hyper-V\GuestVM	
Current configuration	D:\Hyper-V\GuestVM	

Add Share ✖ Remove share ☞ Open ☐ Paste ✖ Delete

◢ Cluster Storage	Name	Size
▷ Volume1		

Start   Cancel

FIGURE 1-47 Moving VM storage to a CSV

After the transfer is complete, you can perform a live migration as long as the Hyper-V environments are the same on the source and destination nodes, including the names of virtual switches in both locations. To perform the live migration, in Failover Cluster Manager, right-click the clustered VM, point to Move, point to Live Migration, and then click Select Node from the shortcut menu, as shown in Figure 1-48.

FIGURE 1-48 Performing a live migration in a failover cluster

In the Move Virtual Machine dialog box that opens, shown in Figure 1-49, select the destination node in the failover cluster to which you want to transfer the running VM and click OK to start the process.

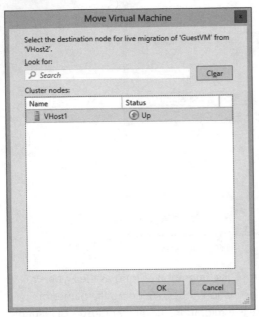

FIGURE 1-49 Selecting a destination node for live migration

You can keep track of the migration status in Failover Cluster Manager, as shown in Figure 1-49.

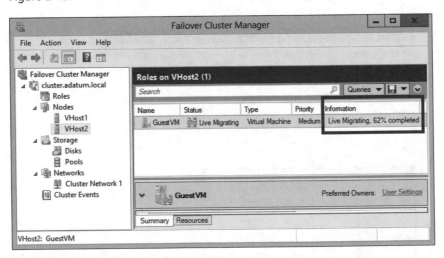

FIGURE 1-50 Viewing live migration status

During and after migration, the VM continues to operate without interruption.

Performing live migration outside a clustered environment

Nonclustered live migration is a new feature in Windows Server 2012 in which you can move a running VM from one Hyper-V host to another, with no downtime, outside of a clustered environment. The feature does require that the source and destination Hyper-V hosts belong to domains that trust each other. However, it doesn't require SAN storage or a clustered environment. It's also worth noting that a disadvantage of nonclustered live migration, compared to clustered live migration, is that the process takes much longer because all files are copied from the source to the destination host. (An exception to this rule is if the VM and its storage are kept on a file share and do not need to be copied from one host to the other during the migration process.)

After you have configured live migration settings in Hyper-V Manager on the source and destination computers, you can perform the live migration. It's a simple procedure. In Hyper-V Manager, right-click the running VM you want to live migrate and select Move from the shortcut menu, as shown in Figure 1-51.

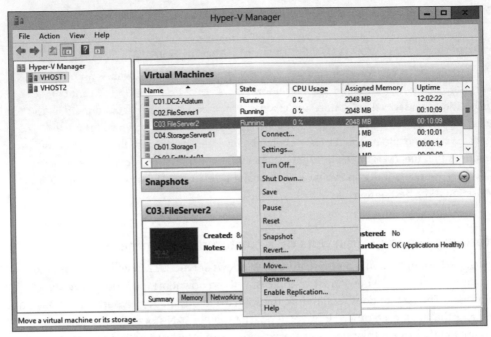

FIGURE 1-51 Initiating a live migration outside of a clustered environment

In the wizard that opens, select the Move The Virtual Machine option, as shown in Figure 1-52.

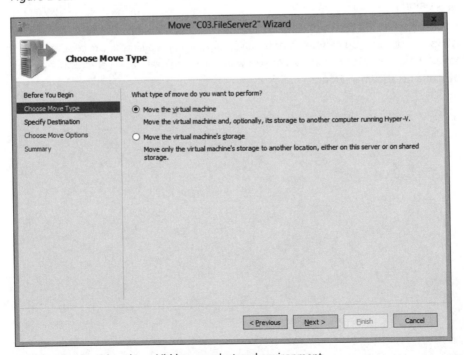

FIGURE 1-52 Live migrating a VM in a nonclustered environment

Then, specify the destination server, as shown in Figure 1-53.

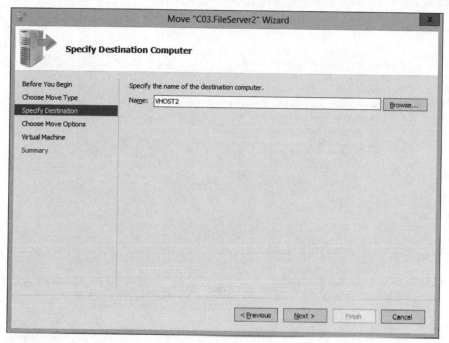

FIGURE 1-53 Choosing a destination host for live migration in a nonclustered environment

You have three options for how you want to move the VM's items when you perform the live migration, as shown in Figure 1-54. First, you can move all of the VM's files and storage to a single folder on the destination computer. Next, you can choose to move different items to different folders in a particular way that you specify. Finally, you can migrate just the VM while leaving the storage in place. Note that this option requires the VM storage to reside on shared storage such as an iSCSI target, a fact that could easily serve as the basis for an incorrect answer choice on a test question.

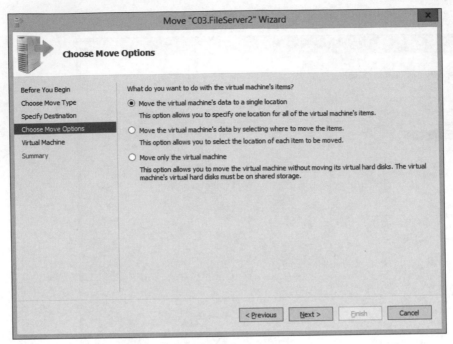

FIGURE 1-54 Moving a VM to a single destination folder

Additional migration considerations

When planning virtual machine migrations, there are additional factors to take into account; these factors determine whether the migration occurs successfully or whether it stalls, leaving the virtual machine on the original host.

Enabling processor compatibility

One potential problem that can arise when you perform a live or quick migration is that the processor on the destination Hyper-V host supports different features than does the processor on the source host. In this case, you might receive the error message shown in Figure 1-55 and the migration fails. (A failed migration does not negatively affect the running VM. The result of the failure is simply that the VM is left running on the source computer.)

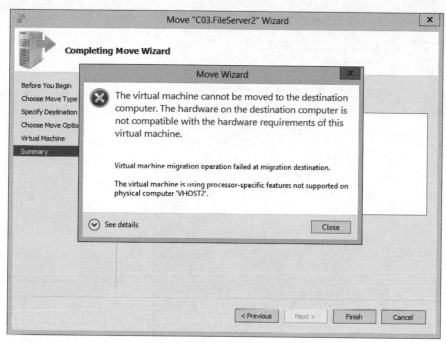

FIGURE 1-55 An error indicating processor feature incompatibility

Neither live migration nor quick migration is supported between hosts with processors from different manufacturers. However, if the processors on the source and destination computers are from the same manufacturer and are found to support incompatible features, you have the option of limiting the virtual processor features on the VM as a way to maximize compatibility and improve the chances that the migration will succeed. (Again: This setting does not provide compatibility between different processor manufacturers.)

To enable processor compatibility, expand the Processor settings in the VM's settings dialog box and select the Compatibility node, as shown in Figure 1-56. Then select the Migrate To A Physical Computer With A Different Processor Version check box. Alternatively, you can run the following command at a Windows PowerShell prompt:

```
Set-VMProcessor VMname -CompatibilityForMigrationEnabled $true
```

It's worth noting that this setting is unusually easy to construct a test question around. If you see a question about live migration in which you receive an error indicating trouble related to processor-specific features, you now know how to handle it: Just enable the processor compatibility setting.

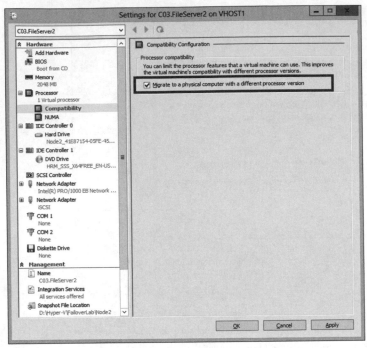

FIGURE 1-56 Enabling processor compatibility for migration

EXAM TIP

Look for questions in which you have to migrate a VM between servers and the fact that the source and destination hosts have different processor manufacturers is buried somewhere in the middle of a table or list. When the processor manufacturers are different, your best option for migration is to manually export it from the source machine and import it on the destination machine. You can't use live migration or quick migration.

Matching names of virtual switches

Another common problem that can occur when you attempt to perform a live migration is that the destination Hyper-V environment doesn't provide virtual switches with names that exactly match those in the Hyper-V environment on the source computer. This problem is detected as you complete the Move Wizard. For each snapshot of the source VM that defines a virtual switch without an exact equivalent on the destination Hyper-V host, you are given an opportunity to choose another virtual switch on the destination that the VM should use in place of the original. This step is shown in Figure 10-57.

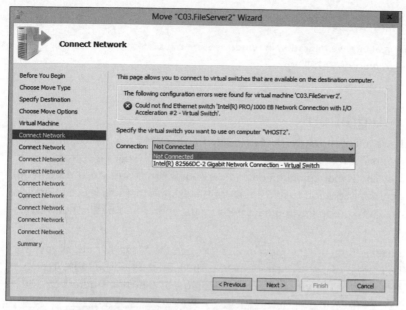

FIGURE 1-57 Matching a virtual switch on a destination host for live migration

After you make the required substitutions, the wizard begins the live migration when you click Finish on the final page, as shown in Figure 1-58.

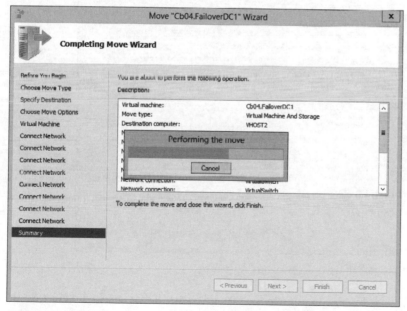

FIGURE 1-58 A live migration in progress in a nonclustered environment

Using storage migration

Storage migration allows you to move the data associated with a VM from one volume to another while the VM remains running. This option is useful if storage space is scarce on one volume or storage array and is more plentiful on another source of storage. An important advantage of storage-only live migration to remember for the exam is that unlike live migration, it can be performed in a workgroup environment because the source and destination servers are the same.

To perform storage migration, use the Move option to open the Move Wizard, as you would do to begin the process of live-migrating the VM. Then, on the Choose Move Type page of the wizard, select Move The Virtual Machine's Storage, as shown in Figure 1-59.

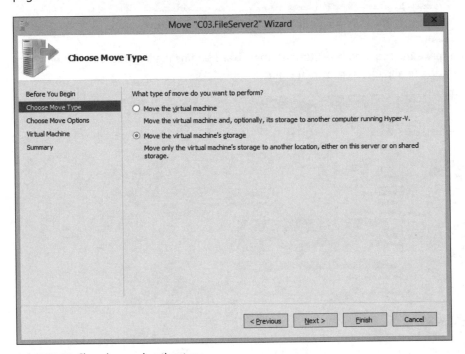

FIGURE 1-59 Choosing a migration type

You have three options for how to migrate the storage of the VM, as shown in Figure 1-60. The first option is to move all storage to a single folder on the destination volume.

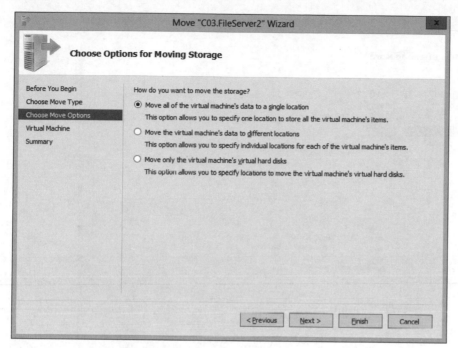

FIGURE 1-60 Moving storage to a single folder

The second option allows you to select which particular storage items you want to migrate, such as snapshot data or the smart paging folder, as shown in Figure 1-61. The third and final option allows you to specify particular VHDs to migrate only.

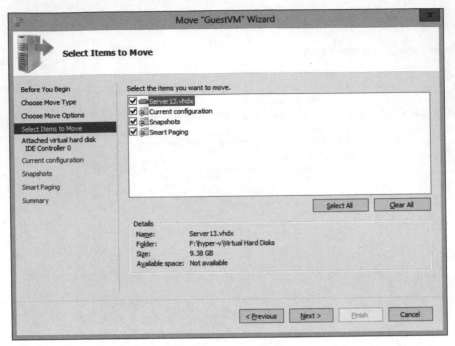

FIGURE 1-61 Selecting VM items to migrate to a new volume

For the exam, the most important fact to remember about storage migration is that this feature provides an option that is often the best way to solve a problem. If space runs out for a running VM, it's not necessarily a good idea to migrate that VM to another server. No other server might be available, for example, and you might want to spare your organization the unnecessary expense of buying a new one. In this case, it's often more prudent simply to attach a new disk array to the server and move the VM storage to this newly available space.

> **MORE INFO   LIVE MIGRATION AND STORAGE MIGRATION**
>
> For a good review of Live Migration and Storage Migration, see the TechEd Australia session on the topic at *http://channel9.msdn.com/Events/TechEd/Australia/2012/VIR314*.

Configuring virtual machine network health protection

Network health protection allows you to configure a virtual machine so that if its connection to an external network configured for protection is lost, the virtual machine is automatically live-migrated to a new host where that protected external virtual network is available. For example, if the network adapter connecting a virtual machine to the Internet fails and the external virtual network associated with that adapter is configured as protected, then the virtual machine will automatically live-migrate to a host where the external virtual network still retains connectivity. Network health protection requires multiple network paths between cluster nodes. This feature is new to Windows Server 2012 R2 and is not available in Windows Server 2012.

Configuring drain on shutdown

Drain on shutdown is a feature new to Windows Server 2012 R2 that ensures that virtual machine workloads are automatically migrated off a cluster node if the cluster node is shut down without being put into maintenance mode. Best practice is still to ensure that the node is put into maintenance mode before shut down; this feature will simply migrate workloads away from the node if you forget to take this step before initiating a shutdown or restart. This feature is not available to Hyper-V host cluster nodes running Windows Server 2012.

Thought experiment
Configuring high availability at Proseware

In this thought experiment, apply what you've learned about this objective. You can find answers to these questions in the "Answers" section at the end of this chapter.

You are a network administrator for Proseware.com, a software company with offices in several cities. You are designing high availability for certain applications and services at the Philadelphia branch office. You have the following goals:

- You want to ensure that two domain controllers from the Proseware.com domain remain online with high availability in the Philadelphia branch office, even if one server experiences a catastrophic failure or is brought down for maintenance. (The domain controllers will not host any operations master roles.)

- You want to ensure that a heavily used LOB application can withstand the failure of one server without experiencing any downtime or file-handling errors, even during failover. The LOB application is not cluster-aware. It also frequently reads and writes data stored on a network share.

With these details in mind, answer the following questions.

1. How many physical servers will you need to support your requirements, at a minimum?

2. How can you best provide high availability for file sharing?

3. How can you best provide high availability for the LOB application?

4. Which of your goals requires Windows Server 2012, as opposed to an earlier version of Windows Server?

Objective summary

- Live migration is a feature in which a running VM is transferred from one host computer to another without any downtime. In Windows Server 2012, live migration can be performed inside or outside a failover cluster, but live migration within a failover cluster is much faster.

- When configuring servers for live migration outside of a failover cluster, you must choose an authentication protocol, CredSSP or Kerberos. CredSSP needs no configuration, but it requires you to trigger the live migration while logged in to the source host. Kerberos allows you to trigger the live migration from a remote host, but it requires you to configure constrained delegation for the source and destination hosts.

- Windows Server 2012 introduced storage migration for VMs. With storage migration, you can move all of the storage associated with a running VM from one disk to another without any downtime.

- Virtual machine network health protection is a Windows Server 2012 R2 feature that ensures that a virtual machine will migrate to a host where an external virtual network is available if the current host loses connectivity to that external virtual network.

- Virtual machine drain on shutdown is a Windows Server 2012 R2 feature that will automatically migrate virtual machines away from a Hyper-V host cluster node if the node is shut down or restarted without being put into maintenance mode.

Objective review

Answer the following questions to test your knowledge of the information in this objective. You can find the answers to these questions and explanations of why each answer choice is correct or incorrect in the "Answers" section at the end of the chapter.

1. You are a network administrator for Contoso.com. You have recently upgraded all of your servers to Windows Server 2012 R2. Your manager has indicated that he wants to start testing the live migration feature in a nonclustered environment so that you can eventually take advantage of this functionality in production.

    You create a small test network consisting of two Hyper-V servers running Windows Server 2012 R2 named Host1 and Host2. The hardware and software settings on these two physical servers exactly match those of two physical servers in your production network. Host1 is currently hosting a guest VM named VM1.

    You enable live migration on both servers and configure CredSSP as the authentication protocol. You then log on locally to Host1 and initiate a live migration of VM1 from Host1 to Host2. You receive an error message indicating that the VM is using processor-specific features not supported on the destination physical computer.

You want to perform a live migration successfully in your test network so that you will know what is required to use this feature successfully in production. What should you do?

A. Configure constrained delegation for Host1 and Host2.

B. Disable VM monitoring on VM1.

C. Configure Kerberos as the authentication protocol on Host1 and Host2.

D. On Host1, run the following command:

```
Set-VMProcessor VM1 -CompatibilityForMigrationEnabled $true
```

2. You are a network administrator for Adatum.com. You have recently upgraded all of your servers to Windows Server 2012 R2. Your manager has indicated that she wants to start testing the live migration feature so that you can eventually take advantage of this functionality in production.

You create a small test network consisting of two Hyper-V servers running Windows Server 2012 R2 named VHost1 and VHost2. The hardware and software settings on these two physical servers exactly match those of two physical servers in your production network. VHost2 is currently hosting a guest VM named VM2.

You enable live migration on both servers and configure Kerberos as the authentication protocol. You then log on locally to Host1 and initiate a live migration of VM1 from VHost2 to VHost1. The live migration fails, and you receive an error indicating "No credentials are available in the security package."

You want to perform a live migration successfully in your test network so that you will know what is required to use this feature successfully in production. You also want to initiate live migrations when you are not logged on to the source host server. What should you do next?

A. Configure constrained delegation for VHost1 and VHost2.

B. Disable VM monitoring on VM2.

C. Configure CredSSP as the authentication protocol on VHost1 and VHost2.

D. On VHost1, run the following command:

```
Set-VMProcessor VM2 -CompatibilityForMigrationEnabled $true
```

3. You are a network administrator for Proseware.com. One of your servers is named HV1 and is running Windows Server 2012 R2 with the Hyper-V role. HV1 is hosting 10 virtual machines on locally attached storage. It is not a member of any domain.

   The available storage used by the 10 guest VMs on HV1 is close to being depleted. At the current rate of growth, the current physical disks attached to HV1 will run out of space in three months.

   You want to provide more space to your guest VMs. How can you solve the storage problem with a minimum financial expense and minimum impact on users?

   A. Perform a quick migration of the VMs on HV1 to a new server with more space.

   B. Perform a live migration of the VMs on HV1 to a new server with more space.

   C. Perform a storage migration of the VMs on HV1 to a new storage array with ample storage space.

   D. Attach a new storage array with ample storage space to HV1 and expand the VHD files used by the guest VMs.

Answers

This section contains the solutions to the "Thought experiments" and the "Objective review" questions in this chapter.

Objective 1.1: Thought experiment

1. You can make the IIS server highly available by deploying Network Load Balancing.

2. You use the drainstop function to ensure that connections to the highly available servers are terminated gracefully.

3. You would configure multiple host filtering with single affinity to accomplish the goal of ensuring that a client is directed to the same node for the duration of its session.

Objective 1.1: Review

1. **Correct Answer:** A

   A. **Correct:** The Affinity-None setting improves load balancing by increasing the likelihood that the server workload will be distributed equitably among all nodes in the NLB cluster. By default, the Affinity-Single setting is enabled, which returns clients to the same node in an NLB cluster on subsequent visits. If some clients connect to the NLB cluster much more often than others, the distribution of the workload can be very uneven by default. Enabling the Affinity-None setting ensures that each client can connect to different NLB nodes on subsequent visits.

   B. **Incorrect:** The question states that port rule settings have not been modified from the defaults. The Affinity-Single setting is enabled by default, so enabling this setting will have no effect. In addition, Affinity-Single generally does not improve load balancing.

   C. **Incorrect:** The Affinity-Network setting ensures that all client requests originating from the same /24 network address are handled by the same node in the NLB cluster. This setting generally does not improve load balancing.

   D. **Incorrect:** The Load Weight setting allows you to configure a node to handle a disproportionate number of incoming client requests. This setting is useful if one NLB host is much more or less powerful than the average host in the NLB cluster. By default, the Load Weight setting ensures that each node will be weighted equally, so if the default settings have not been modified, Affinity settings and not Load Weight settings are very likely responsible for the uneven distribution of client requests among NLB nodes.

2. **Correct Answer:** D

   A. **Incorrect:** The Load Weight setting allows you to configure a specific node to handle a disproportionate number of client requests for the service hosted in the NLB cluster. It would not reduce the likelihood that items will disappear from users' shopping carts.

   B. **Incorrect:** Single Host filtering mode eliminates load balancing for a specific type of traffic defined in a port rule and directs all client requests for that service toward a single host in the NLB cluster. Enabling this setting would not reduce the likelihood that items will disappear from users' shopping carts.

   C. **Incorrect:** Multiple Host filtering mode enables load balancing for a specific type of traffic defined in a port rule. This mode is enabled by default in a new port rule. Re-enabling Multiple Host filtering mode would not reduce the likelihood that items will disappear from users' shopping carts.

   D. **Correct:** Timeout settings extend affinity between a client and NLB node during periods of convergence, which occurs after a node is added to or removed from an NLB cluster. Without enabling and configuring the Timeout setting, a user can have his session redirected to another NLB node after convergence and lose any items he or she has placed in a shopping cart. The value you configure for Timeout determines the number of minutes that a client will retain affinity with a specific node during and after convergence and be able to retain items in the cart.

3. **Correct Answer:** C

   A. **Incorrect:** Load weight affects only traffic that is caught by a port rule. It allows you to configure a specific node to handle a disproportionate number of client requests for the service hosted in the NLB cluster.

   B. **Incorrect:** Single Host filtering mode is a setting in a port rule that applies only to traffic caught by that port rule. Single Host filtering mode avoids load balancing for the traffic and directs all client requests for that traffic toward a single host in the NLB cluster.

   C. **Correct:** Host priority settings apply to the entire NLB cluster. They determine which host in the cluster will receive traffic not caught by any port rule.

   D. **Incorrect:** The Handling priority is set for a particular port rule and affects traffic caught by that port rule. The Handling priority determines which host will handle traffic for which Single Host filtering mode is enabled.

Objective 1.2: Thought experiment

1. Node majority is appropriate given that there is an odd number of cluster nodes.

2. Cluster Aware Updating (CAU) will ensure that updates are applied to cluster host nodes sequentially.

3. You can use shared virtual hard disks to provide shared storage to guest clusters without using iSCSI or Fibre Channel.

Objective 1.2: Review

1. **Correct Answer:** C

A. **Incorrect:** A cluster storage pool can only be created from SAS disks.

B. **Incorrect:** A cluster storage pool can only be created from SAS disks. In addition, a cluster storage pool is incompatible with external RAIDs.

C. **Correct:** To create a cluster storage pool, you need three independent SAS disks that are not configured with any RAID or governed by any disk subsystem.

D. **Incorrect:** You cannot create a cluster storage pool from disks that are configured as part of a RAID or governed by any disk subsystem.

2. **Correct Answer:** B

A. **Incorrect:** Creating a storage pool by itself might simplify management of SAN storage, but it won't minimize downtime in case of node failure. In addition, the SAN storage cannot be configured as a storage pool for the cluster because it is iSCSI based. Only SAS storage can be used for a cluster storage pool.

B. **Correct:** Keeping VM storage on a cluster shared volume (CSV) will optimize live migration of the VM in case of node failure and minimize downtime. Cluster-shared volumes will also simplify management of SAN storage by allowing multiple failover cluster nodes to share LUNs.

C. **Incorrect:** If you provision volumes from a SAS array, you will later be able to create a storage pool for the cluster, which might simplify management of storage. However, using a SAS array will not minimize downtime in case of node failure.

D. **Incorrect:** Assigning a mirrored volume to the cluster might prevent node failure if one disk fails, but it will not minimize downtime if a node does fail. In addition, it will not simplify management of SAN storage.

3. **Correct Answer:** A

A. **Correct:** You can adjust the Quorum configuration to include a witness. A disk or file share witness will enable the cluster to run without a clear majority of active nodes.

B. **Incorrect:** A storage pool will not affect how the many nodes need to remain active for the cluster to run.

C. **Incorrect:** Cluster-aware updating (CAU) does not affect how many nodes need to remain active for the cluster to run.

D. **Incorrect:** Cluster-shared volumes (CSVs) do not affect how many nodes need to remain active for the cluster to run.

Objective 1.3: Thought experiment

1. Scale out file servers use cluster-shared volumes (CSVs) for storage

2. You would configure a File Server For General Use as the file server type as the DFS workload is not supported on a Scale Out File Server

3. Configure SYD-HA-1 as the clustered application's preferred owner

Objective 1.3: Review

1. **Correct Answers:** B, D

   A. **Incorrect:** A traditional file server for general use is best suited for users, not resource-intensive applications. In addition, a traditional file server would not easily allow you to handle an increased load as the usage of the file share increased.

   B. **Correct:** A Scale-Out File Server allows an application to maintain file handles even during failover, which minimizes application errors. In addition, an SoFS allows you to keep all nodes active and to add additional nodes as needed to handle an increased load.

   C. **Incorrect:** A Scale-Out File Server requires CSV storage. Choosing this storage type would not allow you to meet your requirements or reducing errors and maintaining high performance.

   D. **Correct:** A Scale-Out File Server requires CSV storage.

2. **Correct Answers:** A, C, D

   A. **Correct:** A File Server for general use is the more suitable role to provide high availability for a file share that users (as opposed to applications) will use for file storage. In addition, only the File Server role is compatible with Data Deduplication and BranchCache.

   B. **Incorrect:** An SoFS is not compatible with Data Deduplication or BranchCache, two features that will help you meet your requirements for the share.

   C. **Correct:** Data Deduplication will help minimize storage space requirements.

   D. **Correct:** BranchCache will minimize the amount of data transferred over WAN links and prevent file conflicts.

3. **Correct Answer:** C

   A. **Incorrect:** VM monitoring does indeed require Windows Server 2012 to be running on the host Hyper-V server and failover cluster node.

   B. **Incorrect:** VM monitoring requires Windows Server 2012 to be running on the clustered VM.

   C. **Correct:** The host and guest do not need to be members of the same domain. However, the two domains need to trust each other.

   D. **Incorrect:** The firewall rules in the Virtual Machine Monitoring group do need to be enabled on the clustered VM.

4. **Correct Answer:** C

   A. Incorrect: This solution performs updates once on Node1 only, not the entire cluster.

   B. Incorrect: This solution updates the cluster only once. It doesn't minimize administrative effort because you would need to do it repeatedly.

   C. Correct: This solution configures Cluster1 to perform Windows Updates automatically and regularly on both nodes in the cluster.

   D. Incorrect: This solution performs updates only on Node1, not the entire cluster.

Objective 1.4: Thought experiment

1. Three. You need to have two highly available domain controllers even after one server is brought down. You can provide high availability for all workloads on those three servers.

2. Use an SoFS with CSVs so that the LOB application can remain connected to files even during failover.

3. You should host the LOB application in a highly available VM because the application itself isn't cluster-aware.

4. A virtualized domain controller is not recommended in older versions of Windows Server. In addition, an SoFS is available only in Windows Server 2012.

Objective 1.4: Review

1. **Correct Answer:** D

   A. Incorrect: Constrained delegation is required for Kerberos authentication. You have configured CredSSP as the authentication protocol. In addition, you have received an error related to processor compatibility, not authentication.

   B. Incorrect: VM monitoring isn't incompatible with live migration, so it wouldn't generate an error such as this one.

   C. Incorrect: There is no reason to change the authentication protocol to Kerberos under these circumstances. CredSSP allows you to initiate a live migration when you are logged on locally to the source host.

   D. Correct: If you enabled processor compatibility on the VM, the virtual processor will use only the features of the processor that are available on all versions of a virtualization-capable processor by the same processor manufacturer. You would see the error described if each host server used a different processor from the same manufacturer.

2. **Correct Answer:** A

   A. **Correct:** When you choose Kerberos as the authentication protocol, you need to configure constrained delegation on the computer accounts for the source and destination computers.

   B. **Incorrect:** VM monitoring is not incompatible with live migration and would not generate an error such as the one described.

   C. **Incorrect:** CredSSP as an authentication protocol would not enable you to initiate live migrations when you are not logged on to the source host server.

   D. **Incorrect:** The error received was not related to processor compatibility, so this step would not fix the problem.

3. **Correct Answer:** C

   A. **Incorrect:** A quick migration is possible only in a failover cluster environment. In addition, purchasing a new server with ample new storage is unnecessarily costly compared to purchasing only new storage.

   B. **Incorrect:** You cannot perform a live migration from a computer outside of a domain environment. In addition, purchasing a new server with ample new storage is unnecessarily costly compared to purchasing only new storage.

   C. **Correct:** This option avoids the unnecessary expense of purchasing a new server and lets you transfer storage to the new storage array live, without taking your VMs offline.

   D. **Incorrect:** This option will not solve your problem. If you purchase a new disk array, you need to find a way to move the VMs onto the new storage. You will be able to expand the size of the VHD files only to the point that they will use up the space on the old disks.

Configure file and storage solutions

This domain deals with advanced features related to network shares, file access permissions, SAN storage, and storage optimization. Understanding the topics covered in this domain requires a deep understanding of new technologies that you might not have implemented in your own environment. You should supplement the information in this chapter with some hands-on practice so that you can develop an understanding of how you can use these technologies to address real-world scenarios and solve problems in an advanced server environment.

Objectives in this chapter:

- Objective 2.1: Configure advanced file services
- Objective 2.2: Implement Dynamic Access Control (DAC)
- Objective 2.3: Configure and optimize storage

Objective 2.1: Configure advanced file services

This objective deals primarily with BranchCache, File Server Resource Manager, File Access Auditing, and Server for NFS. Each technology allows you to extend the traditional role of the file server beyond simply sharing files, allowing you to speed up access in remote offices, apply quotas, remove old files, audit file access, and provide file services to clients running the UNIX and Linux operating systems.

> **This objective covers how to:**
> - Configure NFS data storage
> - Configure BranchCache
> - Configure File Classification Infrastructure (FCI) using File Server Resource Manager (FSRM)
> - Configure file access auditing

What is BranchCache?

BranchCache is a feature in Windows Server 2012 and Windows Server 2012 R2 that uses file caching to reduce network traffic across WAN links. Here's how BranchCache works: Let's say an employee working on Client1 at a branch office connects across a WAN link to a Branch-Cache-enabled server at a main office, as illustrated in Step 1 of Figure 2-1. If BrancheCache is also enabled on the branch office network, any BranchCache-enabled content (such as a file) that the employee downloads from the remote server will be cached locally at the branch office, as shown in Step 2 of Figure 2-1. If a second employee working on Client2 at the branch office later attempts to download the same content from the same server across the WAN link (Step 3), the content will actually be retrieved from the branch office cache—as long as this content has not been updated. This final step is illustrated in Step 4 of Figure 2-1.

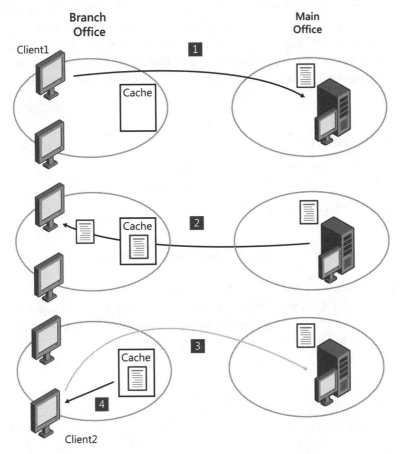

FIGURE 2-1 BranchCache provides a branch office with a local copy of content retrieved from a server at a remote office

Where is this local branch office cache, exactly? The answer depends on the BranchCache mode.

BranchCache can operate in one of two modes: Hosted Cache mode or Distributed Cache mode.

Hosted Cache mode

In *Hosted Cache mode*, you configure a server as the hosted cache server at the branch office. Whenever a client at the branch office attempts to retrieve BranchCache-enabled content at the main office, the client first (and transparently to the user) checks the hosted cache server to see if the content is available locally. If the content is not available on the hosted cache server, the client retrieves the content from the main office and this content is then stored on the hosted cache server. If the content is available on the hosted cache server, the hosted cache server provides the content to the local client. This process is illustrated in Figure 2-2. Here Client1 attempts to access the file. In Step 2 the file is made available to Client1 and also placed in the cache on the hosted cache server. When Client2 attempts to access the file (Step 3), the file is retrieved from the hosted cache server (Step 4).

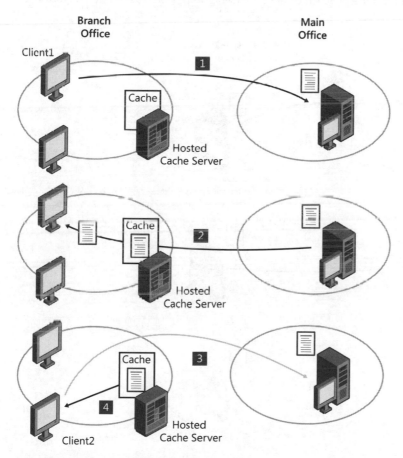

FIGURE 2-2 File retrieval through BranchCache in Hosted Cache mode

Distributed Cache mode

In Distributed Cache mode, no hosted cache server is present. Instead, all BranchCache-enabled clients act as cache servers for other clients on their local subnet. (Note that BranchCache clients must be running Windows 7 Enterprise or Ultimate edition, or Windows 8 Enterprise or Windows 8.1 Enterprise edition.)

In Distributed Cache mode, whenever a client at the branch office attempts to retrieve BranchCache-enabled content at the main office, the client first (and transparently to the user) broadcasts the local subnet to see if the content is already available locally on another client. If the content is not available on the local subnet, the client retrieves the content from the main office, and this content is then stored in its local cache. If a second client later attempt to retrieve the same content, the first client that has cached the data provides this content to the second client.

This process is illustrated in Figure 2-3. Step 1 shows the broadcast check for content, Step 2 shows retrieval from the head office file server, and Step 3 shows the retrieval of the content form the cache.

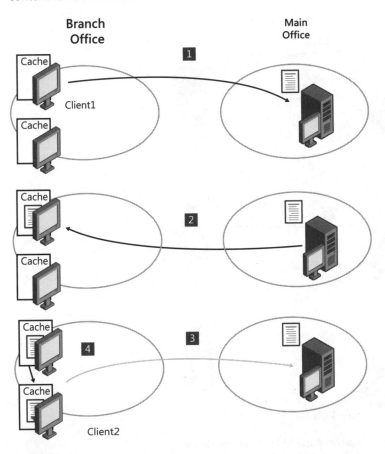

FIGURE 2-3 File retrieval through BranchCache in Distributed Cache mode

Configuring BranchCache

BranchCache can be configured to cache three types of data: web data, file server data, and data from applications based on the Background Intelligent Transfer Service (BITS). Examples of BITS applications are Windows Server Update Services (WSUS) and System Center Configuration Manager.

To configure BranchCache, you first need to configure the content servers. Then, if you're going to configure BranchCache in Hosted Cache mode, you need to configure the hosted cache servers. Finally, you need to configure the clients.

Configuring the content servers

If the content server is a web server or BITS application server, you need to install the Branch-Cache feature on the server, shown in Figure 2-4. To install the feature by using Windows PowerShell, use the following command:

```
Install-WindowsFeature BranchCache -IncludeManagementTools
```

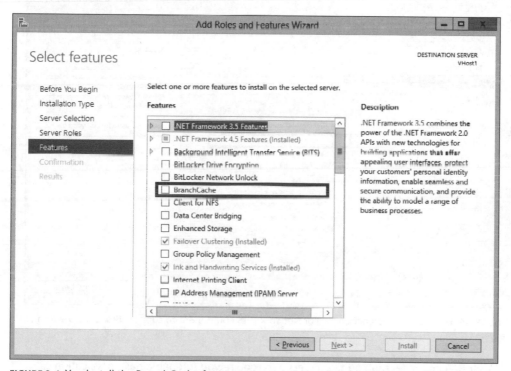

FIGURE 2-4 You install the BranchCache feature to support BranchCache for web servers or BITS application servers

If the content server is a file server, you need to install a different component altogether: the BranchCache For Network Files component (role service) of the File Server role, as shown in Figure 2-5. To install this component by using Windows PowerShell, use the following command:

```
Install-WindowsFeature FS-BranchCache -IncludeManagementTools
```

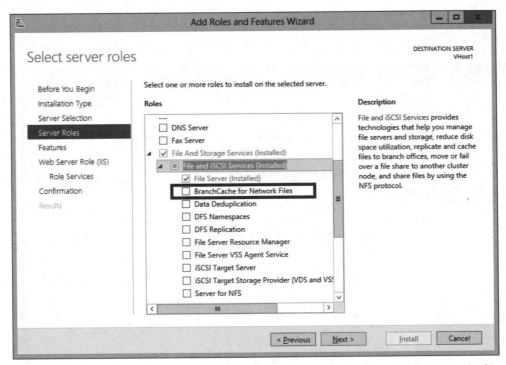

FIGURE 2-5 You install the BranchCache For Network Files component to support BranchCache for file servers

Your BranchCache-enabled file servers also require you to enable hash publication through local policy or Group Policy. You can find this policy setting in the following location, shown in Figure 2-6: Computer Configuration\Policies\Administrative Templates\Network\ Lanman Server\Hash Publication For BranchCache.

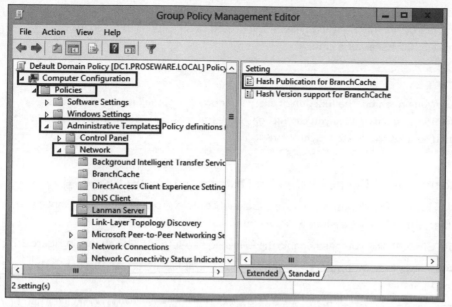

FIGURE 2-6 You need to enable hash publication for BranchCache on BranchCache file servers

Configuring the hosted cache servers (optional)

To configure a hosted cache server at a branch office, first install the BranchCache feature on a server running Windows Server 2012 or Windows Server 2012 R2. Next, run the Enable-BCHostedServer cmdlet in Windows PowerShell. If the server is joined to a domain, you must also add the -RegisterSCP switch, as follows:

```
Enable-BCHostedServer -RegisterSCP
```

To verify that the local server has been configured as a hosted cache server, use the Get-BCStatus cmdlet.

At this point, it's advisable to preload the web or file content information from Branch-Cache-enabled web and file servers to your hosted cache server or servers. To do so, you first have to generate hashes of the content to stage the data on each content server, then export the staged data into a package, and then import the package on each hosted cache server. You perform these three steps by using Windows PowerShell:

1. For each folder and file you want to preload, on each content server, first generate hashes to stage the data for export by running either the Publish-BCFileContent or the Publish-BCWebContent cmdlet (depending on whether the BranchCache content is file content or web content).

2. After you've generated hashes to stage the data, you need to produce a package of this staged data by using the Export-BCCachePackage cmdlet.

3. Transfer the package to the hosted cache server by using the method of your choice. Then, import the data package file on the hosted cache server. To do so, use the Import-BCCachePackage cmdlet.

EXAM TIP

Make sure you remember the function of every Windows PowerShell cmdlet mentioned in this section. Also, make sure you can recognize the proper sequence of cmdlets used in preloading content to a hosted cache server.

Configuring BranchCache clients for Distributed Cache mode

Configuring clients for Distributed Cache mode is fairly simple. To configure the clients, you can use either Group Policy or Windows PowerShell.

If you use Group Policy, you need enable the following two settings, also shown in Figure 2-7:

- Computer Configuration\Policies\Administrative Templates\Network\BranchCache\ Turn On BranchCache

- Computer Configuration\Policies\Administrative Templates\Network\BranchCache\Set BranchCache Distributed Cache Mode

If you use Windows PowerShell instead of Group Policy, you need to run the Enable-BCDistributed cmdlet on every Windows 7, Windows 8 or Windows 8.1 client on which you want to enable BranchCache in Distributed Cache mode.

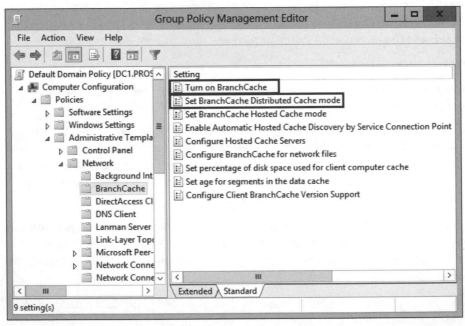

FIGURE 2-7 Enable these Group Policy settings to configure BrancheCache clients in Distributed Cache mode

If a question about configuring BranchCache clients does not refer to hosted cache servers in any way, you should assume that the clients are supposed to be configured in Distributed Cache mode. Such a question is unlikely to mention Distributed Cache mode by name because the question would then be too easy: If you look at Figure 2-7, you can see that only one policy setting includes the term "Distributed Cache Mode."

Configuring BranchCache clients for Hosted Cache mode

You can configure BranchCache clients by using Group Policy or Windows PowerShell.

If you want to use Group Policy and the clients are running Windows 7, Windows 8, or Windows 8.1, you need to configure two policy settings, also shown in Figure 2-8.

- Computer Configuration\Policies\Administrative Templates\Network\BranchCache\ Turn On BranchCache

  (This is the same policy setting enabled for Distributed Cache mode.)

- Computer Configuration\Policies\Administrative Templates\Network\BranchCache\ Configure Hosted Cache Servers

If you use Windows PowerShell instead of Group Policy, you need to run the Enable-BCHostedClient cmdlet on every Windows 8 client on which you want to enable BranchCache in Hosted Cache mode.

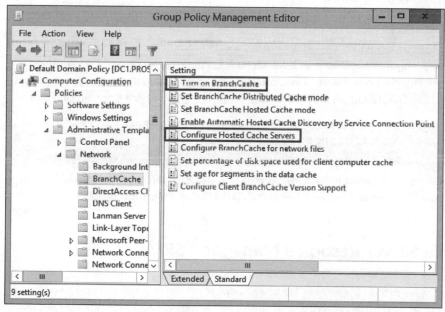

FIGURE 2-8 Enable these Group Policy settings to configure BrancheCache clients running Windows 8 in Hosted Cache mode

WINDOWS 7 COMPATIBILITY

Both the Enable-BCHostedClient cmdlet and the Configure Hosted Cache Servers policy setting allow you to configure a list of hosted cache servers for computers running the Windows 8, Windows 8.1, Windows Server 2012, or Windows Server 2012 R2 operating systems. These policies don't apply to Windows 7 or Windows Server 2008 R2 clients. Another policy setting visible in Figure 2-8, Set BranchCache Hosted Cache Mode, enables Windows 7, Windows 8, or Windows 8.1 clients (and the corresponding server versions) for Hosted Cache mode. However, this policy setting has a limitation: It lets you specify only a single hosted cache server, as opposed to specifying a list of servers.

So what should you remember about these two similar Group Policy settings—Configure Hosted Cache Servers and Set BranchCache Hosted Cache mode—on the 70-412 exam? If a question asks you how to configure clients with more than one hosted cache server, the answer is to enable the Configure Hosted Cache Servers policy setting. If a question requires you to configure both Windows 7 and Windows 8 clients with a single hosted cache server, the answer is to enable the Set BranchCache Hosted Cache Mode policy setting. Keep in mind, however, that questions on Microsoft exams typically favor settings that apply only to the most current operating systems.

HOSTED CACHE SERVER DISCOVERY

There's one other Group Policy setting for Hosted Cache mode that's good to remember. If you want to configure your Windows 8, Windows 8.1, Windows Server 2012 or Windows Server 2012 R2 BranchCache clients to automatically discover hosted cache servers, then configure this setting: Enable Automatic Hosted Cache Discovery By Service Connection Point.

> **MORE INFO BRANCHCACHE GROUP POLICY SETTINGS**
>
> For more information about BranchCache Group Policy settings, search for "What's New in BranchCache" on TechNet (or visit *http://technet.microsoft.com/en-us/library/jj127252. aspx*) and read the section entitled "New BranchCache Group Policy Settings."

Using File Server Resource Manager (FSRM)

File Server Resource Manager (FSRM) is a tool that allows you to perform advanced file management tasks such as implement file screens, apply per-folder quotas, configure file classification tasks, run storage reports, and configure file management tasks. FSRM allows you to exercise greater control over the content stored on file servers, allowing you to block certain types of files from being written to the server and allowing you to determine which data stored on the file server is no longer being regularly accessed and therefore can be removed or archived.

File screens

File screens allow you to block users from saving files with specific names to specific folders. For example, you could create a file screen to stop users saving .mp3 files to the c:\accountingdocs folder, which serves as the host folder for the Accounting_Documents share. File screens work based on file name matches rather than performing a check on file content. This means it's possible for a user to rename a file with an allowed extension and save a file that way, but the vast majority of users aren't likely to figure out this trick.

File screens work on the basis of file groups. A *file group* is a set of preexisting patterns based on common file name extensions. For example, the Audio and Video File Group contains commonly used audio and video file extensions. When configuring file groups, you can also configure an exclusion. For example, you might want to block all audio and video files except those that match the *.avi pattern. It's also possible to configure file groups as a way of enforcing file name policies. This allows you to block users from saving files unless they use a specific naming format.

A file screen template allows you to apply one or more file groups to a specific path. The advantage of using templates is that you can apply the same template in multiple locations. If you want to change the files that are being blocked, you can update the template. When configuring a template, you need to choose whether the template will actually block files or whether to simply report that a user has saved a file that meets a specific file name pattern.

When configuring a template, you can configure the following actions to occur:

- **Perform active screening or passive screening**   *Active screening* blocks files from being written. *Passive screening* allows files to be written. Use Passive screening when you want to monitor when specific file types have been written to a specific path.

- **Send an email message**   You can configure an email message to be sent to the user who attempted to save the file, to an administrator, or both. The email address used for the user is located by querying the user's Active Directory account.

- **Run a script or command**   You can configure a script or command to be run when a user attempts to save a file that has a name that matches a pattern in the file group.

- **Generate an event log item**   When a user attempts to save a file with a name that matches the pattern in the file group, an item will be written to the System event log.

- **Create a report**   Create a storage report that can be sent to the user who triggered the file screen, to an administrator, or to both.

You can apply file screen templates either directly or as exceptions to a path. For example, you might apply a template to block compressed files from being written to the path c:\accountingdocs but then apply the same template as an exception to the path c:\accountingdocs\archive folder. This would block compressed files from being written to all locations under the c:\accountingdocs folder except the c:\accountingdocs archive folder.

Quotas

Quotas allow you to apply storage limits based on a specific folder path. You can apply different quotas to different paths on the same volume, which makes quotas applied through FSRM superior to NTFS quotas, which could only be configured on a per-volume basis. By configuring quota templates, you can apply the same quota to multiple paths. If you want to update all quotas applied on existing paths, you need only to update the template.

You can configure two types of quota:

- **Hard quota**   A user cannot exceed a hard quota. Once they reach that limit, they will be unable to store additional data in the path to which the quota applies.
- **Soft quota**   Users are able to exceed a soft quota limit. You use this primarily to determine the number and identities of users that store a certain amount of data in a path.

In addition to hard and soft quotas, you can configure different notification thresholds. When a threshold is exceeded, you can configure the quota template so that an event is written to the event log, a command or script is run, or a report is generated and sent to designated recipients.

> **MORE INFO QUOTAS**
>
> To learn more about quotas, visit *http://technet.microsoft.com/en-us/library/cc733029.aspx.*

Storage reports

Storage reports allow you to view information about files that are stored in particular paths. You can use FSRM to create the following reports:

- **Duplicate Files**   Allows you to locate duplicate files within a path.
- **File Screening Audit**   Allows you to view file screen information
- **Files by File Group**   Allows you to determine the number of files for a specific file group.
- **Files By Owner**   Allows you to generate and view a report detailing the number of files on the basis of file owner.
- **Files By Property**   Allows you to generate and view a report of files based on a property of the file. This can be a file classification property or be based on file name.
- **Folders By Property**   Allows you to generate and view a report on folders based on a property of the folder. This property can be a file classification property or be based on folder name.
- **Large Files**   Allows you to generate and view a report detailing all files that exceed a specific size.

- **Least Recently Accessed Files**   Allows you to generate and view a report detailing all files that have not been accessed for a specific number of days. The default is 90 days.
- **Most Recently Accessed Files**   Allows you to generate and view a report detailing files that have been accessed within a specific number of days. The default is 7 days.
- **Quota Usage**   Allows you to generate and view a quota usage report.

File management tasks

File management tasks allow you to automate the process of finding files that have a set of properties, usually applied through file classification, and performing tasks against those files. For example, you could configure a file expiration task that looks for files that haven't been accessed for a specific number of days and then automatically move those files to a folder where they can be archived. You can configure file management tasks based upon the following properties:

- Location
- Classification Properties
- Creation Time
- Modification Time
- Last Accessed Time

> **MORE INFO** **FILE SERVER RESOURCE MANAGER**
>
> To learn more about File Server Resource Manager, visit *http://technet.microsoft.com/ en-us/library/hh831701.aspx.*

Implementing file access auditing

You implement file access auditing when you want a record of when and how users access specific files and folders. You configure file access auditing by first enabling auditing in Group Policy and then configuring the items that you want to track so that they will be audited. You have two options when configuring group policy:

- You can audit object access generally by enabling the Audit Object Access policy located in the Computer Configuration\Policies\Windows Settings\Security Settings\ Local Policies\Audit Policy node. This will enable auditing for other objects as well as for file and folders.
- You can audit file and folder access specifically by enabling the Audit File System Policy located in the Computer Configuration\Policies\Windows Settings\Security Settings\ Advanced Audit Policy Configuration\Audit Policies\Object Access node. This only allows auditing of file and folders.

Once you have enabled auditing through Group Policy, you configure the auditing entry on the object you want to track. When you configure an auditing entry, you choose the following:

- The security principal (user, computer, group) that you want to track.
- Whether to audit success, failure, or both.
- Whether to audit just the file or a single folder or whether you want to audit all folders, all subfolders, and all files.
- Whether to limit the scope of the auditing (for example, limiting auditing so that it occurs only when files are accessed from computers that are members of a specific security group).

> **MORE INFO** FILE ACCESS AUDITING
>
> To learn more about file access auditing, visit *http://technet.microsoft.com/en-us/library/ hh831382.aspx*.

Installing the Server for NFS component

Windows networks natively use the Server Message Block (SMB) protocol to support file and folder sharing, but UNIX and Linux use another protocol called Network File System (NFS) for the same purpose. To support UNIX and Linux clients on file shares, you can install the Server for NFS component (role service) of the File And iSCSI Services role, shown in Figure 2-9. If you prefer to use Windows PowerShell to install the feature, you can use the following command:

```
Install-WindowsFeature FS-NFS-Services -IncludeManagementTools
```

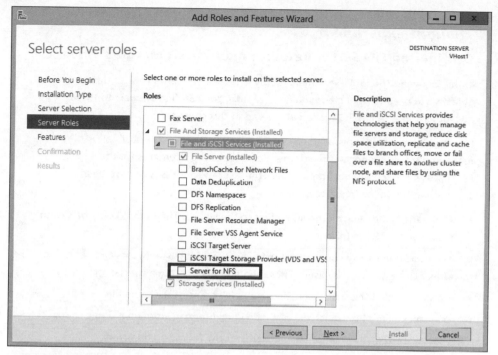

FIGURE 2-9 Installing Server For NFS

You can also configure Windows clients to be NFS-compatible by installing the Client For NFS feature.

Windows Server has included some version of Server for NFS for many years. However, Windows Server 2012 introduces a couple of interesting capabilities with Server for NFS. First, NFS shares are now fully compatible with failover clustering, meaning that a user experiences no downtime when connected to an NFS share during failover. In addition, just as you can store Hyper-V VMs and storage on SMB shares, you can now do the same with VMWare ESX VMs and NFS shares.

On the 70-412 exam, it's unlikely you'll need to know many details about how to configure Server for NFS. The main thing is that you remember what it's for and when you need to install and configure it.

> **MORE INFO CONFIGURING SERVER FOR NFS**
>
> For more information about configuring Server for NFS, search for "Deploy Network File System" on TechNet or visit *http://technet.microsoft.com/en-us/library/jj574143.aspx*.

Thought experiment
Configuring File Server Resource Manager at Margie's Travel

In the following thought experiment, apply what you've learned about this objective to predict what steps you need to take. You can find answers to these questions in the "Answers" section at the end of this chapter.

You are a network administrator for Margie's Travel. You are responsible for managing several important file shares. The storage requirements for these file shares has been growing rapidly over the last few months. You have been considering the following factors:

- Users tend to be saving large audio files to the shares. They should only be saving documents in Office format.

- Some documents have been stored on file servers for several years and yet do not appear to be accessed by users. These should be moved to a special archive share.

- You suspect that the share is hosting multiple copies of the same file.

- You want to limit how much data an individual user can store on a single share.

With the preceding information in mind, answer the following questions.

1. How should you stop users from storing audio files on the file share?

2. How can you determine which files can be moved to the archive share?

3. How can you determine which files are stored more than once on the share?

4. How can you limit the amount of data a user stores on a single share?

Objective summary

- BranchCache is a feature that uses file caching to improve network performance for clients that retrieve content from a server across a WAN link. BranchCache can be configured in Hosted Cache mode or Distributed Cache mode. In Hosted Cache mode, a server at a branch office is used to cache all data that local clients retrieve from BranchCache-enabled servers at a main office. In Distributed Cache mode, Branch-Cache clients cache their own retrieved content and serve other local clients requesting the same content.

- To configure a content server for BranchCache, install the BranchCache feature if the content server is a web server or a BITS application server. If the content server is a file server, you need to install the BranchCache For Network Files component of the File Server role and then enable hash publication on the server by using local policy or Group Policy.

- To configure a hosted cache server, install the BranchCache feature and then run the Enable-BCHostedServer cmdlet. To preload content from the Branch Cache server, first generate hashes of the desired folders to prestage the data with the Publish-BCFileContent or Publish-BCWebContent cmdlet. Then export the prestaged data to a package by using the Export-BCCachePackage cmdlet. Finally, import the package to the hosted cache server by using the Import-BCCachePackage cmdlet.

- To configure clients for BranchCache in Distributed Cache mode, enable the Turn On BranchCache policy setting and the Set BranchCache Distributed Cache mode policy setting. To configure clients for BranchCache in Hosted Cache mode, enable the Turn On Branch Cache policy setting and the Configure Hosted Cache Servers policy setting.

- File Server Resource Manager allows you to configure file screens, quotas, storage reports, and file management tasks.

- File Access Auditing allows you to track access to files and folders.

- Server for NFS is a component (role service) of the File and iSCSI Services role. This component allows you to configure file shares for UNIX and Linux clients. To configure Windows clients to connect to NFS shares, you can install the Client for NFS feature on those clients.

Objective review

Answer the following questions to test your knowledge of the information in this objective. You can find the answers to these questions and explanations of why each answer choice is correct or incorrect in the "Answers" section at the end of the chapter.

1. You are a network administrator for Proseware, which has a main office and a branch office. The company network consists of a single Active Directory domain, Proseware.com. All servers are running Windows Server 2012 R2 and all clients are running Windows 8.1.

   You configure a file server at the main office as a BranchCache content server and configure two servers at the branch office as hosted cache servers.

   You create a new Group Policy Object (GPO) for the branch office. Which of the following Group Policy settings do you need to configure in the GPO to enable the clients at the branch office to use the hosted cache servers? (Choose all that apply.)

   A. Turn on BranchCache

   B. Set BranchCache Hosted Cache Mode

   C. Enable Hosted Cache Discovery by Service Connection Point

   D. Configure Hosted Cache Servers

2. You work as a network administrator for Adatum.com. Adatum has a main office and a branch office. You configure a file server named FS1 in the main office as a Branch-Cache content server and you configure a server named HC1 at the branch office as a hosted cache server.

   You have selected file shares on FS1 that you want to preload on HC1. You now want to generate hashes for these file shares to stage the data for a cache package.

   Which cmdlet should you run?

   A. Publish-BCFileContent

   B. Publish-BCWebContent

   C. Export-BCCachePackage

   D. Import-BCCachePackage

3. You are a network administrator for Proseware, which has a main office and a branch office. The company network consists of a single Active Directory domain, Proseware.com. All servers are running Windows Server 2012 R2, and all clients are running Windows 8.1.

   You configure a file server at the main office as a BranchCache content server. You now want to configure clients at the branch office for BranchCache.

   You create a new GPO for the branch office. Which of the following Group Policy settings do you need to configure in the GPO to enable the clients for BranchCache? (Choose all that apply.)

   A. Turn On BranchCache

   B. Set BranchCache Distributed Cache Mode

   C. Set BranchCache Hosted Cache Mode

   D. Configure BranchCache For Network Files

Objective 2.2: Implement Dynamic Access Control (DAC)

Dynamic Access Control (DAC) relies on file classifications (which is descriptive metadata about files), on user and device attributes called claims, and on rules and policies built from all of these elements. Through DAC you can configure access to files based on a user's Active Directory attribute and the file's contents. For example, you can configure DAC to only allow access to files that contain the text TOP_SECRET to users whose Active Directory accounts have an attribute that indicates they have a clearance level of "TOP SECRET".

> **This objective covers how to:**
> - Configure user and device claim types
> - Implement policy changes and staging
> - Perform access-denied remediation
> - Configure file classification
> - Create and configure central access rules and policies
> - Create and configure resource properties and lists

Introducing DAC

DAC doesn't replace NTFS and share permissions but is sometimes combined with them. When DAC permissions are combined with the NTFS and share permissions, the most restrictive permissions always apply to the account requesting access.

You can think of DAC as being based on *access rules*. These rules are if-then statements built on the attributes of files, users, and devices. An example expression to serve as the basis for an access rule could be "If a user is a member of the finance department with an office on Floor 10 and is connecting from a device that is located in the company HQ, then that user can access finance files and folder designated as having a high business impact." Before you can even create such an access rule, you need to create and assign the needed attributes to all the objects mentioned in that rule. The user and device attributes are called *claims*. The file attributes are called *classifications* (or *resource properties*).

The way these three attribute types relate to an access rule is illustrated in Figure 2-10.

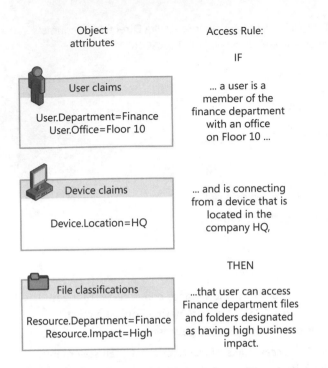

Object attributes	Access Rule:
	IF
User claims User.Department=Finance User.Office=Floor 10	... a user is a member of the finance department with an office on Floor 10 ...
Device claims Device.Location=HQ	... and is connecting from a device that is located in the company HQ,
	THEN
File classifications Resource.Department=Finance Resource.Impact=High	...that user can access Finance department files and folders designated as having high business impact.

FIGURE 2-10 Access rules refer to the attributes of users, devices, and files

DAC is advantageous for a number of reasons. First, it allows administrators to manage file access centrally, in a way that impacts all file servers in the organization. (It should be noted, however, that you cannot enforce access rules centrally through DAC; you can only make access rules available for enforcement.) Another advantage of DAC is that it allows you to dramatically reduce the number of user groups you would otherwise need to create and manage to implement a particular access policy. A third advantage of DAC is that it allows you to construct access rules in a way that is much more flexible and much more likely to correspond to the needs of your organization. Instead of access control lists (ACLs) based only on user and group accounts, you can create rules based on location, office, country/region, telephone number, or any other parameter that is most useful to you.

To implement DAC, you need at least one Windows Server 2012 or Windows Server 2012 R2 file server, at least one Windows Server 2012 or Windows Server 2012 R2 domain controller (one recommended at each site), and Windows 7 clients or higher. In addition, specific features such as access-denied assistance require Windows 8 or Windows 8.1. The domain functional level must also be set to Windows Server 2012 or higher.

Configuring claims-based authentication

Kerberos is the authentication protocol used by Active Directory Domain Services (AD DS). With Kerberos, users are provided with a token when they are authenticated. The token essentially determines user permissions.

DAC relies on an expanded Kerberos token. This Kerberos token includes more than the usual data, which is the user's ID and group memberships. In addition to this information, the expanded Kerberos token used in DAC includes certain attribute values (called *claims*) about the user, additional claims about the device to which the user is signed on, and the same device's own group memberships. The expanded Kerberos token used in DAC is illustrated in Figure 2-11.

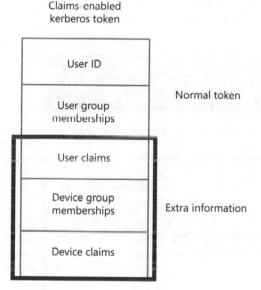

FIGURE 2-11 The Kerberos token used in DAC

To configure a DAC policy, perform the following steps:

1. Define the types of claims about users and devices you want to include in Kerberos tokens.

2. Configure Active Directory Domain Services to use the expanded Kerberos tokens that include these claims.

Defining user and device claims types

In this step, you choose the specific user and device properties that will be presented as claims in the Kerberos token whenever access permissions are evaluated. User and device claim types correspond to names of Active Directory attributes (such as "Department" or "City") for user and computer account objects. The actual claim values included in a token are copied from the corresponding Active Directory attribute values. Because access rules refer to these claim types in their specifications about who is allowed or denied access to a given resource, you want to define claims types you will need later when you create access control rules.

You can use Active Directory Administrative Center to configure the user and device claim types. In the console tree, select tree view and then navigate to Dynamic Access Control\ Claim Types. Right-click Claim Types, click New, and then select Claim Type, as shown in Figure 2-12.

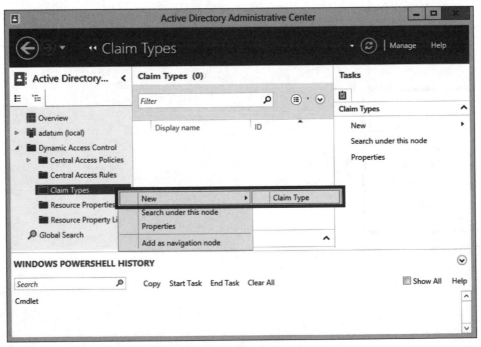

FIGURE 2-12 Creating a new claim type for a user or device

The Create Claim Type page that opens is shown in Figure 2-13.

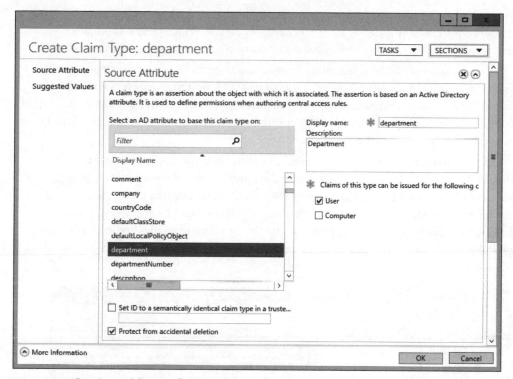

FIGURE 2-13 Creating a claim type for a user object

In the Source Attribute section, click the Active Directory object attribute name that you want to use as the basis of the claim type. You can also specify whether you want this claim type to be issued for users, for computers (devices), or both. For example, if you plan to define rules that include references to the department of either the user or the device to which a user is signed on, you should select both User and Computer when you create the Department claim type.

In the Suggested Values section, you can provide a list of suggested matching values that you will later be able to supply in access rules. For example, if you plan to create access rules that specify user or device Department values such as "Finance," "Engineering," "Operations," "Marketing," and "Sales," you can precreate those same strings as suggested values now, when you are creating the claim type. Note that if you define any suggested values, those values you supply will be the only ones available to select when you create rules that refer to the claim type.

Enabling Kerberos support for claims-based access control

The next step to take is to configure Group Policy to enable Kerberos support for claims on domain controllers. This step ensures that Kerberos tokens include claims information and that this information can then be evaluated by domain controllers for access authorization.

In the Group Policy Management Console, create or edit a Group Policy Object (GPO) linked to the domain controllers organizational unit (OU), and then enable the following setting: Computer Configuration/Policies/Administrative Templates/System/KDC/KDC Support For Claims, Compound Authentication And Kerberos Armoring. (Within the Policy Setting dialog box, leave selected the default option of Supported.)

The requirement that you set this policy for claims-based authorization, and that you should do so at the domain controllers' container level, is one of the most likely aspects about DAC that you'll be tested on during the 70-412 exam. Learn to recognize not only the full name of this policy but the possible ways its name might be shortened. (For example, an answer choice might say simply "Use Group Policy to enable Kerberos armoring on the domain controllers' OU.") The location of this policy setting within a GPO is shown in Figure 2-14.

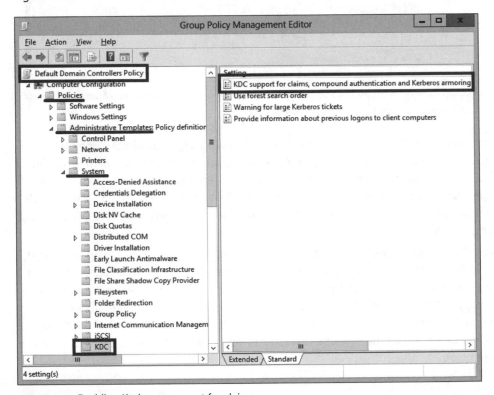

FIGURE 2-14 Enabling Kerberos support for claims

Configuring file classification

File classification refers to the process of adding attributes to the properties of files and folders. These attributes allow you to construct access rules that apply to these resources. The steps to configuring file classification are as follows:

1. Enable or create selected resource properties.

2. Add resource properties to a resource property list.

3. Update Active Directory file and folder objects.

4. Classify files and folders.

Enabling or creating selected resource properties

You enable or create selected resource properties on a domain controller running Windows Server 2012 or later using Active Directory Administrative Center. To perform this task, in the console tree, select tree view (the right tab) and then click the Resource Properties container, as shown in Figure 2-15.

Resource properties correspond to attribute categories, such as Department, that you can make appear on the Classification tab of the Properties dialog box of files and folders. You make a resource property appear on this Classification tab by first enabling the property and then performing steps 2 and 3 described later in this section. Generally, you should enable only the resource properties you plan to use later in access rules. For example, if your eventual goal is to create and apply the access rule shown in Figure 2-15, you should enable the Department and Impact resource properties.

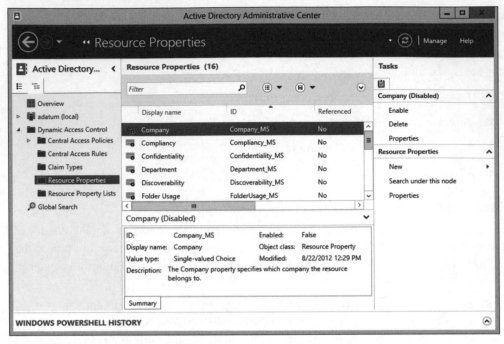

FIGURE 2-15 Creating resource properties

Windows Server 2012 and Windows Server 2012 R2 include 16 predefined resource properties, including Department, Impact, Compliancy, Intellectual Property, and Confidentiality. These resource properties include predefined suggested values you can eventually assign to objects, values such as the specific names of departments; High, Medium, or Low; and Yes or No. However, if a resource property you need isn't predefined (such as City or Country/Region), you can create it and define suggested values you need, such as London, New York, UK, US, and so on. Any new resource properties you create are automatically enabled.

Adding resource properties to a resource property list

After you enable your desired resource properties, you have to add them to a resource property list before they can be applied to objects. Begin by selecting the Resource Property Lists container in Active Directory Administrative Center. One predefined list is available, named Global Resource Property List. If you want the same classifications to be available for all objects, use this list. To add the resource properties you have enabled, right-click the list and Add Resource Properties, as shown in Figure 2-16. In the Select Resource Properties dialog box that opens, add the desired resource properties that you have enabled and click OK.

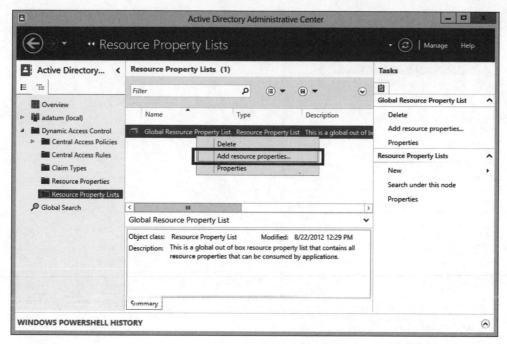

FIGURE 2-16 Adding resource properties to a resource property list

Updating Active Directory file and folder objects

To update Active Directory Domain Services with the new classifiable properties, you now need to run the following cmdlet on a file server on which the File Server Resource Manager (FSRM) component of the File Server role has been installed.

```
Update-FSRMClassificationPropertyDefinition
```

After you perform this step, the resource properties you chose in Step 1 appear on the Classification tab of every file and folder on that file server. The Classification tab is shown in Figure 2-17.

EXAM TIP

This cmdlet is one of the most likely items related to DAC to appear on the 70-412 exam. Make sure you understand its function.

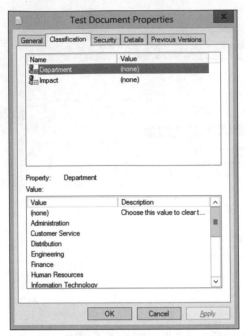

FIGURE 2-17 Resource properties on the Classification tab

Classifying files and folders

Objects in the file structure can be classified manually or automatically. The following sections provide instructions about how to classify files by using both of these strategies.

MANUAL CLASSIFICATION

To classify file objects manually, you can select and apply a resource property value on the Classification tab directly on selected files or on their parent folder. For example, for the folder shown in Figure 2-18, the Finance value and the High value have been selected for the Department property and the Impact property, respectively. When you click Apply, these classifications will automatically be applied to all child objects within the folder.

Child objects keep these classification settings until they are reapplied. Files do not automatically inherit the values of other parent folders when they are moved into those other folders. In fact, the classifications remain applied to those objects even when you copy them from computer to computer. However, you can only see and read these classifications that have been applied to objects after you install FSRM and run the Update-FSRMClassification-PropertyDefinition cmdlet.

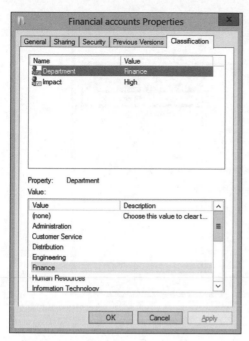

FIGURE 2-18 Classification values set on a parent folder

AUTOMATIC CLASSIFICATION

Windows Server 2012 and Windows Server 2012 R2 include a built-in file classifier that can be configured to automatically classify files within targeted folders. You can automatically classify all files within targeted folders or you can restrict this function to a subset of the files, limiting classification to those Microsoft documents with contents that include a match of a specified expression. You can also restrict classification to the files selected by a custom Windows PowerShell script. Besides this built-in functionality, automatic classification (and DAC in general) can be greatly extended through third-party applications.

To start configuring automatic file classification, you first need to install the FSRM component of the File Server role. Then, in the File Server Resource Manager console tree, navigate to Classification Management\Classification Rules. In the Actions pane, click Create Classification Rule, as shown in Figure 2-19.

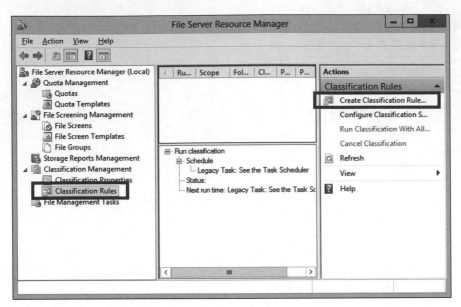

FIGURE 2-19 Creating a classification rule

This step opens the Create Classification Rule dialog box. On the General tab, type a name and description for the new rule. The General tab also includes an Enabled check box, which is selected by default.

On the Scope tab, shown in Figure 2-20, click Add to select the folders where this rule will apply. The classification rule applies to all folders and their subfolders in the list. Alternatively, you can target *all* folders that store *any* of the following selected classifications of data: Application Files, Backup And Archival Files, Group Files, or User Files.

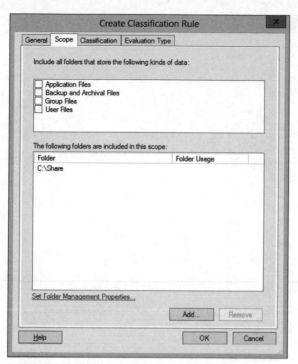

FIGURE 2-20 Setting the scope for a classification rule

On the Classification tab, shown in Figure 2-21, choose a classification method along with the classification value for one selected property that the rule will assign.

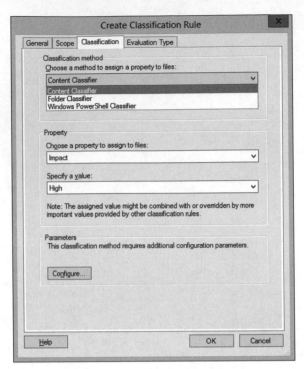

FIGURE 2-21 Configuring a classification method and property value

For a classification method, there are three options:

- The Folder Classifier option assigns the property value to all files that fall within the scope of the rule.

- The Windows PowerShell Classifier prompts you to specify a script to determine the target files within the scope of the rule.

- The Content Classifier option searches Microsoft documents for a text or regular expression string. Click Configure to further configure this option with the Classification Parameters dialog box, shown in Figure 2-22.

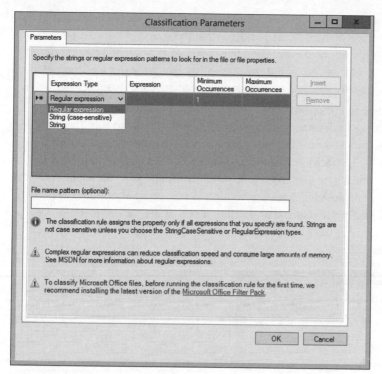

FIGURE 2-22 Configuring a content search for automatic classification

This dialog box lets you specify an expression that will be searched for in the content of Microsoft documents that fall within the scope of the rule. If the content search results in a match for the specified expression, the file is tagged with the property value specified on the Classification tab of the Create Classification Rule dialog box.

You can choose one of three expression types to search for: string, case-sensitive string, or regular expression. A regular expression, sometimes called a *regex*, is used in programming to match patterns of text strings as opposed to exact sequences of specific numbers or letters. A regular expression is often a useful matching mechanism to classify files that include sensitive numbers, such as credit card numbers.

The following is an example of a regular expression. It matches credit card numbers from most vendors:

```
^((4\d{3})|(5[1-5]\d{2})|(6011)|(34\d{1})|(37\d{1}))-?\d{4}-?\d{4}-?\d{4}|3[4,7][\d\s-]
{15}$
```

The Evaluation Type tab is the final tab of the Create Classification Rule dialog box. On this tab, you choose how to handle files that already exist within the scope of the rule. By default, the classification rule does not apply to preexisting files. You can choose, however, to run the rule against existing files. If matches are found, you can either overwrite any existing classification that conflicts with the new value or attempt to aggregate them if possible.

After you create the desired classification rule, click Configure Classification Schedule in File Server Resource Manager to determine how often you want the rule to run. This step opens the File Server Resource Manager Options dialog box. On the Automatic Classification tab, shown in Figure 2-23, select the Enable Fixed Schedule check box. You must then specify days and times at which you want the rule to run. In addition, you can select the Allow Continuous Classification For New Files check box to run the rule on newly created or edited files that fall within the scope of the rule and on existing files that are moved to a new location that falls within the scope of the rule. (Be sure to remember the option for continuous classification for the exam.)

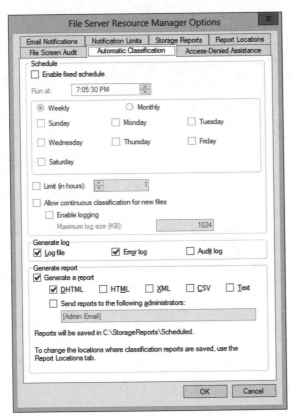

FIGURE 2-23 Configuring a schedule for a classification rule

After configuring the schedule, you can click Run Classification With All Rules Now in the Actions pane of File Server Resource Manager. This step will run all rules immediately and classify the targeted files.

ACCESS-DENIED ASSISTANCE

The File Server Resource Manager Options dialog box shown in Figure 2-23 also includes an Access-Denied Assistance tab. You can use this tab to enable the local file server to provide helpful information to a user whose access to a file or folder has been denied.

To enable this functionality, on the Access-Denied Assistance tab, select the Enable Access-Denied Assistance check box. In the Display The Following Message text box, you can type a custom message that users will see when they are denied access to a file or folder. You can also add certain variables in brackets that will insert customized text, such as:

- **[Original File Path]**   The original file path that was accessed by the user.
- **[Original File Path Folder]**   The parent folder of the original file path that was accessed by the user.
- **[Admin Email]**   The administrator email recipient list.
- **[Data Owner Email]**   The data owner email recipient list.

You can also configure the file server to provide in access denied messages a Request Assistance button, which allows the user who was denied access to send an email to a pre-defined user. To configure this option, click Configure Email Requests, select the Enable Users To Request Assistance check box, and then click OK.

You can also use Group Policy to configure access-denied assistance on all file servers that fall within the scope of a GPO (as opposed to just one server). You use these two policy settings, both found in Computer Configuration\Policies\Administrative Templates\System\Access-Denied Assistance:

- **Enable Access-Denied Assistance On Client For All File Types**   Use this policy setting to enable Windows clients for access-denied assistance of all types.
- **Customize Message For Access Denied Errors**   Use this policy setting to customize the message that users see when access is denied. These message customization options are the same as those you see when you customize access-denied messages by using File Server Resource Manager.

For the 70-412 exam, you need to remember the general steps of how to configure access-denied assistance by using either File Server Resource Manager or Group Policy. For more detailed information about the configuration process, search for "Deploy Access-Denied Assistance (Demonstration Steps)" on TechNet or visit *http://technet.microsoft.com/en-us/library/hh831402.aspx*.

REAL WORLD **RMS ENCRYPTION**

If your network environment includes an Active Directory Rights Management Service server, you can use FSRM to automatically apply RMS encryption to files in designated folders. This feature is configured through the File Management tasks node. For more information, visit *http://technet.microsoft.com/en-us/library/hh831572.aspx*.

Configuring access policies

Finally, you are ready to create access policies after you have assigned attributes to users, devices, and files. To configure access policies, perform the following steps:

1. Create a claims-based central access policy.

2. Use Group Policy to deploy this central access policy to your file servers.

Creating a central access policy that includes claims

This step consists of two parts, both of which you can perform in Active Directory Administrative Center. First, you create one or more central access rules that include claims. Then you add those rules to a central access policy.

CREATING A NEW CENTRAL ACCESS RULE

A *central access rule* is similar to an ACL in that it describes which conditions must be met for access to be granted to a resource. To create a new central access rule, in Active Directory Administrative Center, select tree view in the console tree and then select Central Access Rules. In the Tasks pane, click New and then click Central Access Rule. This step opens the Create Central Access Rule page, shown in Figure 2-24.

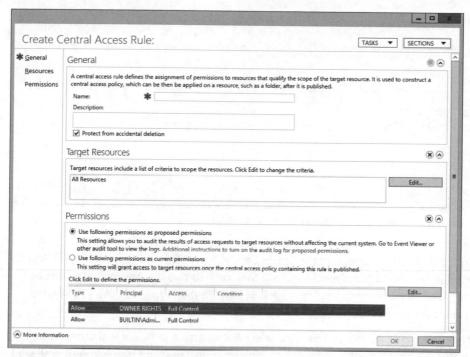

FIGURE 2-24 Creating a new central access rule

Follow these steps to complete the page:

1. In the Name text box, type the name you want to give to the rule.

2. In the Target Resources section, click Edit, and In the Central Access Rule dialog box, add the conditions that match the target resources for which you want to define access. For example, if your goal is to define access permissions to resources that have been configured with a Department classification property of Finance and with an Impact classification property of High, then you want to add the two conditions configured as shown in Figure 2-25.

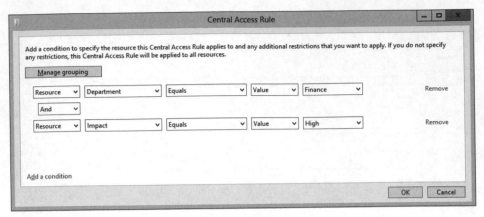

FIGURE 2-25 Configuring matching conditions for target resources

3. In the Permissions section of the Create Central Access Rule page, select Use Following Permissions As Current Permissions and then click Edit. In the Advanced Security Settings For Permissions dialog box, click Add to open the Permission Entry For Permissions dialog box, shown in Figure 2-26.

4. Near the top of the dialog box, click Select A Principal. A *principal* is another name for a user or group account. To configure DAC, you normally want to select Authenticated Users as the principal. (Remember this point both for the real world and the exam.)

5. In the middle of the dialog box, beneath Basic Permissions, select the permissions that you want to assign to users who match the conditions in your rule.

6. Near the bottom of the dialog box, add conditions that match the users for whom you want to define access. For example, if you want to provide access only to users whose accounts in Active Directory have defined a Department value of Finance and an Office value of Floor 10, and who are signed on to computers whose accounts in Active Directory have defined a Location value of HQ, then you want to add the three conditions configured as shown in Figure 2-26. Remember that if Authenticated Users attempt to access the target resource and do *not* match these conditions, the users will be completely denied access (with the exception of the file owner).

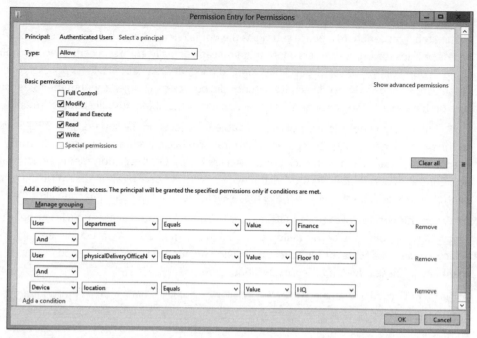

FIGURE 2-26 Configuring permissions and matching conditions for users and devices

7. Click OK three times to finish and return to Active Directory Administrative Center.

ADDING CENTRAL ACCESS RULES TO A CENTRAL ACCESS POLICY

In the console tree of Active Directory Administrative Center, click Central Access Policies. In the Tasks pane, click New and then click Central Access Policy. On the Create Central Access Policy page that opens, perform the following steps:

1. In the Name text box, type the name you want to assign to the policy.

2. In Member Central Access Rules, click Add and then add the desired central access rules you have created. Click OK twice to return to Active Directory Administrative Center.

> **REAL WORLD** **MULTIPLE CENTRAL ACCESS RULES**
>
> When you include multiple access rules in a policy, all the rules will be applied along with that policy when the policy is applied. The most restrictive access permissions always take effect when two rules provide different levels of access to the same user.

Deploying central access policy to file servers

In this step, you configure a policy setting at the domain level that will deliver chosen central access policies to your file servers. Note that you can't actually enforce a central access policy by using Group Policy. You use Group Policy only to make desired central access policies available for selection in the Advanced Security Settings dialog box of all objects within the folder structure on file servers. The policy must then be applied to the object (usually a folder) manually.

To make your central access policies available to objects on file servers, in a GPO linked to the domain, navigate to Computer Configuration/Policies/Windows Settings/Security Settings/File System and then click Central Access Policy. On the Action menu, select Manage Central Access Policies. In the Central Access Policies Configuration dialog box, add the central access policies that you want to make available to file servers and then click OK.

When this Group Policy policy setting is enforced, the central access policies appear on a new Central Policy tab of this dialog box, shown in Figure 2-27. A particular central access policy applies to a folder or file object only when an administrator selects and applies it manually in these advanced security settings.

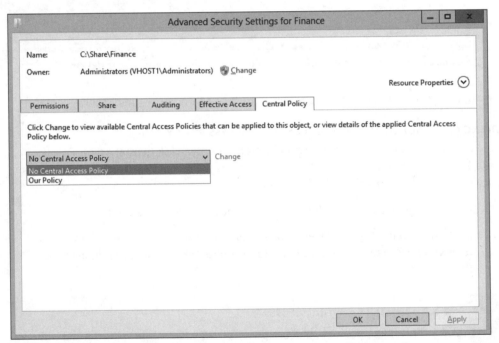

FIGURE 2-27 The Central Policy tab of the Advanced Security Settings dialog box

> **MORE INFO** **PRACTICE IMPLEMENTING DAC**
>
> For more practice implementing DAC, you can perform the DAC walkthrough named "Deploy a Central Access Policy (Demonstration Steps)" at *http://technet.microsoft.com/ en-us/library/hh846167.aspx.*

Thought experiment

Configuring Dynamic Access Control at Tailspin Toys

In the following thought experiment, apply what you've learned about this objective to predict what steps you need to take. You can find answers to these questions in the "Answers" section at the end of this chapter.

You are a network administrator for Tailspin Toys. Tailspin Toys designs revolutionary remote control aircraft. Recently Tailspin Toys suffered a security breach and details of their new secret remote control aircraft were leaked to a rival company. This was traced to incorrectly applied NTFS permissions. With this in mind, you want to use Dynamic Access Control to manage access to sensitive files and folders. Specifically you want to accomplish the following:

- Ensure that users have access only to projects that they are associated with.

- Have the projects that users are associated with represented as a user account property in Active Directory rather than security group membership.

- Have files classified automatically based on the projects they are associated with when project keywords are contained within the file text.

- Provide information to users on why they have been blocked from accessing specific files.

With the preceding information in mind, answer the following questions. You can find the answers to these questions in the "Answers" section at the end of the chapter.

1. How can you ensure that files are assigned a classification that associates them with a specific project based on keywords within the file?

2. After configuring Active Directory attributes to represent projects that users are associated with, what do you need to configure so that you can use this information in a rule?

3. What method do you use to deploy a central access policy to a file server?

4. How can you provide users with a way to automatically request access to files they are unable to open?

Objective summary

- Dynamic Access Control is a new option for setting access permissions to file and folder objects in Windows Server 2012 and Windows Server 2012 R2. DAC works by assigning file classifications to target resources, configuring user and device claims, and then creating rules that describe conditions for access.

- DAC relies on a modified form of Kerberos in which user tokens are expanded to include extra information called claims about the user and the device from which the user is connecting. To support this functionality, you need to enable Key Distribution Center (KDC) support for claims-based authentication in Group Policy at the Domain Controllers OU level. You also need to define the claims types that you will include in the Kerberos token for each user.

- To assign file classifications, first enable chosen resource properties in Active Directory and then add the properties to a property list. Afterward, run the Update-FSRMClassificationPropertyDefinition cmdlet. Then configure classification values of desired file or folder objects on the Classification tab of the Properties dialog box. You can also use File Server Resource Manager (FSRM) to configure file classification rules that classify files automatically, for example, on the basis of an expression found in the contents of the file.

- A central access rule includes one or more conditional expressions that match target resources and one or more conditional expressions that match users or devices and defines permissions to the target resources. One or more central access rules must be added to a central access policy before it can be deployed to file servers.

- You use Group Policy to make central access policies available to file and folder objects. A central policy must be selected and enforced manually on a file or folder.

Objective review

Answer the following questions to test your knowledge of the information in this objective. You can find the answers to these questions and explanations of why each answer choice is correct or incorrect in the "Answers" section at the end of the chapter.

1. You are a network administrator for Adatum.com. The Adatum.com network consists of a single domain that spans branch offices in New York and London. Within the Adatum.com domain, the users and computers within the New York office are contained in an OU named US; the users and computers within the London office are contained in an OU named UK.

   You want to be able to classify data as originating from either the New York office or the London office. You create a resource property named Country/Region and configure the suggested values "US" and "UK." You want administrators in both the New

York and London offices to see the Country/Region resource property appear on the Classification tab of files and folder properties.

What should you do next?

A. Run the Update-FSRMClassificationPropertyDefinition cmdlet.

B. Enable the Country/Region resource property.

C. Create a classification rule.

D. Add the Country/Region property to a resource property list.

2. Your organization's network consists of a single Active Directory domain. All servers are running Windows Server 2012 R2 and all clients are running Windows 8.1.

   You want to enable claims-based access authorization for users in your domain. Which of the following steps should you take to take to achieve this goal?

   A. Enable the policy setting KDC Support For Claims, Compound Authentication And Kerberos Armoring in a GPO at the domain controllers OU level.

   B. Enable the policy setting KDC Support For Claims, Compound Authentication And Kerberos Armoring in a GPO at the domain level.

   C. Enable the policy setting Kerberos Support For Claims, Compound Authentication And Kerberos Armoring in a GPO at the domain controllers OU level.

   D. Enable the policy setting Kerberos Support For Claims, Compound Authentication And Kerberos Armoring in a GPO at the domain level.

3. You are a network administrator for Proseware.com. The Proseware.com network consists of a single Active Directory domain. All servers in the network are running Windows Server 2012 R2 and all clients are running Windows 8.1

   On a file server named FileSrv1, your manager has created five new file shares named Finance, Marketing, Sales, Operations, and Legal. On each share, your manager has assigned Full Control to Authenticated Users for both the NTFS and share permissions.

   Your manager now asks you to configure permissions to the contents of each departmental file share so that Full Control access is restricted to members of the corresponding department and that no other users are allowed any access. Your manager also wants you to ensure that files within each departmental share can be traced to their origin even when they are moved from their original share location.

   Which of the following steps will allow you to meet these stated goals? (Choose two. Each answer represents part of the solution.)

   A. On each new shared folder, remove all currently configured NTFS permissions and then grant Full Control NTFS permissions to a security group that includes all the members of the corresponding department only.

B. On each new shared folder, remove all currently configured share permissions and then grant Full Control share permissions to a security group that includes all the members of the corresponding department only.

C. On each department's shared folder, configure a Department classification property value that corresponds to the name of the department.

D. On each department's shared folder, apply a central access policy that assigns to members of the appropriate department Full Control permissions on files assigned with a matching Department value classification.

Objective 2.3: Configure and optimize storage

This objective relates to certain advanced features that allow you to optimize the use of storage in Windows Server 2012 and Windows Server 2012 R2. This involves the topics of iSCSI, Features on Demand, Data Deduplication, and storage tiering.

> **This objective covers how to:**
> - Configure iSCSI Target and Initiator
> - Configure Internet Storage Name Service (ISNS)
> - Implement thin provisioning and trim
> - Manage server free space using Features on Demand
> - Configure tiered storage

iSCSI storage

Windows Server 2012 and Windows Server 2012 R2 provides both the client and server components for iSCSI, a SAN protocol that carries SCSI commands over ordinary IP networks. By configuring these iSCSI client and server components, you can provide to multiple remote servers shared storage that is essentially equivalent to directly attached storage.

Why share storage centrally among your servers? First, shared storage is required for failover clusters. But even outside of failover clustering, shared storage offers a huge advantage: It allows you to manage the storage for your servers in a much more flexible and efficient way. With shared storage, you don't worry about configuring every server with the right number of correctly sized physical disks. Your storage capabilities are consolidated for all servers; for each server, you can provision logical disks from central storage as you need them.

Installing the iSCSI Target Server

The server-side portion of iSCSI storage is provided through the iSCSI Target Server component of the File And Storage Services role (shown in Figure 2-28). This component allows you to create virtual iSCSI disks (VHD files) that can be made to appear as locally attached disks to remote iSCSI clients.

Use the following command to add the iSCSI Target Server component to a storage server by using Windows PowerShell instead of Server Manager:

```
Add-WindowsFeature FS-iSCSTarget-Server
```

To install the iSCSI Target Server component, you have to agree also to install the File Server component if it isn't already installed.

MANAGING ISCSI VIRTUAL DISKS

You must use Server Manager to manage iSCSI virtual disks if you choose only the iSCSI Target Server component to install. If you also add the iSCSI Target Storage Provider (VDS And VSS Hardware Providers) component, you can manage iSCSI virtual disks by using older applications (such as the Diskraid command) that rely on a Virtual Disk Service (VDS) hardware provider. This component also enables applications to perform volume shadow copies of iSCSI virtual disks.

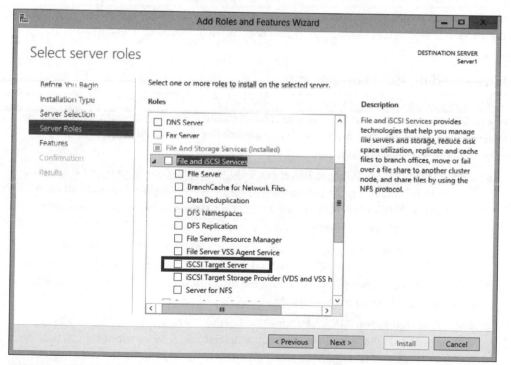

FIGURE 2-28 The iSCSI Target Server component of the File And iSCSI Services role

Enabling iSCSI Initiator

The iSCSI client component included in Windows Server is called *iSCSI Initiator*. iSCSI Initiator is already installed by default, but its associated service (Microsoft iSCSI Initiator service) is not running by default. Before you can begin to configure shared storage, you need to start this service and set it to start automatically in the future.

You can perform this task just by opening iSCSI Initiator in the Tools menu of Server Manager. When you first open it, you get the message shown in Figure 2-29. Clicking Yes starts the service and sets it to start automatically in the future whenever the computer restarts.

To perform the same task at the command line, run the following commands:

```
Start-Service msiscsi
Set-Service msiscsi -StartupType "Automatic"
```

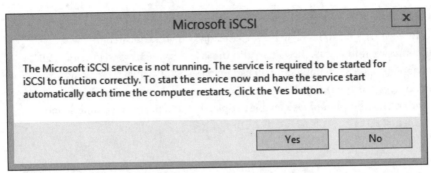

FIGURE 2-29 You need to start the Microsoft iSCSI service before iSCSI Initiator is functional

Understanding iSCSI components

After you install the iSCSI Target Server component on the storage server and start the Microsoft iSCSI Initiator service on the remote server, you are ready to configure iSCSI storage. However, it's a good idea to learn in advance the names of the main iSCSI storage components and how they all work together.

- **iSCSI target** An iSCSI Target Server can include one or more targets. In Windows Server, an iSCSI target is the software interface between a defined set of local iSCSI virtual disks and a defined set of remote iSCSI initiators allowed to use those disks. Every iSCSI target on a server must have a unique name such as "Target1".

- **iSCSI virtual disk** An *iSCSI virtual disk* is a special VHD file that you can add to an iSCSI target. By adding an iSCSI virtual disk to a specific target, you are also indirectly specifying which remote servers can use the disk. (iSCSI targets connect only to the iSCSI initiators defined for the target.)

- **Logical unit number (LUN)** Informally, a LUN refers to a logical disk (such as an iSCSI virtual disk) made available through shared storage. More specifically, a LUN is a unique value that distinguishes one logical disk from another for a shared storage interface such as an iSCSI target. Normally, LUN values are assigned automatically by

Windows, but if you have removed iSCSI virtual disks from a target, you might want to assign or re-assign a LUN value manually so the disks are numbered in an unbroken sequence starting with 0.

- **iSCSI Initiator**   An *iSCSI Initiator* is a software client that allows a server to use storage found at an iSCSI target across an IP network. Before you configure a particular iSCSI Initiator, you first have to configure the target by adding that initiator to the target. Then you configure the initiator to connect to that target. Only after you perform both of these steps will the remote server recognize as local the available disks attached to the target.

- **iSCSI qualified name (IQN)**   An *IQN* is an individual name that networked iSCSI servers and targets use to identify each other. An example of an IQN for an iSCSI target is "iqn.1991-05.com.microsoft:Srv1-MyTarget-target".

  An example of an IQN for an iSCSI Initiator is "iqn.1991-05.com.microsoft:Srv2".

The relationship between all these iSCSI components is illustrated in Figure 2-30.

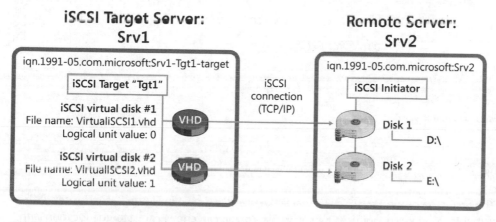

FIGURE 2-30 Two servers configured with an iSCSI target and initiator, respectively.

Configuring iSCSI storage

To configure a local storage server to provide logical disks to a remote server through iSCSI, perform the following steps. (These steps assume that the iSCSI Target Server is already installed on the storage server and that iSCSI Initiator is already enabled on the remote server.)

1. In Server Manager on the storage server, create a new iSCSI virtual disk by using the New iSCSI Virtual Disk Wizard. You will be prompted to add the new virtual disk to an iSCSI target. If no target is yet available, you will be prompted to create a new target in the wizard and to add iSCSI initiators to the target.

2. Configure the iSCSI Initiator on the remote server to connect to the iSCSI target.

3. When the new disk or disks appear in Server Manager on the remote server, bring them online, initialize them, and then create volumes as needed.

These steps are described in more detail in the following sections.

After you install the iSCSI Target Server component, you should start the New iSCSI Virtual Disk Wizard on the storage server. To do this, first click the File and Storage Services page of Server Manager and then click the iSCSI context that appears. Finally, click the link to start the wizard in the iSCSI Virtual Disks area of the details pane. This sequence of steps is shown in Figure 2-31.

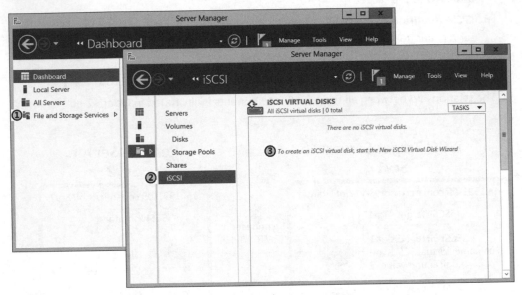

FIGURE 2-31 Starting the New iSCSI Virtual Disk Wizard

The first page of the New iSCSI Virtual Disk Wizard is shown in Figure 2-32. The new iSCSI virtual disk you create is going to be a VHD file, so you can choose any storage location with enough space to support the logical disk size you want to provide to the remote source.

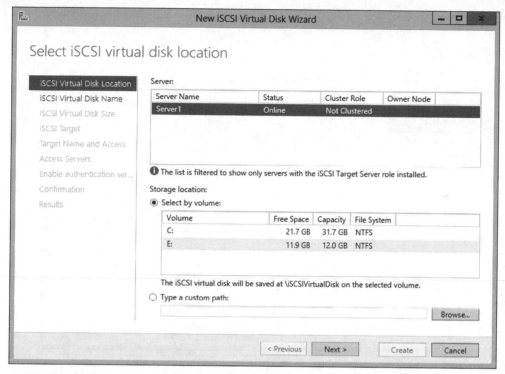

FIGURE 2-32 The Select iSCSI Virtual Disk Location page of the new iSCSI Virtual Disk Wizard

In the next two pages of the wizard, you choose a name and folder location for the new VHD file and then specify a file size. (When choosing a size, remember not to use up all the available space on the volume with the new virtual disk file. Leave more than 10 precent free or you will get errors and poor performance.)

At this point, you get to the Assign iSCSI Target page, shown in Figure 2-33. Here you have to specify an iSCSI target to which the new iSCSI virtual disk will be assigned. If you have not yet created any iSCSI targets, you will have to create one now. If you have previously created other iSCSI virtual disks by using this same wizard, at least one other target will be listed and available.

> **NOTE   CREATING TARGETS**
>
> If you want to precreate an iSCSI target before assigning to it any iSCSI virtual disks (or adding any iSCSI initiators to it), you have to use Windows PowerShell, not the GUI. For example, the following command is (as of this writing) the only way to create an iSCSI target on the local server with the name "Target1," without any other parameters attached:
>
> ```
> New-IscsiServerTarget -Targetname "Target1"
> ```

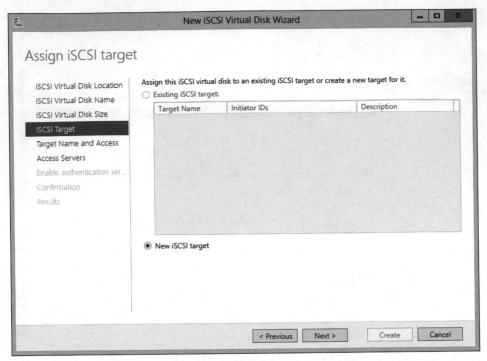

FIGURE 2-33 The Assign iSCSI Target page of the New iSCSI Virtual Disk Wizard

On the following page, you are prompted to provide a name for the target. After that, you get to the Specify Access Servers page, shown in Figure 2-34. On this page, you specify the iSCSI initiators that will be allowed to access the target you are creating.

Click Add to open the Add Initiator ID dialog box, also shown in Figure 2-34. If the desired iSCSI Initiator is not already listed and available for selection, select the option (at the bottom) to enter a value for the selected type.

By default, IQN is selected as the Type (parameter) by which to specify the remote iSCSI Initiator. In general, you can determine the IQN of an iSCSI Initiator on a Windows Server by running the Iscsicli command on that server or by reading the Initiator Name text box on the Configuration tab of the iSCSI Initiator tool. However, in the Add Initiator ID dialog box, it's easier to specify the desired iSCSI Initiator by something other than an IQN. For example, you can change the Type selection to DNS Name or IP Address. Then in the Value text box you can simply type the corresponding name or address of the remote server.

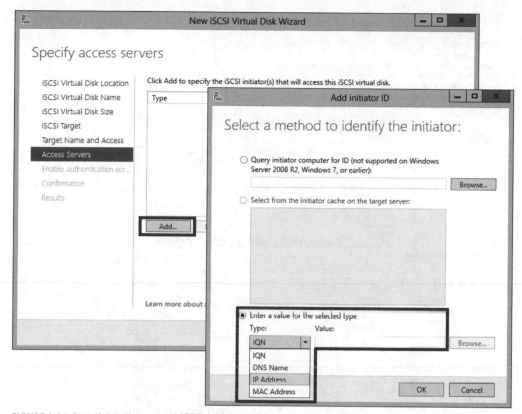

FIGURE 2-34 Specifying the remote iSCSI initiators that will be attached to the iSCSI target

The subsequent page in the wizard allows you to enable CHAP authentication between the iSCSI target and initiator if desired. Finally, after confirming your selections, the wizard creates the new iSCSI virtual disk and its connected target.

Configuring the iSCSI Initiator

After you create the iSCSI virtual disk and target and have specified one or more iSCSI initiators for the target, you have to point the same initiator(s) toward that same target. Begin by opening the iSCSI Initiator tool on the remote server. (You can use the Tools menu or type **Iscsicpl** at a command prompt.) On the Targets tab, shown in Figure 2-35, type the IP address of server hosting the target and then click Quick Connect. If (and only if) the initiator has been added to the target, the target should be discovered, identified by its IQN. Click Done and then click OK to approve the target.

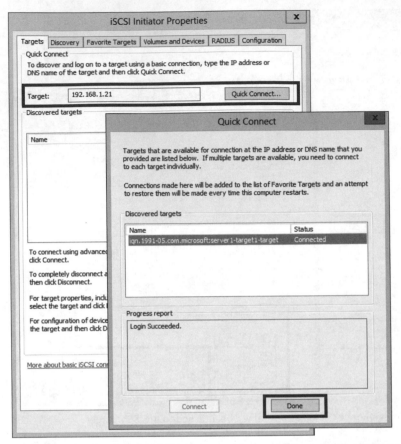

FIGURE 2-35 Configuring the iSCSI Initiator tool to connect to an existing iSCSI target

> **MORE INFO** **ISCSI INITIATOR CONFIGURATION OPTIONS**
>
> For more information about the many configuration options available in iSCSI Initiator, search for "Microsoft iSCSI Initiator Step-by-Step Guide" on TechNet or visit *http://technet. microsoft.com/en-us/library/ee338476(v=ws.10).aspx*.

Configuring the new disk on the remote server

On the remote server connecting to the iSCSI target, the new disk or disks made available through that target should now be visible in Server Manager. In Server Manager, click File and Storage Services and then click Disks. (If Server Manager is already open, you might need to refresh the screen manually. The Disks context doesn't update dynamically.)

In the Disks context, the new disk will appear in an offline state. Use the shortcut menu for the disk to bring the disk online, initialize it, and then create volumes as desired. Only after you create a new volume can the new storage appear as a drive letter in Windows Explorer.

You need to know the sequence of steps required to configure a remote server with storage through iSCSI. Remember above all that you need to add an initiator to a target before you can configure the initiator to connect to that target.

Managing existing iSCSI virtual disks and targets

You can use Server Manager on the iSCSI target server to modify iSCSI virtual disks and targets that have already been created. For example, the shortcut menu of an iSCSI virtual disk, shown in Figure 2-36, allows you to assign or re-assign an iSCSI virtual disk to an iSCSI target, to extend the disk, to disable the disk, or to remove the disk from its target. The properties dialog box of the iSCSI virtual disk allows you to modify the LUN value assigned to the disk. The Tasks menu provides an option to import an existing VHD file that is not yet managed by Server Manager.

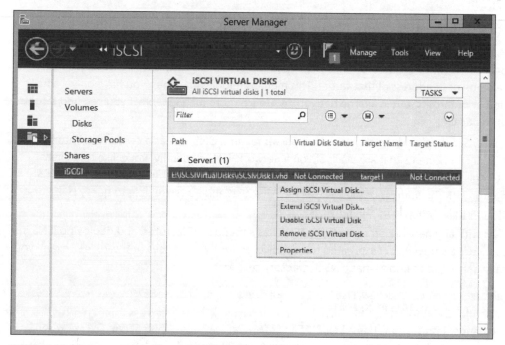

FIGURE 2-36 Management options for an iSCSI virtual disk

If in Server Manager you scroll down from the iSCSI Virtual Disks area, you will see an iSCSI Targets area. Here you can adjust the properties of targets by adding or removing the initiators to which they are connected. You can also adjust the security options for a target, or disable or remove a target.

EXAM TIP

You need to know the management and configuration options for iSCSI virtual disks and targets that are available through Server Manager. Make sure you spend some time looking at all these options so you get a feel for them.

MORE INFO CONFIGURING ISCSI STORAGE

For more information about configuring iSCSI storage, search for "Introduction of iSCSI Target in Windows Server 2012" on TechNet or visit *http://blogs.technet.com/b/filecab/archive/2012/05/21/introduction-of-iscsi-target-in-windows-server-2012.aspx*.

It is also recommended that you review the Windows PowerShell cmdlets for the iSCSI target. For a reference on these cmdlets, search for "iSCSI Target Cmdlets in Windows PowerShell" on TechNet or visit *http://technet.microsoft.com/en-us/library/hh826097*.

Using Internet iStorage Name Service (iSNS) Server

Let's say you're deploying a new application server and want to add storage from your network's iSCSI target. In the way described in the previous sections, you'd need to know the name or IP address of that target. This method might work when you have only a small number of targets, but in a large network, it's much more manageable if you can find targets automatically.

iSNS Server is an installable Windows Server feature. iSNS acts as a central repository of iSCSI components that are available on a network. iSNS generally works like this: First, you register iSCSI initiators and targets with the iSNS server. You then configure each iSCSI Initiator with the address of the iSNS server. After that, initiators are able to query iSNS for a list of targets available on the network.

As with any networking technology, iSNS has a number of features, and deploying iSNS in practice is a somewhat complicated topic. However, for the purposes of the 70-412 exam, you really only need to know what iSNS Server service is for.

MORE INFO ISNS SERVER FEATURE

For more information about the iSNS Server feature, search for "iSNS Server Overview" on TechNet or visit *http://technet.microsoft.com/en-us/library/cc772568.aspx*.

Using Features on Demand

A copy of the binary files for all features and roles that are installed during Windows Setup is stored in a directory called the *side-by-side store*, located in Windows\WinSxS. Keeping a copy of the feature files available on disk in this way allows you to add a role or enable a feature after Windows Server installation without needing to access Windows Server media.

In previous versions of Windows Server, these features files remained on disk for the life of the operating system. The disadvantage of this approach was that these files took up space on the disk even if you never wanted to install its associated feature or role. In addition, you weren't able to reduce the size of the installation image, as you might want to do when creating custom installation media for your organization.

In Windows Server 2012 or Windows Server 2012 R2, you can reduce the footprint of your installation by deleting the files for features you're not using from the side-by-side store. This ability to delete feature files is called *Features on Demand*. To later reinstall a role or feature for which files have been deleted, you need to have access to the Windows Server 2012 or Windows Server 2012 R2 source files.

To completely remove all files for a role or feature from disk, use the Uninstall-WindowsFeature cmdlet of Windows PowerShell and specify the name of the feature using the -Remove option. For example, to delete the DHCP server binaries from server storage, run the following Windows PowerShell command:

```
Uninstall-WindowsFeature DHCP -Remove
```

Figure 2-37 shows the result after this procedure when you run the Get-WindowsFeature cmdlet. The DHCP Server install state is described as Removed.

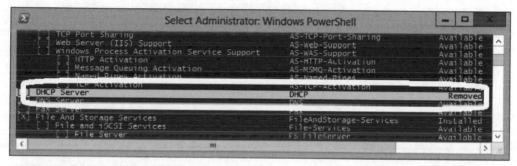

FIGURE 2-37 Removing feature files

You can reinstall these feature files at any point. To install a role or feature for which the binaries have been deleted, you can use the Install-WindowsFeature cmdlet in Windows PowerShell with the –Source option to specify any of the following:

- A path to a local WIM file (e.g. the product DVD).

   The path for a WIM file should be in the following format: WIM:[*drive letter*]:\sources\install.wim:[*image index*] (for example, WIM:e:\sources\install.wim:4.)

- A UNC path to a WIM file on a network share, using the "WIM:" prefix before the path.

- A UNC path to a network share that contains the WinSxS folder for the appropriate version of WS2012.

If you do not specify a –Source option, Windows will attempt to access the files by performing the following tasks in order:

1. Searching in a location that has been specified by users of the Add Roles And Features Wizard or Deployment Image Servicing and Management (DISM) installation commands.

2. Evaluating the configuration of the Group Policy setting: Computer Configuration\Administrative Templates\System\Specify settings for optional component installation and component repair.

3. Searching Windows Update. (Note that this can be a lengthy process for some features.)

Alternatively, you can reinstall the feature using Server Manager. When you get to the final page of the Add Roles And Features Wizard, choose the Specify An Alternate Source Path option, as shown in Figure 2-38. Then provide a path to source files when prompted.

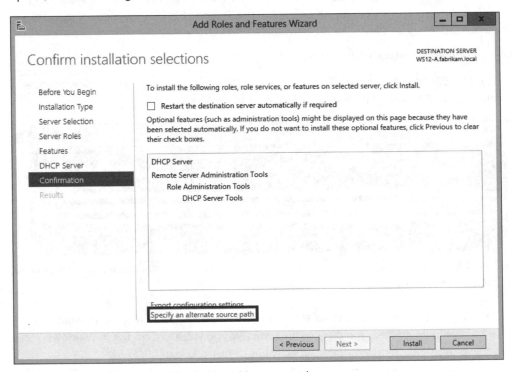

FIGURE 2-38 Reinstalling feature files that have been removed

The source path or file share must grant Read permissions either to the Everyone group (not recommended because of security reasons) or to the computer account of the destination server; granting user account access is not sufficient.

MORE INFO **FEATURES ON DEMAND**

For more information on Features on Demand, visit *http://technet.microsoft.com/en-us/library/jj127275.aspx*.

Installing the Data Deduplication component

Data Deduplication is an installable component of the File And Storage Services role, as shown in Figure 2-39. When you install the Data Deduplication component, you can enable Windows to reduce redundant (duplicate) chunks of data saved in storage. The purpose of data deduplication in general is to reduce the storage footprint and your data and increase your storage capacity without reducing performance. Space savings you can get from configuring this feature range from 30 percent to as much as 90 percent.

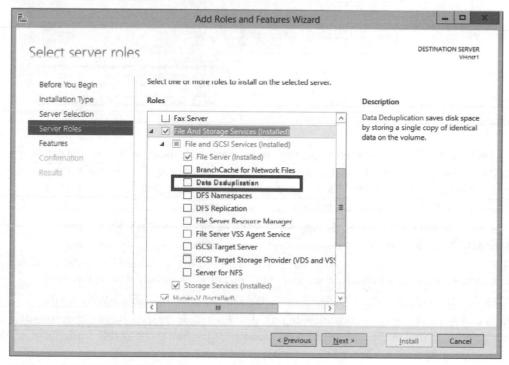

FIGURE 2-39 Data Deduplication is a component (role service) of the File And Storage Services role

You configure the Data Deduplication component through the File and Storage Services page in Server Manager. In File and Storage Services, click Volumes. Right-click any volume on which you want to configure data deduplication and then select Configure Data Deduplication, as shown in Figure 2-40.

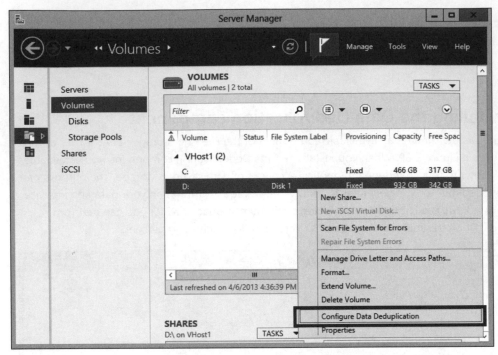

FIGURE 2-40 You configure data deduplication in File and Storage Services in Server Manager

Figure 2-41 shows the main configuration options available. Begin in the Deduplication Settings dialog box by enabling data deduplication on the volume. You can also set the minimum age for files targeted for deduplication and define any files that you want to be excluded from the deduplication process.

Next, you can customize the deduplication schedule by clicking Set Deduplication Schedule. To understand why a deduplication might be scheduled, remember that deduplication isn't instantaneous. It requires a process, usually running in the background, to scan and alter the data for optimal storage. (It's similar to defragmentation in this way.)

By default, only the Enable Background Optimization option is selected. With this default option, data deduplication runs with no defined schedule. Instead, it runs frequently at low priority as long as the system isn't busy. However, if you select the Enable Throughput Optimization option, you can define a start time and length of time during selected days of the week that you want deduplication to run at normal priority instead of low priority. For more flexibility, you can also configure a second schedule.

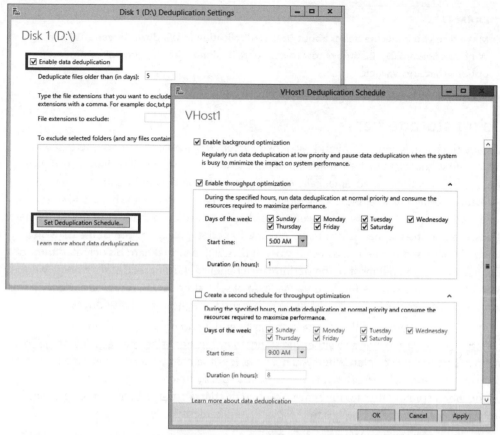

FIGURE 2-41 Configuring deduplication settings

One final note about the Data Deduplication functionality in Windows Server 2012: If you want to evaluate the space savings you'll get from data deduplication without enabling the feature, you can use the Deduplication Data Evaluation Tool (DDPEval.exe), which is found in the \Windows\System32\ directory.

> **MORE INFO** **DATA DEDUPLICATION**
>
> For more information about the Data Deduplication functionality in Windows Server 2012, search for "Introduction to Data Deduplication in Windows Server 2012" on TechNet or visit *http://blogs.technet.com/b/filecab/archive/2012/05/21/introduction-to-data-dedupli-cation-in-windows-server-2012.aspx.*

Using storage tiers

Storage tiers allows you to configure Windows Server 2012 R2 storage spaces so that you
can create virtual disks that are made up of both solid state and magnetic hard disk drives.
Storage tier functionality automatically moves data based on how frequently that data is
accessed. Frequently accessed data is moved onto the part of the virtual hard disk stored on
solid state drive while less frequently accessed data is moved onto the part of the virtual hard
disk stored on the magnetic disk drives. In many scenarios, only a fraction of the data on a
volume is accessed frequently. By using storage tiers with a virtual hard disk created through
storage spaces, you get most of the performance benefits of using solid state storage without
requiring all of the storage fabric to be made up of solid state drives. A typical storage tiering
configuration involves having 4 solid-state drives and 8 magnetic hard disk drives.

Data is moved between the standard and fast tier depending on how often it is accessed. You can also pin files to either the standard or fast tier using the Set-FileStorageTier
Windows PowerShell cmdlet. When you pin a file, it will remain associated with the selected
tier independently of how often it is accessed. You specify that a storage space will support
tiering when creating the storage space. You cannot enable storage tiering on an existing
storage space. Storage tiering has the following requirements:

- Only supported on Windows Server 2012 R2
- When creating a storage space with storage tiers, the virtual disk must use fixed
  provisioning
- The number of columns must be identical (a two column, two-way mirror with storage
  tiers requires four solid state and four magnetic hard disk drives)
- Ensure that volumes created on storage tier virtual disks are the same size as the virtual
  disk

MORE INFO **STORAGE TIERING**

You can learn more about storage tiering by consulting the following TechNet link:
*http://blogs.technet.com/b/josebda/archive/2013/08/28/step-by-step-for-storage-spaces-
tiering-in-windows-server-2012-r2.aspx.*

Thought experiment

Managing storage at Adventure Works

In the following thought experiment, apply what you've learned about this objective to predict what steps you need to take. You can find answers to these questions in the "Answers" section at the end of this chapter.

You are a network administrator for Adventure Works, Inc., a rapidly growing company based in Seattle that has just opened its first branch office in Denver. The network consists of a single Active Directory domain, Adventureworks.com. All servers are running either Windows Server 2008 R2 or Windows Server 2012 and all clients are running either Windows 7 or Windows 8. The two sites are linked by a site-to-site VPN.

The Seattle office and the Denver office each includes a main file server (named FSSeattle1 and FSDenver1, respectively) that is shared by all users in the local office location. DFS has been configured so that the same five shares are available to authorized users in both offices. Each share is used by one company-wide department, including Finance, Sales and Marketing, Operations, Human Resources, and Research and Development.

Each office location includes employees from each of the five departments.

A goal for the IT department is to address security concerns about confidential information while making all other information available to members of each department.

With the preceding information in mind, answer the following questions.

1. If you wanted to limit access to some files within each department share to members of each office site, how can you best achieve this goal by using NTFS file permissions?

2. Given the information provided about the network, what changes might you need to make to ensure that DAC can be implemented on the network?

3. You want to make sure that when employees at one office designate a file in their department share as highly confidential, the file can be viewed only from computers with account properties in Active Directory that indicate the same physical delivery office name as that of the user. How might you achieve this goal by using DAC permissions only? (Describe or list resource properties, claims types, and the central access rules you would need to create. You can assume that all informational fields are filled out in the properties of both user and computer accounts at both locations.)

4. What changes must you make to the network before you can configure detailed assistance to all users who are denied access to a resource?

Objective summary

- You can provide iSCSI SAN storage to clients on a network by installing and configuring the iSCSI Target Server available in Windows Server 2012.

- Windows Server 2012 includes iSCSI Initiator, which is an iSCSI client that connects to iSCSI targets and provisions storage from those targets as apparently local disks.

- To create iSCSI storage on a target server, run the New iSCSI Virtual Disk Wizard. This wizard creates a VHD file that you must attach to a local iSCSI target. When a remote initiator later connects to this target, the VHD appears to the iSCSI client as a local disk.

- You need to add an initiator to a target before you can establish a connection from the initiator to the target.

- Features on Demand is the name of a functionality in Windows Server 2012 that allows you to reduce the footprint of your Windows Server installation by removing all of the files associated with unneeded features. To remove an unneeded feature completely from a Windows Server 2012 installation, use the Uninstall-WindowsFeature cmdlet with the -Remove option.

- Data Deduplication is a component of the File And Storage Services role that reduces the amount of space taken up by data on your disks without adversely affecting performance. When installed and enabled, Data Deduplication runs as a background process by default. You configure Data Deduplication on a per-volume basis in the File And Storage Services page of Server Manager.

- Storage tiering allows you to improve performance by including both solid state and traditional magnetic media hard disks in a storage pool. Frequently accessed data is automatically moved to the solid state disks with less frequently access data moved to the magnetic media hard disks.

Objective review

Answer the following questions to test your knowledge of the information in this objective. You can find the answers to these questions and explanations of why each answer choice is correct or incorrect in the "Answers" section at the end of the chapter.

1. You are a network administrator for Adatum.com. You are deploying a new application server named App1, and you need to provision storage for App1 from an active iSCSI target on a server named Storage1.

   You enable the iSCSI Initiator service on App1. What should you do next?

   A. Run the Iscsicli command.

   B. Run the Iscsicpl command.

   C. Add App1 to the iSCSI target on Storage1.

   D. Point the iSCSI Initiator on App1 to the iSCSI target on Storage1.

2. You work as a network administrator for Fabrikam.com. The Fabrikam.com network includes approximately 50 servers and 600 clients. New iSCSI resources are frequently added to the network to support increased storage demands. Locating these iSCSI resources on the network is becoming increasing difficult.

   You want to improve the manageability of your iSCSI resources on the network by using a central repository.

   Which feature should you configure?

   A. An iSCSI Target

   B. An iSNS Server

   C. An iSCSI Initiator

   D. A storage pool

3. Data Deduplication is enabled on the E:/ volume of a server named VHost1. You want to modify the deduplication schedule so that deduplication can run at a higher priority during the overnight hours.

   Which tool should you use to configure this setting on VHost1?

   A. Server Manager

   B. Computer Management

   C. Windows Explorer

   D. File Server Resource Manager

Answers

This section contains the solutions to the "Thought experiments" and the "Objective review" questions in this chapter.

Objective 2.1: Thought experiment

1. You can configure a file screen to stop users from storing audio files on the file share.

2. You can run a report to determine which files haven't been accessed after a specific number of days. You can then move these files to the archive share.

3. You can run a duplicate files report to determine when multiple copies of a file are being stored.

4. You can use quotas to limit the amount of data a user stores on a single share.

Objective 2.1: Review

1. **Correct Answers:** A, D

   A. **Correct:** You need to enable this policy setting to enable BranchCache on clients that fall within the scope of the policy.

   B. **Incorrect:** You can use this policy setting to specify only a single hosted cache server.

   C. **Incorrect:** You use this policy setting to enable hosted cache discovery. You want to configure clients with two specific hosted cache servers, not enable hosted cache discovery.

   D. **Correct:** You use this policy setting to configure clients running Windows 8 or Windows Server 2012 with the names of one or more hosted cache servers.

2. **Correct Answer:** A

   A. **Correct:** This cmdlet lets you generate hashes for content on BranchCache-enabled file shares to stage the data for a cache package used for preloading.

   B. **Incorrect:** This cmdlet lets you generate hashes for content on BranchCache-enabled web servers to stage the data for a cache package.

   C. **Incorrect:** This cmdlet lets you generate a cache package containing all the staged data.

   D. **Incorrect:** This cmdlet lets you import a cache package to a hosted cache server.

3. **Correct Answers:** A, B

   A. **Correct:** You need to use this policy setting to enable BranchCache on clients that fall within the scope of the policy.

   B. **Correct:** You need to use this policy setting to enable clients for BranchCache if no hosted cache server is present in the branch office.

   C. **Incorrect:** This policy setting is used to enable clients with the name of a single hosted cache server. It is not used to configure BranchCache clients to use Distributed Cache mode.

   D. **Incorrect:** This policy setting is used to define the network latency threshold beyond which clients will attempt to retrieve content from a local cache instead of from a remote source over a WAN link. You can't use this policy setting to configure BranchCache clients to use Distributed Cache mode.

Objective 2.2: Thought experiment

1. Create a file classification rule that assigns a specific classification when a keyword is located within the file.

2. You need to configure a user claim that will allow you to create a rule based on the user's Active Directory attribute.

3. You use Group Policy to deploy central access policies to file servers.

4. You can configure access denied assistance to allow users to automatically request access to files they are unable to open.

Objective 2.2: Review

1. **Correct Answer:** D

   A. **Incorrect:** You should run this cmdlet after you add the new resource property to a resource property list.

   B. **Incorrect:** You don't need to enable new resource properties that you create. They are already enabled when you create them.

   C. **Incorrect:** Optionally, you can create a classification rule to classify files and folders automatically. However, you can take this step only later, after you have updated file and folder objects.

   D. **Correct:** After you create or enable a resource property, you need to add it to a resource property list. Only then can you update file and folder objects so that they include this resource property on the Classification tab.

2. **Correct Answer:** A

   A. **Correct:** To enable claims-based authorization in your domain, you should enable this policy setting at the domain controller level.

   B. **Incorrect:** You should enable this policy setting at the domain controller level, not at the domain level.

   C. **Incorrect:** This policy setting enables computers to request claims. It is used for policy auditing, not for enabling claims-based authorization.

   D. **Incorrect:** This policy setting enables computers to request claims. It is used for policy auditing, not for enabling claims-based authorization.

3. **Correct Answers:** C, D

   A. **Incorrect:** Changing the NTFS permissions will restrict access to members of the appropriate department, but it will not provide any information about files that will allow them to be traced when they are moved outside of the shared folder.

   B. **Incorrect:** Changing the share permissions will restrict access to members of the appropriate department when they connect over the network, but it will not provide any information about files that will allow them to be traced when they are moved outside of the shared folder.

   C. **Correct:** Configuring a Department property value will allow you to classify the files in each departmental shared folder as belonging to that department, even when they leave that folder.

   D. **Correct:** Applying this type of central access policy to each shared folder will configure the files within these folders with appropriate access permissions.

Objective 2.3: Thought experiment

1. You should create a security group for members of each site-specific department, such as Seattle-Finance and Denver-Finance. Then you could create a folder in each department share to which only members of each site-specific department had access.

2. You might need to install a Windows Server 2012 domain controller at each site.

3. You can configure the following:

   - Resource property: Confidentiality

   - Claims types: Office name (Physical-Delivery-Office-Name) for both users and computers

   - Access rule, target resource conditional expression: Resource.Confidentiality Equals High

   - Access rule, permissions: Authenticated users = Full Control. Conditional expression: Device.physicalDeliveryOfficeName Equals User.physicalDeliveryOfficeName.

4. You must first upgrade all clients to Windows 8.

Objective 2.3: Review

1. **Correct Answer:** C

   A. **Incorrect:** Iscsicli is a command-line utility used to manage iSCSI Initiator. Used without any parameters, the command will provide the IQN of the local iSCSI Initiator. However, the next step you need to take is to add the local initiator to the iSCSI target.

   B. **Incorrect:** Running the Iscsicpl command will launch the iSCSI Initiator tool in the GUI. However, your next step is not to configure the local iSCSI Initiator but to configure the iSCSI target (by adding the initiator to the target).

   C. **Correct:** You need to modify the properties of the target by adding App1 to its list of iSCSI initiators. Only then should you point the initiator to the target.

   D. **Incorrect:** You need to add the initiator to the target on Storage1 before you point the initiator toward the target on App1.

2. **Correct Answer:** B

   A. **Incorrect:** An iSCSI target does not provide a central repository. It provides one source of logical disks to remote iSCSI initiators.

   B. **Correct:** An iSNS server is a central repository of iSCSI services on network.

   C. **Incorrect:** An iSCSI Initiator is an iSCSI client. An iSCSI Initiator provisions storage from an iSCSI target. It doesn't provide a central repository of iSCSI resources on a network.

   D. **Incorrect:** A storage pool is a Windows Server feature that allows you to consolidate physical disks for one server into a single flexible source of storage for that one server. A storage pool doesn't provide a central repository of iSCSI resources on a network.

3. **Correct Answer:** A

   A. **Correct:** You configure the Data Deduplication feature in File and Storage Services in Server Manager.

   B. **Incorrect:** You can't configure Data Deduplication in Computer Management. You have to use the File and Storage Services page Server Manager.

   C. **Incorrect:** You can't configure Data Deduplication in Windows Explorer. You have to use the File and Storage Services page Server Manager.

   D. **Incorrect:** You can't configure Data Deduplication in File Server Resource Manager. You have to use the File and Storage Services page Server Manager.

Implement business continuity and disaster recovery

This domain refers to the essential functions of backing up, restoring, and recovering servers. Understanding the topics covered in this domain requires a deep understanding of new technologies that you might not have implemented in your own environment. You should supplement the information in this chapter with some hands-on practice so that you can develop an understanding of how you can use these technologies to address real world scenarios and solve problems in an advanced server environment.

Objectives in this chapter:

- Objective 3.1: Configure and manage backups
- Objective 3.2: Recover servers
- Objective 3.3: Configure site-level fault tolerance

Objective 3.1: Configure and manage backups

This objective deals with preparing for data loss. Performing backups with the Windows Server Backup feature is the simplest and most obvious way to prepare for disaster recovery, but that doesn't mean that it's the most likely topic in this objective to appear on the exam. Windows Server Backup—at least at the basic level in which people most often use it— is actually too simple to lend itself well to exam questions. If you see a question about Windows Server Backup on the 70-412 exam, the question will address deeper configuration issues, such as configuring VSS or performance settings.

The exam question writers will likely have an easier time creating questions at an appropriate level of difficulty for the other topics covered in this objective, such as backup user rights, VSSAdmin, and Windows Azure Backup.

Using the Windows Server Backup feature

Windows Server Backup is the server backup feature in Windows Server 2012 and Windows Server 2012 R2. Its graphical console (Wbadmin.msc) is installed by default, but you can't use this console perform any local backups until you actually install the feature itself. To install the Windows Server Backup feature, you can, of course, use the Add Roles and Features Wizard, but if you prefer to use Windows PowerShell, type the following at a Windows PowerShell prompt:

```
Install-WindowsFeature Windows-Server-Backup
```

After you install Windows Server Backup, two backup wizards become available in the Windows Server Backup console: The Backup Schedule Wizard and the Backup Once Wizard. The links to open these wizards are shown in Figure 3-1. To prepare for Objective 3.1 on the 70-412 exam, you need to understand (among other things) all of the configuration options available in these two wizards. Fortunately, the wizards are very similar, and there aren't many options to learn.

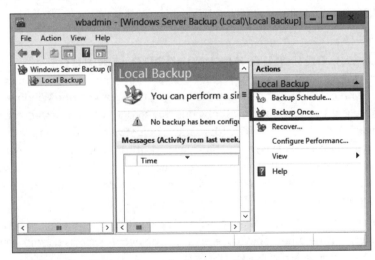

FIGURE 3-1 The Windows Server Backup console

Backup Options page

The Backup Options page appears only in the Backup Once Wizard, not the Backup Schedule Wizard. This first page gives you two options for performing a backup now: The first option is available only if you've already configured a scheduled backup for the local server. When available, this option lets you make an immediate backup of the same items you've already configured for the scheduled backup. All settings you've configured for that scheduled backup are also used, including the location at which you've chosen to save the backup data. The second backup option is to perform an immediate backup with options that haven't been configured for the scheduled backup on the local server. In Figure 3-2, the option to choose the scheduled backup options is, in fact, grayed out because no scheduled backup has been configured for the local server.

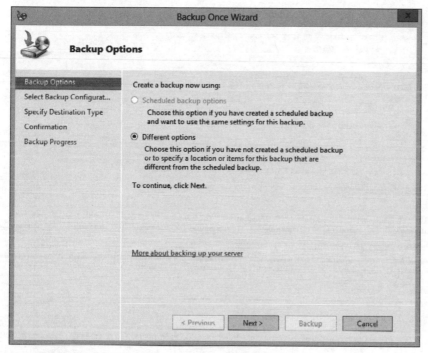

FIGURE 3-2 General options for immediate backup

Select Backup Configuration page

This page is shown in in the top left portion of Figure 3-3. Here you decide whether to perform a full server backup or a custom backup. As you might expect, a full server backup, includes all data on the system and lets you perform any type of recovery, including a system state or bare metal recovery. A custom backup can be a full backup or any subset of volumes, folders, or files. A custom backup also allows you to make some advanced configuration choices, such as creating exclusions or changing VSS settings for the backup.

If you are testing backup functionality for the purpose of exam preparation, make sure you choose the Custom option so that you can see all available backup options.

Select Items For Backup page

The Select Items For Backup page is shown in the bottom-right portion of Figure 3-3. On this page, click Add Items to choose which items to back up. Click Advanced Settings to adjust some default configuration settings for the backup.

FIGURE 3-3 Choosing a backup type and items for backup

Add Items

Clicking Add Items on the Select Items For Backup page opens the Select Items dialog box, shown in Figure 3-4.

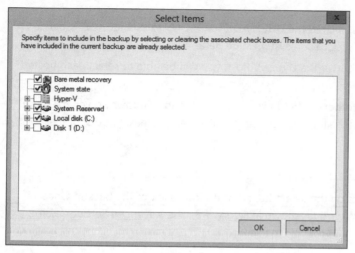

FIGURE 3-4 Selecting items to back up

Of these options, make sure you understand the following:

- **Bare Metal Recovery**   This item in the Select Items dialog box is not a data component but a shortcut that selects the components required for a bare metal recovery. When you select Bare Metal Recovery, as shown in Figure 3-4, the System State and system disk (typically C:) are automatically selected, along with any System Reserved partition that the local system might include. Backing up these Bare Metal Recovery components lets you later boot a restored version of the local system on a server that is not loaded with any software at the outset. The bare metal server can be the original system with newly formatted disks or it can be another, identical system.

- **System State**   System State contains only the system files and configuration data of the local server. By restoring these files, you would restore the configuration state of the server as it existed at the time the backup was performed. If the operating system on your server becomes corrupted, you can also use the system state data to repair a system and get it to a bootable state. System state always includes the following components:

  - Registry
  - COM+ class registration database
  - Boot files, including system files
  - System files under Windows File Protection

If the server is a domain controller, the following two components are also included in the system state:

- Active Directory service
- SYSVOL directory
- Certain server roles, such as the DHCP, AD CS and DNS roles and their associated databases, are also included in system state data.
- **Hyper-V** If the local server is a Hyper-V host, you will be able to select each hosted VM for backup.
- **Individual files and folders** Windows Server Backup in Windows Server 2012 and Windows Server 2012 R2 allows you to select individual volumes, folders, or files for backup.

Advanced Settings

If you click Advanced Settings on the Select Items For Backup page of the Backup Once Wizard or Backup Schedule Wizard (as shown in Figure 3-3), the Advanced Settings dialog box opens.

CONFIGURING EXCLUSIONS

It's possible that you'll see a question on the 70-412 exam that requires some understanding of backup exclusions. Such a question might set up a scenario in which you need to perform a backup more quickly, or with less space, or with less network traffic, than the current backup set. The "correct answer" might be to exclude a folder or files that match a particular filename pattern with some unneeded data in the current backup set. You do this on the Exclusions tab of the Advanced Settings dialog box, as shown in Figure 3-5.

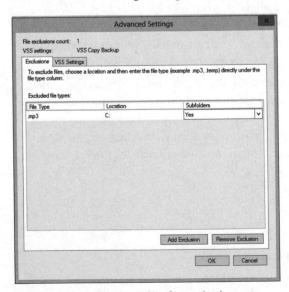

FIGURE 3-5 Excluding .mp3 files from a backup set

CONFIGURING VSS SETTINGS

The other tab—VSS Settings—is shown in Figure 3-6. *Volume Shadow Copy Service (VSS)* is the background service that, among other important functions, allows Windows Server Backup to create backups of all files, even ones which are locked by applications. All backups performed by Windows Server Backup are VSS backups, so these settings are always applied when the backup you're currently defining is performed.

The two options are:

- **VSS Full Backup**   With this setting, the files you back up are marked as backed up in the application log file. This option is appropriate when you are not using any other backup application.

- **VSS Copy Backup**   This is the default selection. With this option, the backed-up files are not marked up as backed up, so the backup doesn't interfere with any other backup applications.

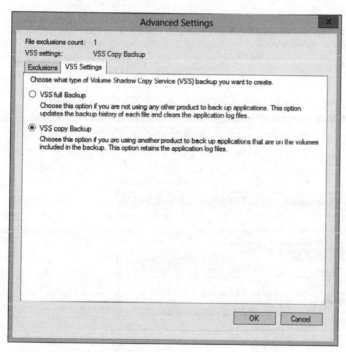

FIGURE 3-6 Choosing the type of VSS backup

Destination type

After you choose which items to back up and make any desired exclusions and changes to VSS settings, you need to specify a location to store the backup.

- **Back Up To A Dedicated Hard Disk**   This option is available only for scheduled backups. If you have a spare physical hard disk, this option offers the best performance for storing backups. Writing to the dedicated disk doesn't interfere with any other I/O operations.

- **Back Up To A Volume**   This option is also available only for scheduled backups and applies to non-dedicated volumes and mapped network drives, not optical drives such as DVD drives.

- **Local Drives**   This option is available only with the Backup Once option. It is similar to the Back Up To A Volume option, except that you can also burn the backup to an optical drive.

- **Remote Shared Folder**   This option is available for both the scheduled backups and immediate backups. An important limitation of saving to a remote shared folder is that you can only store one backup at the remote location. Any existing backups found at the network path are overwritten by the new backup.

EXAM TIP

Remember that backing up to a remote shared folder overwrites the previous backup.

Performance settings

Performance settings are configured in the Windows Server Backup console, not the Backup Schedule Wizard or the Backup Once Wizard. The performance settings allow you to make backup operations quicker, at the expense of a longer restore operation. To view performance settings, click Configure Performance Settings in the Actions pane of the console, as shown in Figure 3-7. This opens the Optimize Backup Performance dialog box, shown in Figure 3-8.

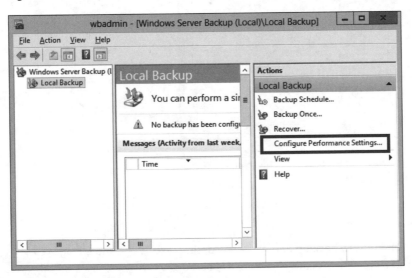

FIGURE 3-7 Configuring performance settings

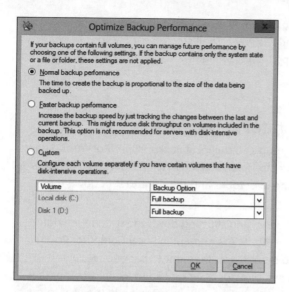

FIGURE 3-8 Configuring performance settings

By default, Normal Backup Performance is selected. With this option, full backups are performed. (The complete source data is backed up to the destination storage location, regardless of whether the blocks of data have changed.)

If you select Faster Backup Performance, incremental backups are performed 14 times in a row or 14 days in a row (whichever is sooner) before each full backup is performed. With incremental backups, only the blocks of data that have been modified since the last backup are copied to the destination storage location. The backup procedure is usually faster as a result, but the restore operation is typically longer.

To apply different backup methods to different volumes, select the Custom option. The choice for each volume is displayed as Full Backup or Incremental Backup.

Command-line tools for backup

Although backups you've reviewed where backup options are found in the GUI, it's also a good idea to look at how you can perform or configure backups from the command line. Windows Server 2012 and Windows Server 2012 R2 include two command-line tools to configure and perform backups: the *Wbadmin.exe* utility and Windows PowerShell.

Wbadmin.exe offers basic backup functionality and is installed when you install the Windows Server Backup feature of Windows Server 2012 and Windows Server 2012 R2. To see the commands available in Wbadmin.exe, type **Wbadmin /?** at a command prompt after you've installed Windows Server Backup feature.

Windows PowerShell includes a much more complete command-line administration interface for server backups. To see the Windows PowerShell cmdlets for backups in Windows Server 2012 or Windows Server 2012 R2, type the following at a Windows PowerShell prompt:

```
Get-Command -Module WindowsServerBackup
```

Understanding Backup Operators

Only members of the local Administrators group and the local Backup Operators group have the right to perform backups of files and directories on a given machine. Backup Operators are also granted the rights to restore files and directories and the right to shut down the system.

All three of these rights (backing up, restoring, and shutting down the system) are rights that can be assigned separately through User Rights Assignment in Local Computer Policy or Group Policy. If, for example, you want to grant a user the right to back up files and directories but not the right to restore files and directories, you need to assign the user that specific user right through Local Computer Policy or Group Policy. Don't add the user to the Backup Operators group because you will be granting that user unwanted privileges.

EXAM TIP

For the 70-412 exam, remember that Backup Operators have more rights than just backing up a system. They can back up, restore, shutdown the system, log on locally, and access the computer from the network. If you want to assign a user just a few of those privileges, you should assign that user those rights through Local Computer Policy or Group Policy instead of adding her to the Backup Operators group.

Using the Shadow Copies feature (Previous Versions)

The Volume Shadow Copy Service provides the software framework not only for Windows Server backups but for the Shadow Copies feature and its related Previous Versions feature.

You can enable shadow copies of volumes in the properties of those volumes, after which snapshots of the volume are taken regularly (twice per day by default). You can also access these settings by right-clicking a volume and selecting Configure Shadow Copies on the shortcut menu. After you have enabled shadow copies on a volume, users can use the Previous Versions feature to restore to a previous snapshot any file or folders the users own on that volume. This functionality is shown in Figure 3-9. In the figure, shadow copies are enabled on volume D:\. When you then right-click a file on that volume, the shortcut menu shows an option to restore previous versions.

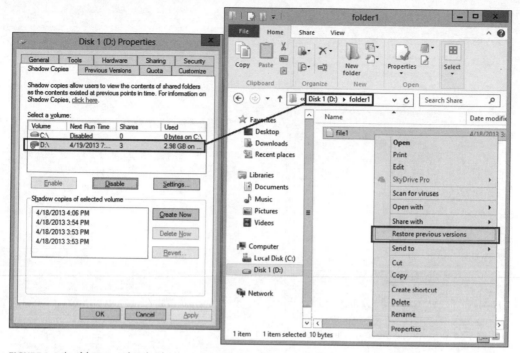

FIGURE 3-9 In this example, shadow copies are enabled on Volume D:\, allowing a user to restore a previous version of a file stored on that same volume

If you select the Restore Previous Versions option shown in Figure 3-9, the Previous Versions tab of the File Properties dialog box opens. This tab is shown in Figure 3-10. To restore a previous snapshot of the file, users can select the desired file version and then click the Restore button.

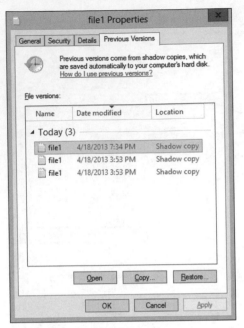

FIGURE 3-10 Restoring a previous version of a file

VSSAdmin is the command-line utility used for managing shadow copies and the Previous Versions feature. For example, you can create a new shadow copy (snapshot) of a volume by typing **VSSAdmin Create Shadow** at an elevated command prompt. To list available snapshots, type **VSSAdmin List Shadows**. To revert a volume to a previous snapshot, type **VSSAdmin Revert Shadow**. To delete a snapshot, type **VSSAdmin Delete Shadow**. To review other administrative options made available through VSSAdmin, type **VSSAdmin /?**.

EXAM TIP

You need to remember that VSSAdmin is the command-line tool used to manage shadow copies and the Previous Versions feature.

Configuring Windows Azure Backup

Microsoft provides an online backup feature—*Windows Azure Backup*—that lets you perform individual server backups to the cloud. Because it's an online service, Windows Azure Backup is capable of changing more than built-in features of Windows Server 2012 are. Make sure you consult online references about this service before you take the exam, so you know you have the most up-to-date information.

Create a Windows Azure account

The first step in configuring online backups is to create Windows Azure account and then create a backup vault. You can create a backup vault directly through the Windows Azure management console at *http://manage.windowsazure.com*, as shown in Figure 3-11.

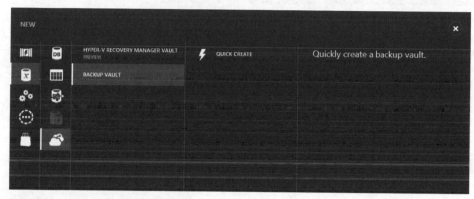

FIGURE 3-11 Creating a backup vault

Create a vault and add a certificate

In your Windows Azure portal, navigate to the recovery services and create a recovery vault in which to store your backups. After you create a vault, you need to upload management certificate to Windows Azure. You can obtain this certificate from a public certification authority (CA) or from a CA managed by your organization (such as Active Directory Certificate Services). Alternatively, you can create a self-signed client certificate by using the Makecert.exe command line utility. Makecert.exe is included in Microsoft Visual Studio Express, the most recent version of which is a free download at *http://microsoft.com/download*.

> **NOTE** MAKECERT.EXE SYNTAX
>
> If you use Makecert.exe to create a self-signed certificate, use the following syntax:
>
> ```
> makecert.exe -r -pe -n CN=<certName> -ss my -sr localmachine -eku
>    1.3.6.1.5.5.7.3.2 -e 12/12/2018 -len 2048 <CertificateName>.cer
> ```

Download and install the Windows Azure Backup Agent

After you create an account on the Windows Azure Backup website, create your vault, and upload your client certificate, you can download the Windows Azure Backup Agent and install it locally on the server. The Backup Agent appears similar to the Windows Server Backup console and is shown in Figure 3-12. This agent can be used to back up a single server to Windows Azure or it can be used to allow System Center 2012 R2 Data Protection Manager to perform backups to Windows Azure.

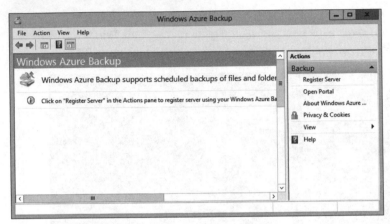

FIGURE 3-12 Using the Windows Azure Backup console

Register your server

The next step is to register your server. Registering a server enables you to perform backups from that same server only, though you can register multiple servers with the same recovery vault hosted with the same Windows Azure account.

The Register Server Wizard includes a few configuration steps. First, you are given an opportunity to specify a proxy server if desired. Second, you are asked to specify the certificate again and choose the Windows Azure vault to which you want to save your backups, as shown in Figure 3-13.

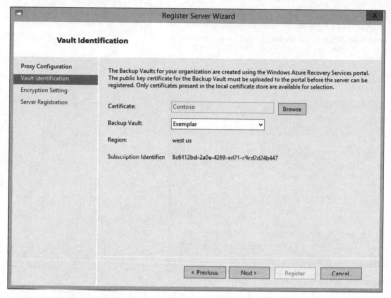

FIGURE 3-13 Registering a server

Finally, you need to specify a passphrase that will be used to encrypt your backup data. You must also specify a location to save this passphrase in a file. You need to provide this passphrase when you perform a restore operation, so it's essential that you don't lose it. (Microsoft doesn't maintain a copy of your passphrase.) A Generate Passphrase option creates the passphrase for you automatically.

After you register a server, new options for online backups appear in the Actions pane, including Schedule Backup, Recover Data, Change Properties, and Open Portal.

EXAM TIP

Remember this sequence of configuration steps: Create a Windows Azure account, upload the management certificate, download and install the agent, and then register the server.

Create a schedule

To start the Schedule Backup Wizard, click Schedule Backup in the Actions pane. The items you can select to backup in the Schedule Backup Wizard are shown in Figure 3-14.

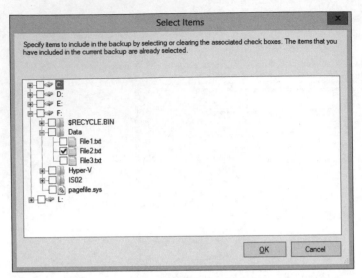

FIGURE 3-14 Selecting backups for an online backup

SPECIFYING RETENTION SETTINGS

Another feature especially relevant for the exam can be found on the Specify Retention Setting page of the Schedule Backup Wizard, shown in Figure 3-15. The *retention setting*, also called the *retention range*, is simply the number of days that the backup cannot be overwritten or deleted to make space for another backup. You can set the retention range for a backup at 7 days (the default), 15 days, or 30 days.

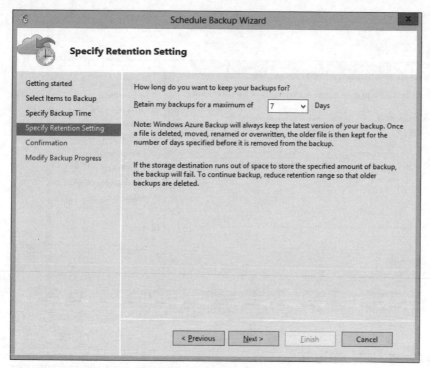

FIGURE 3-15 Configuring backup retention settings

Configure the Back Up Now option

The Back Up Now option appears in the Actions pane for online backups, as shown in Figure 3-16, but it does so only after you first complete the Schedule Backup Wizard. As stated earlier, Back Up Now for online backups allows you to perform additional online backups only of online backup sets that have been previously defined and scheduled. You *can't* use this option to select a new set of volumes, folders, or files and then perform an online backup of that new set.

Aside from this critical difference, the Back Up Now option for online backups resembles the Back Up Once option for local backups.

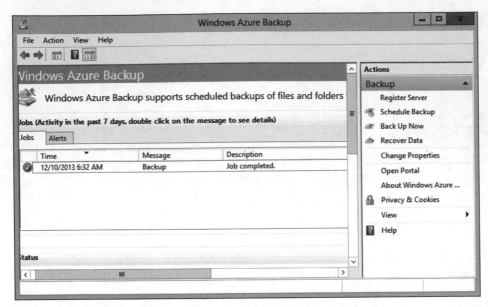

FIGURE 3-16 Viewing a backup job in the Windows Azure Backup console

Choose a Recover Data option

To restore data that has been backed up, choose the Recover Data option in the Actions pane. As Figure 3-17 shows, there isn't anything new or unusual about this option that would likely confuse you in the real world or in the exam world. However, it's worth remembering that you can restore online backups to another server.

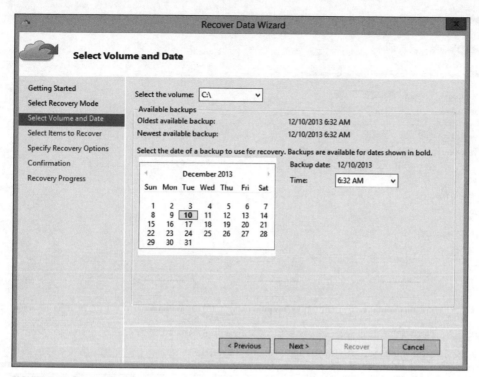

FIGURE 3-17 Recovering data

Enable bandwidth throttling

You can restrict the amount of bandwidth used during your online backup operations in a way that depends on when the backup occurs. To enable bandwidth throttling, click Change Properties in the Actions Pane, select the Throttling tab, and then select Enable Internet Bandwidth Usage Throttling For Backup Operations, as shown in Figure 3-18.

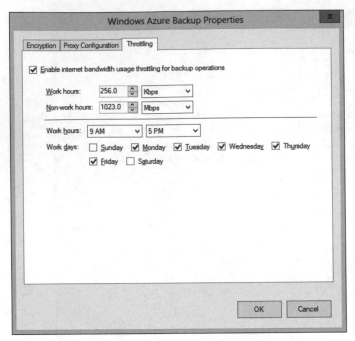

FIGURE 3-18 Configuring bandwidth throttling for online backups

Bandwidth throttling works by letting you set different bandwidth speeds for work and non-work hours. First you define the hours that should be considered work hours and for which days of the week. Then you specify how much Internet bandwidth you want to use for online backup operations during both these work hours and during the remaining non-work hours.

Bandwidth throttling might be the most likely feature about online backups to appear on the exam. For example, you could see a question that displays the Throttling tab and an accompanying scenario in which you need to adjust these settings in a way that reduces the impact of online backups on your users. In such a case, you might need to redefine the work hours (perhaps by lengthening the work day). Alternatively, you might need to decrease the bandwidth currently assigned to work hours if you want to prevent workday disruption. Or you might want to increase the bandwidth currently assigned to non-work hours if you want the online backups to be performed as quickly as possible.

Thought experiment

Using Windows Azure Backup at Adatum's branch offices

In the following thought experiment, apply what you've learned about this objective to predict what steps you need to take. You can find answers to these questions in the "Answers" section at the end of this chapter.

You are in the process of developing a solution to ensure that important server data hosted at remote Adatum branch offices is backed up in a reliable manner. In the last few years, backups have been written to attached USB storage devices. The problem is that these devices have been found to be unreliable, with the failure of the device only becoming apparent when an attempt to restore data has been performed. One solution that you are investigating is using Windows Azure Backup so that backed up data is stored within Windows Azure. With this in mind, you need to answer several questions before you proceed with the pilot program.

1. What steps do you need to take prior to downloading the Windows Azure Backup agent?

2. What is the maximum retention period for data backed up to Windows Azure using Windows Azure Backup?

3. In addition to your Windows Azure account, what do you need access to if you want to recover data from Windows Azure Backup?

Objective summary

- Windows Server Backup is the GUI-based backup tool in Windows Server 2012. Windows Server Backup lets you back up individual files, folder, and volumes; the system state data; the System Reserved partition; and the individual VMs hosted in Hyper-V. The command-line tool for performing backups in Windows Server 2012 is Wbadmin.exe.

- Backup Operators have the right to back up files and directories, restore files and directories, shut down the system, log on locally, and access the computer from the network.

- You can enable shadow copies on individual volumes. Snapshots of the volumes are then automatically taken by default twice per day. Users connecting to shared folders on these volumes will see previous versions of files in the shares available through the Previous Versions tab of the share properties. You can manage this Shadow Copy feature with the VSSAdmin tool.

- Windows Server 2012 provides an option to let you back up selected volumes, folders, and files of the local server over the Internet to cloud storage on Microsoft-owned premises. This functionality is provided by an optional add-on service called Windows Azure Backup.

- To prepare to use Windows Azure Backup, you first create a Windows Azure account, then create a vault in which to store backups, then upload a certificate, and finally download and install the Windows Azure Backup Agent.

Objective review

Answer the following questions to test your knowledge of the information in this objective. You can find the answers to these questions and explanations of why each answer choice is correct or incorrect in the "Answers" section at the end of the chapter.

1. Your network includes a file server named FileSrv1 that is running Windows Server 2012. You want to allow a user named User1 to back up FileSrv1. You also want to minimize the administrative privileges assigned to User1.

   What should you do?

   A. Assign User1 to the Backup Operators group on FileSrv1.

   B. Assign User1 to the Power Users group on FileSrv1.

   C. Assign User1 the user right to back up files and directories.

   D. Assign User1 the user rights to back up and restore files and directories.

2. Your network includes a file server named FileSrv2. FileSrv2 is running as a server core installation of Windows Server 2012. You want to create an immediate snapshot of volume E:\ so that users connecting to file shares will be able to revert files to the now-current version of the files in those shares. You want to perform this task with the least amount of administrative effort.

   Which tool should you use?

   A. VSSAdmin

   B. Shadow

   C. Get-VMSnapshot

   D. Wbadmin

3. You configure a Hyper-V host running Windows Server 2012 named VHost01 to perform a Windows Azure Backup at 11 P.M. every Wednesday. The organization's Internet connection isn't used for any other operations until 8 A.M. the following day. After running the online backup for the first time, you discover that the backup operation completes at 10:00 A.M. Thursday, after the start of the workday. You open the bandwidth throttling settings for the server and see the configuration shown in Figure 3-19.

   You want the online backup of VHost01 to complete before 8 A.M. on Thursday. Which of the following solutions is most likely to help you accomplish your goal with a minimum disruption for workers?

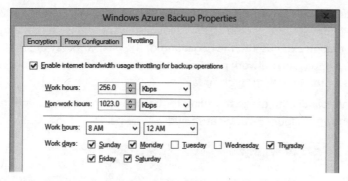

FIGURE 3-19 Configuring bandwidth throttling settings on FS01

A. Change the bandwidth setting assigned to work hours.

B. Change the bandwidth setting assigned to non-work hours.

C. Change the hours defined as work hours.

D. Change the days defined as work days.

4. You have a Windows Azure Backup account with a storage quota of 300 GB. You use this account to configure a single weekly backup of a file server running Windows Server 2012 named FileSrv01. The total amount of data on FileSrv01 does not significantly change from week to week. No other backups are configured with your account.

The online backup of FileSrv01 completes successfully on the first week, but on the second week, the backup fails. You receive an error indicating that the usage associated with your Windows Azure Backup account has exceeded its quota.

The Windows Azure Backup console displays the information shown in Figure 3-20 about the backup.

FIGURE 3-20 Viewing backup settings and destination usage

You want to be able to perform the weekly backup of FileSrv01 without failure. Which of the following actions is most likely to allow you to accomplish your goal?

A. Configure an exclusion for C:\Windows\Temp and choose to exclude its subfolders.

B. Configure an exclusion for C:\Windows\Temp and choose not to exclude its subfolders.

C. Change the retention range to 7 days.

D. Change the retention range to 30 days.

5. You want to configure a file server running Windows Server 2012 and named FS02 to perform a daily Windows Azure Backup at 3 AM. You also want to ensure that if the online backup operation extends into the beginning of the next workday at 9 AM, it will have a minimal impact on network performance for users. The workweek in your organization runs from Monday through Friday.

    You enable Internet bandwidth usage throttling for backup operations and find the default settings shown in Figure 3-21. What should you do next?

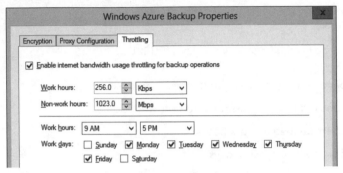

FIGURE 3-21 Configuring bandwidth throttling settings on FS02

A. Leave the default settings.

B. Increase the bandwidth setting assigned to work hours.

C. Increase the bandwidth setting assigned to non-work hours.

D. Change the selected workdays.

Objective 3.2: Recover servers

You have three topics to learn about for this objective, all of which are straightforward. First, learn the purpose of every advanced boot option and how to select these options. Then learn when and how to perform a system image recovery. Finally, learn a few command-line tools useful for troubleshooting in the Windows Recovery Environment.

> **This objective covers how to:**
> - Use the Advanced Boot Options menu
> - Recover servers with the Windows installation media

Using the Advanced Boot Options menu

The Advanced Boot Options menu gives you an important set of troubleshooting tools to fix a faulty Windows installation if the system at least begins the process of loading. Advanced Boot Options is especially useful when Windows doesn't start successfully, but it also provides options to repair the system if the system boots but behaves erratically (for example, after an application or driver install).

To get the menu to appear, press F8 just as the system is starting. If you are already in Windows and want to access the Advanced Boot Options menu the next time the system starts without pressing F8, you can use the **Shutdown /r /o** command or hold down the Shift key as you click Restart. These last two options shut down the system and then open a special Choose An Option screen, as shown in Figure 3-25. To restart the system into the Advanced Boot Options menu, click Troubleshoot, Startup Settings, Restart.

The Advanced Boot Options menu is shown in Figure 3-22.

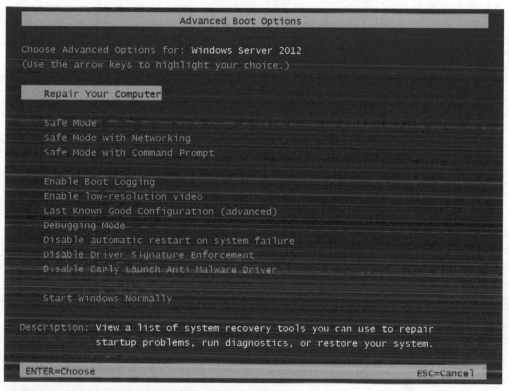

```
                        Advanced Boot Options

Choose Advanced Options for: Windows Server 2012
(Use the arrow keys to highlight your choice.)

     Repair Your Computer

     Safe Mode
     Safe Mode with Networking
     Safe Mode with Command Prompt

     Enable Boot Logging
     Enable low-resolution video
     Last Known Good Configuration (advanced)
     Debugging Mode
     Disable automatic restart on system failure
     Disable Driver Signature Enforcement
     Disable Early Launch Anti-Malware Driver

     Start Windows Normally

Description: View a list of system recovery tools you can use to repair
             startup problems, run diagnostics, or restore your system.

ENTER=Choose                                              ESC=Cancel
```

FIGURE 3-22 The Advanced Boot Options menu

EXAM TIP

For the 70-412 exam, you need to understand when to use all of the advanced boot options, but some options are more important to know for the exam than others. The most important advanced boot options for the exam are all three Safe Mode options (including the alternative methods to open them with Bcdedit and Msconfig), Last Known Good Configuration, and Disable Driver Signature Enforcement.

The available options are:

- **Repair Your Computer** Use this option to perform system image recovery. With this option, you can completely restore your computer from an earlier backup or image file.

- **Safe Mode** This option lets you boot the operating system with only minimal drivers, files, and services. The only drivers loaded are for the mouse, keyboard, storage, and video. This limited footprint allows you to get into the GUI operating system to remove applications or drivers or change any settings that are otherwise disrupting the system.

- **Safe Mode With Networking** This option is almost the same as Safe Mode, but it also adds networking drivers and services. With this option you can connect to the Internet or the local network to download files needed to fix the system.

- **Safe Mode With Command Prompt** This option is almost the same as Safe Mode, but the system boots into a command prompt instead of a GUI. No networking capabilities are provided.

- **Enable Boot Logging** This option attempts a normal boot into Windows Server 2012 and logs the boot procedure. For example, you can use this option to see which file is the last to load before a system freezes. The log file generated is named Ntbtlog.txt and is found in the Windows directory. If you can't boot into Windows, you can access and open Ntbtlog.txt if you boot with another operating system, such as a Windows PE 5.0 disk.

> **MORE INFO WINDOWS PE 5.0**
>
> To learn more about Windows PE 5.0, visit *http://technet.microsoft.com/en-us/library/hh825110.aspx.*

- **Enable Low-Resolution Video** This option starts the system with 640x480 display resolution. You might use this feature when the display settings you chose in the operating system are incompatible with your hardware and prevent you from seeing anything on the screen.

- **Last Known Good Configuration** This option is useful when a configuration change has prevented the system from starting. When you select this option, the system boots with the set of registry settings that were in place the last time the system booted successfully.

  For example, you could use this option when you install a device driver or application and you cannot successfully start the system immediately afterwards.

- **Debugging Mode** This mode can be used by developers who are troubleshooting operating system bugs.

- **Disable Automatic Restart on System Failure** This option prevents the system from rebooting after a system crash. It is useful when you want to prevent an endless loop of system restarts.

- **Disable Driver Signature Enforcement**   By default, Windows Server 2012 will not load any kernel-mode software that isn't digitally signed. *Kernel mode software* refers to programs or drivers that run in the most protected parts of the operating system. *Digitally signed software* refers to programs and (especially) drivers that have been tested by Microsoft and whose bits have not been altered since they were approved.

  Windows will normally warn you before you install unsigned software, but in some cases, you might need to install and use unsigned drivers or applications. For example, your organization might develop software that is not yet signed but that needs to be used temporarily.

  For such occasions, choose the Disable Driver Signature Enforcement option to allow the software to load. Make sure you understand this option for the 70-412 exam.

- **Disable Early Launch Anti-Malware Driver**   Malicious software that can load transparently before the operating system has proliferated in recent years. Instances of such malware, called *rootkits*, are difficult for traditional anti-malware software to detect. To remedy this problem, Windows Server 2012 introduces a new feature called Secure Boot. *Secure Boot* keeps unauthorized firmware, operating systems, and drivers from running at boot time by requiring the boot manager to be signed and pre-approved. If a problem is detected with the boot manager on the system and cannot be fixed, you will see a message indicating a Secure Boot Violation and the system will not start.

  Secure Boot is enabled by the early launch anti-malware driver. When you choose Disable Early Launch Anti-Malware Driver from the Advanced Boot Options menu, the computer will start in Safe Mode without first running the system's early-launch malware detection.

> *MORE INFO*   **SECURE BOOT**
>
> To learn more about Secure Boot, search for "Secure Boot" on TechNet or visit *http://technet.microsoft.com/en-us/library/hh824987.aspx*.

Booting into Safe Mode: Alternatives with Bcdedit and Msconfig

If you are already in Windows, you can configure the system to boot into any of the three Safe Modes the next time the system starts. You can use either the Bcdedit command at the command prompt or the System Configuration Utility (Msconfig) in the GUI of Windows Server 2012 to make this configuration change.

In Bcdedit, type one of the following commands to boot the system on the next startup into Safe Mode, Safe Mode with Networking, or Safe Mode with Command Prompt, respectively:

```
Bcdedit /Set SafeBoot Minimal
```

```
Bcdedit /Set SafeBoot Network
```

```
Bcdedit /Set SafeBootAlternateShell True
```

To return to normal booting, then type the following:

```
Bcdedit /DeleteValue SafeBoot
```

To accomplish the same thing in Msconfig, select the Boot tab and then check Safe Boot, as shown in Figure 3-23. The next time the system starts, it will boot into the option you select here. Minimal is Safe Mode, Alternate Shell stands for Safe Mode with Command Prompt, and Network refers to Safe Mode with Networking. (The Active Directory Repair option refers to Directory Services Restore Mode, which is used on domain controllers to bring the Active Directory database offline for repairs.)

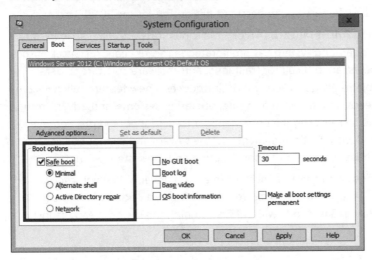

FIGURE 3-23   Booting into Safe Mode from Msconfig

Recovering servers with the Windows installation media

The Advanced Boot Options menu discussed in the previous section presents useful recovery options when Windows Server 2012 or Windows Server 2012 R2 can at least begin the process of loading. Other times, however, Windows doesn't even begin to load. On these occasions, you can boot with Windows Server 2012 or Windows Server 2012 R2 installation media and enter into Setup. When you get to the Windows Setup screen shown in Figure 3-24, choose the Repair Your Computer option. This step launches the Windows Recovery Environment, also called Windows RE. The Windows Recovery Environment (RE) runs on the Windows PE operating system. Windows PE is a version of Windows that is small enough to run on a DVD or a USB drive.

FIGURE 3-24 Recovering a server by using the Windows Server 2012 installation media

The Choose An Option screen of the Windows Recovery Environment is shown in Figure 3-25.

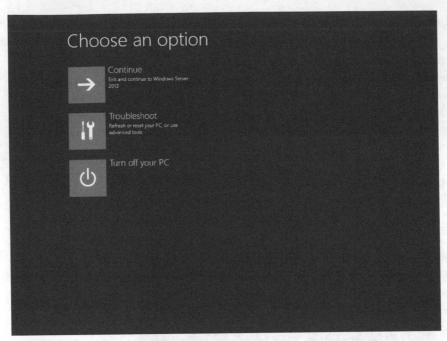

FIGURE 3-25 The Choose An Option screen in Windows RE

Click Troubleshoot to present the default troubleshooting options on the Advanced Options screen, shown in Figure 3-26.

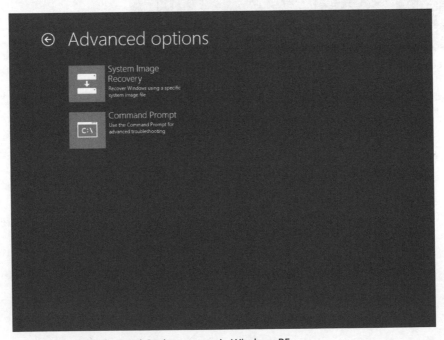

FIGURE 3-26 The Advanced Options screen in Windows RE

As you can see in Figure 3-26, the two built-in troubleshooting tools provided in the Windows Recovery Environment are System Image Recovery and Command Prompt. You can use System Image Recovery to restore a full server backup on a server that doesn't boot. You can use Command Prompt to repair the boot record by using Bootrec, Startrep, or other commands (or to perform any other troubleshooting).

Configuring System Image Recovery

When you select System Image Recovery after booting with Windows installation media, your disks are scanned for a Windows image backup (VHD or VHDX file). If one or more backup is found, you are given an opportunity to restore the most recent. If none is found, you can select one manually, as shown in Figure 3-27.

FIGURE 3-27 Recovering from a backed up system image

You should perform System Image Recovery from Windows installation media when you have a backup of your Windows Server 2012 R2 installation and either of the following is also true:

- You want to move the image to a new computer. (The hardware on the new computer should be identical to the old one so that the drivers contained in the image will work with the new hardware.)

- The disks or disk array on your server has been replaced (for example, because of hardware failure or data corruption).

Using command-line recovery tools

The Windows RE command prompt opens at the X:\Sources path by default. From this prompt, you can use a number of command-line tools to recover a Windows Server installation, such as Startrep, Bootrec, and Bcdedit.

EXAM TIP

Make sure you remember all of these command-line recovery tools for the 70-412 exam.

STARTREP

If the registry has become so corrupted that the system cannot start, you can use Startrep. exe to perform an automatic startup repair. Startrep.exe is located in the X:\Sources\Recovery directory, so you have to enter the command **cd recovery** before you can use Startrep.

BOOTREC

To understand the function of this utility, you first need to understand the difference between the boot sector, the Master Boot Record (MBR), and the Boot Configuration Data (BCD) store.

- The *boot sector* is the first sector of a bootable drive. The boot sector provides instructions about how to boot from that drive.

- The *MBR* is a type of boot sector used only in disks partitioned in the MBR partition style. This record contains information about the partitions on the drive. It also contains instructions about how to load the operating system.

- The *BCD store* is a binary file that contains the boot configuration data in Windows. The BCD maintains a record of the operating systems installed on the local disks and controls how operating systems load, in which order (and in which manner) they are presented in the boot menu, and which operating system is set as the default.

The *Bootrec.exe* utility is useful in performing basic repairs of the boot sector, the MBR, and the BCD store. It's used with four options, described below:

- **Bootrec /FixBoot**   This option writes a new boot sector to the system partition. Use this option if the boot sector has been damaged or if a version of Windows earlier than Windows Vista or Windows Server 2008 has been installed on the system after Windows Server 2012 or Windows Server 2012 R2.

- **Bootrec /FixMbr**   This option should be used only with disks partitioned with an MBR partition style, not with disks partition with a GUID Partition Table (GPT) partition style. (GPT disks are very common in Windows Server 2012 systems.) For MBR-type disks, the /FixMbr option writes an MBR to the system partition. Use this option to repair master boot record corruption issues or to remove nonstandard code from the MBR.

- **Bootrec /ScanOs**   This option scans all disks for Windows installations, including those that aren't currently listed in the BCD store.

- **Bootrec /RebuildBcd**   This option scans all disks for Windows installations and lets you add detected installations to the BCD store.

BCDEDIT

Bcdedit.exe is the main command-line editor of the BCD store. One of the main reasons to use Bcdedit is so you can modify boot entries, which are the options that define each operating system available on the boot menu. You don't normally need to edit the boot entries from Windows RE unless the BCD store has become corrupted or improperly modified. If you've used the Bcdedit /export command to back up a functioning version of the BCD store, you can use the Bcdedit /import command in Windows RE to restore store that backed up version if necessary.

BCDBOOT

You can use Bcdboot to quickly rebuild a new BCD store if the old one has become corrupted and you don't have a backed up version to restore.

Thought experiment

Configuring server recovery at Contoso

In the following thought experiment, apply what you've learned about this objective to predict what steps you need to take. You can find answers to these questions in the "Answers" section at the end of this chapter.

You are in the process of developing documentation to assist in the diagnosis and recovery of servers running the Windows Server 2012 R2 operating system which have been deployed on physical hardware. You are working on the section related to choosing boot options and need to answer the following questions before you can proceed:

1. Which boot option would you enable to determine the last service or driver to load before the system freezes?

2. What is the name of the file that records this information and where is it located?

3. Which boot option should you select to start the system using the configuration that was in place the last time a successful sign-on occurred?

Objective summary

- You can troubleshoot a Windows installation that at least begins the process of loading by using advanced boot options. To access the Advanced Boot Options menu, press F8 as the system is starting.

- The Advanced Boot Options menu includes Safe Mode, which loads only minimal drivers; Last Known Good Configuration, which loads the last version of the Registry that allowed a system to completely start; and Disable Driver Signature Enforcement, which allows Windows to load unsigned drivers.

- If Windows doesn't even begin to start, you can recover the system by booting from Windows Server 2012 or Windows Server 2012 R2 installation media. You can then click Troubleshooting to enter the Windows Recovery Environment.

- If you want to recover your installation from backup onto a bare-metal system in the Windows Recovery Environment, choose the option to perform a System Image Recovery.

- If you want to troubleshoot your installation in the Windows Recovery Environment, choose the Command Prompt option. From there, you can use command-line tools such as Startrep to perform automatic startup repair; Bootrec to repair the boot sector, MBR, or BCD store; Bcdedit to restore a backed up version of the BCD store; or Bcdboot to quickly rebuild the BCD store.

Objective review

Answer the following questions to test your knowledge of the information in this objective. You can find the answers to these questions and explanations of why each answer choice is correct or incorrect in the "Answers" section at the end of the chapter.

1. You want to ensure that a server running Windows Server 2012 R2 boots into Safe Mode the next time it starts.

   Which commands can you use to achieve this goal? (Choose all that apply.)

   A. Bootrec

   B. Bcdedit

   C. Startrep

   D. Msconfig

2. Your company is preparing to migrate a server named Server1 from Windows Server 2003 to Windows Server 2012 R2. A developer at your company is working to update a kernel mode driver installed on Server1 that has been developed in-house. He installs the driver for testing on TestServer1. TestServer1 is running Windows Server 2012 R2 and has hardware that is identical to that of Server1. After he installs the program, TestServer1 fails to start. You need to ensure that he can test the driver on TestServer1. You also want to minimize the security risk on the machine. Which option should you choose from the Advanced Boot Options menu?

   A. Safe Mode

   B. Last Known Good Configuration

   C. Disable Driver Signature Enforcement

   D. Disable Early Launch Anti-Malware Driver

3. You are a network administrator for Contoso.com. All servers in the company network are running Windows Server 2012 R2.

   The disk array fails on a file server named FileSrvA. You replace the disk array. You now need to recover the server as quickly as possible and allow users to connect to the file shares on FileSrvA. What should you do?

   A. Start FileSrvA in the Last Known Good Configuration

   B. Start FileSrvA from the Windows Server 2012 R2 installation media

   C. Start FileSrvA in Safe Mode with Command Prompt

   D. Initiate a network boot of FileSrv to connect to a WDS server.

Objective 3.3: Configure site-level fault tolerance

Hyper-V Replica is a Windows Server 2012 and Windows Server 2012 R2 feature introduced in that allows you to create a replica of a virtual machine running on Hyper-V on either of these platforms. If the primary VM fails, you can fail over to the replica VM. Hyper-V Replica can thus provide fault tolerance for a VM even if an entire host site should go offline.

Unlike a failover cluster, Hyper-V Replica doesn't rely on shared storage between the VMs. The replica VM instead begins with its own copy of the primary VM's virtual hard disk. The primary VM then sends updates of its changes (called *replication data* and this data is repeatedly saved by the replica VM. Replication frequency is every 5 minutes for Hyper-V on Windows Server 2012 and either 30 seconds, 5 minutes, or 15 minutes when Hyper-V is running on Windows Server 2012 R2.

This objective covers how to:

- Configure Hyper-V physical host servers
- Configure VMs
- Perform Hyper-V Replica failover
- Use Hyper-V Replica in a failover cluster
- Configure Hyper-V Replica Extended Replication
- Use Global Update Manager
- Recover multi-site failover clusters

Configuring Hyper-V physical host servers

It's important to understand the sequence of steps in configuring Hyper-V Replica. The first step is to configure the server-level replication settings for *both* physical Hyper-V hosts, called the primary server and the replica server. You can access these settings in Hyper-V Manager by right-clicking a host server in the navigation pane, selecting Hyper-V Settings, and then selecting Replication Configuration in the left column of the Hyper-V Settings dialog box, as shown in Figure 3-28. By default, replication is not enabled, and no options are selected or configured.

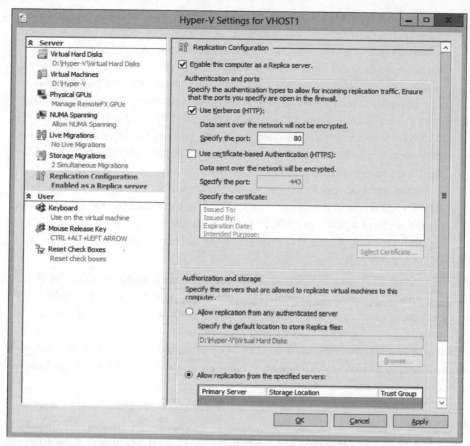

FIGURE 3-28 The host server settings for Hyper-V Replica

To enable a physical host for Hyper-V Replica, first select the Enable This Computer As A Replica Server check box. Then, configure settings in the Authentication And Ports area and the Authorization And Storage area shown in Figure 3-28. You need to repeat these configuration steps on both primary and replica servers before configuring a VM for replication.

- **Authentication And Ports** In this area you choose which authentication methods you want to be available later as options when you configure a locally hosted VM for replication. You can enable Kerberos (HTTP), Certificate-Based Authentication (HTTPS), or both.

  - **Use Kerberos (HTTP)** You can enable Kerberos (HTTP) only if the local server is domain-joined. The advantage of choosing Kerberos is that it requires no further configuration. The two disadvantages are first that it doesn't encrypt data sent over the network, and second that it can be used for authentication only when the remote host server is located in a trusted domain. Note also that when you choose this authentication protocol, you need to enable the firewall rule named Hyper-V Replica HTTP Listener (TCP-In).

■ **Use Certificate-Based Authentication (HTTPS)** You can enable Certificate-Based Authentication (HTTPS) regardless of whether the local server is domain-joined. In fact, when the local server is a standalone server, it is the only authentication protocol option. The two advantages of enabling Certificate-Based Authentication (HTTPS) are that it encrypts replication data and that it allows you to replicate with a remote host when there is no trust relationship with that host through Active Directory. The disadvantage of this authentication method is that it is more difficult to configure: It requires you to provide an X.509v3 certificate for which Enhanced Key Usage (EKU) must support both Client Authentication and Server Authentication (through the Computer certificate template, for example) and that specifies (typically) the fully qualified domain name (FQDN) of the local server in the subject name field. The certificate can be self-signed or issued through a public key infrastructure (PKI). When you choose this authentication protocol, you need to enable the firewall rule named Hyper-V Replica HTTPS Listener (TCP-In).

It's important to remember that Windows Server 2012 doesn't automatically enable the firewall rules you need for the authentication protocols you choose. Depending on which protocol(s) you have enabled, you also need to enable the firewall rule Hyper-V Replica HTTP Listener (TCP-In), Hyper-V Replica HTTPS Listener (TCP-In), or both. You can enable a rule either in Windows Firewall with Advanced Security or by using the Enable-NetFirewallRule -DisplayName command in Windows PowerShell followed by the name of the rule (including quotation marks).

EXAM TIP

Remember that encrypted replication of a VM requires the host servers to have installed a certificate including both Client Authentication and Server Authentication extensions for EKU.

MORE INFO **CONFIGURING CERTIFICATE-BASED AUTHENTICATION WITH HYPER-V REPLICA**

To learn more about configuring certificate-based authentication with Hyper-V Replica, search for Hyper-V Replica - Prerequisites for certificate-based deployments or visit *http://blogs.technet.com/b/virtualization/archive/2012/03/13/hyper-v-replica-certificate-requirements.aspx.*

When configuring replication, you must also configure the following settings:

- **Authorization And Storage** This area allows you to configure security settings on the local server that are used when the local server acts as a replica server. More specifically, your choice here determines the remote primary servers from which the local server will accept replication data. Even if you are configuring your local server as the primary server, the settings here are required so that—if you ever need to fail over to a remote replica—you can later fail back to the local server.

You need to choose one of two security options, both of which also provide a default path you can modify to store replication data:

- **Allow Replication From Any Authenticated Server** This option is somewhat less secure. When you choose this option, the local server can receive replication data from any authenticated server.

- **Allow Replication From The Specified Servers** This option requires you to specify the primary server(s) authorized for the local replica server. You can add multiple entries to authorize different primary servers by DNS name. To add an entry authorizing a primary server address, click Add as shown in Figure 3-29. This step opens the Add Authorization Entry dialog box shown in Figure 3-30.

For each entry, a default storage path (the middle field) is already provided, but the other two fields must be filled in manually. In the Specify The Primary Server field, you enter an FQDN that can include a wildcard character (for example, "*.adatum.com"). You also have to provide a tag called a trust group. If you want to allow replication traffic from a set of primary servers, you should assign those primary servers the same trust group name.

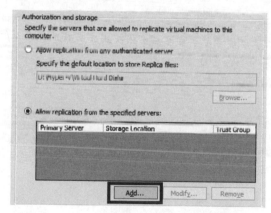

FIGURE 3-29 Authorizing primary servers for the local replica server

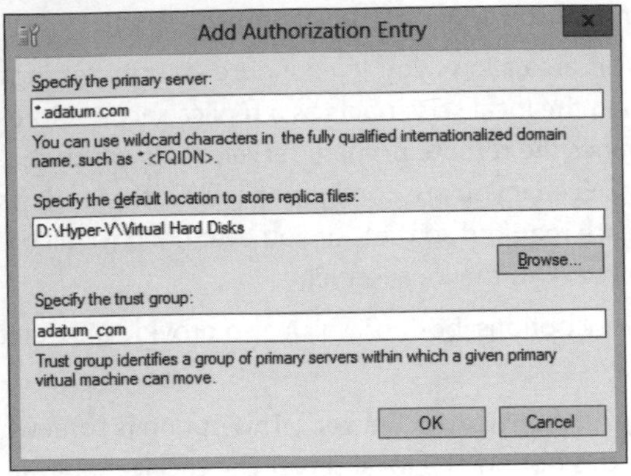

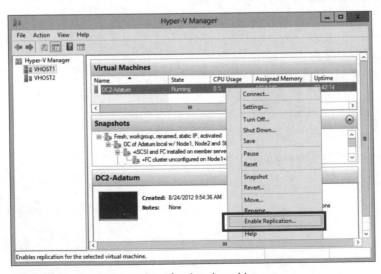

FIGURE 3-30   Adding an authorized primary server address

How might these settings in the Authorization And Storage area appear on the 70-412 exam? One could imagine a question based on an unsuccessful failover. In such a question, authorization settings might not be configured at all on the replica server. Or the FQDN provided in the Specify The Primary Server field in Figure 3-30 might be configured incorrectly, and the correct answer fixes that problem. Another possible question could involve a new organizational requirement that security be tightened on a replica server. Incorrect answer choices might refer to IPSec or other security-tightening methods, but the correct answer will refer to adding an authorization entry on the replica server.

Configuring VMs

After you configure both physical host servers, the next step in configuring Hyper-V Replica is to configure the chosen VM for replication on the primary server. Begin by right-clicking the VM and selecting Enable Replication, as shown in Figure 3-31.

FIGURE 3-31   Creating a replica of a virtual machine

This step opens the Enable Replication wizard. The wizard includes the following five configuration pages:

- **Specify Replica Server**   Use this page to specify the remote replica server by name.
- **Specify Connection Parameters**   This page, shown in Figure 3-32, asks you to specify which of the authentication types enabled at the server level in Hyper-V Settings you want to use to support this replicated VM. If you have enabled only one of these two authentication methods at the server level, that same method is the only option here. Naturally, the replica server must support the same authentication method.

This page also provides an option that lends itself fairly well to an exam question: the Compress The Data That Is Transmitted Over The Network check box. This compression option reduces bandwidth requirements for replication at the expense of increased processor usage. If this option does appear on the exam, this trade-off is likely to be the key to getting the right answer.

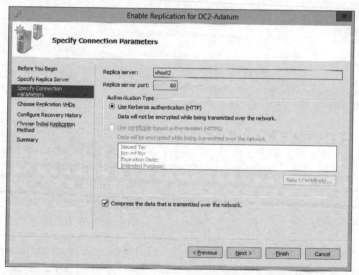

FIGURE 3-32 Selecting authentication and compression settings for a replicated VM

EXAM TIP

If both authentication types are available for the VM and you want to change the authentication type later to certificate-based authentication, you have to remove replication and complete the Enable Replication wizard again. Before you do, however, make sure that certificate-based authentication is also enabled in the Hyper-V Settings on the remote host server.

- **Choose Replication VHDs**   By default, all virtual hard disks (VHDs) attached to the VM are enabled for replication. You can use this page to deselect any VHDs that you don't want to be replicated.

- **Configure Additional Recovery Points**   This page, shown in Figure 3-33, includes the settings to Configure Additional Recovery Points. These are among the most likely of all Hyper-V Replica settings to appear on the 70-412 exam. As shown in the figure, you can configure Only The Latest Recovery Point or Additional Recovery Points.

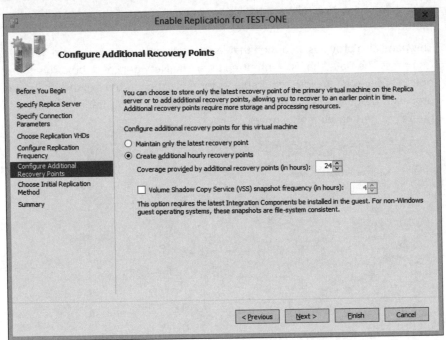

FIGURE 3-33   Configuring additional recovery points

Recovery points are VM snapshots saved on a replica server. Replication traffic sends a new snapshot from the primary to the replica server every 5 to 15 minutes, but only the latest is saved on the replica by default. Selecting the Additional Recovery Points option configures the replica server to keep one extra snapshot per hour. If you later perform a failover operation at the replica server, you then have the option of recovering either the most recent version of the VM, which is always available, or one of these earlier, hourly snapshots. Windows Server 2012 R2 increases the number of maximum recovery points to 24 from the 16 that are available in Windows Server 2012.

A menu of available recovery points on a replica server is shown in Figure 3-34. If the Configure Recovery History page were left at the default setting (Only The Latest Recovery Point), only the first option named Latest Recovery Point would appear in this menu.

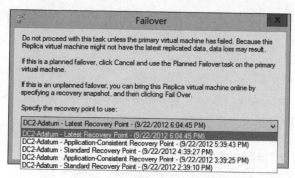

FIGURE 3-34 Specifying the latest recovery point and previous hourly snapshots of a VM that can be restored in a failover on the replica server

When you enable the Additional Recovery Points option on the Configure Recovery History page, the replica server by default will keep an hourly snapshot for each of the past four hours in addition to the latest recovery point. However, you can change this setting if you want to store more (or fewer) of these recovery points on the replica server. The main drawback to keeping many recovery points is the use of storage resources required to do so.

The last configuration settings on the Configure Recovery History page relate to *incremental Volume Shadow Copy Service (VSS) copies*, also known as *application-consistent recovery points*. These are high-quality snapshots taken during moments in which the VM momentarily "quiesces" (gracefully pauses) activity in VSS-aware applications such as Microsoft Exchange and SQL Server. The advantage of these snapshot types is that they help ensure that the failover will be free of errors in these applications. The disadvantage is that they are more processor-intensive and cause important applications to pause briefly. (However, it should be noted that the pause is normally too brief for users to detect.)

You enable Incremental VSS copies by selecting the Replicate Incremental VSS Copy Every check box, and then selecting the frequency of the application-consistent recovery point. (You can see these options in Figure 3-33.) If you leave the default frequency of 1 hour, then every recovery point will be an application-consistent recovery point. If you select a frequency of 2 hours, then the standard recovery point will be replaced by an application-consistent recovery point every 2 hours, and so on. Figure 3-35 shows the snapshots stored on a replica server for which incremental VSS copies are scheduled every two hours.

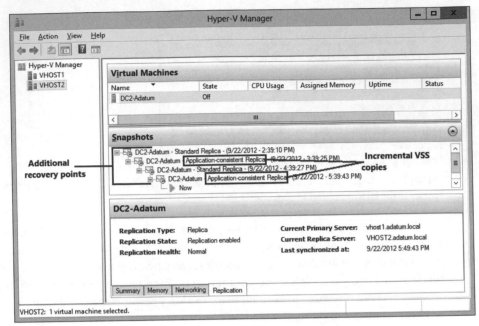

FIGURE 3-35 Viewing incremental VSS copies and standard recovery points

EXAM TIP

Be prepared to answer a question about application-consistent snapshots on the 70-412 exam.

- **Choose Initial Replication Method** This page, shown in Figure 3-36, allows you to specify how the initial copy of the VHDs attached to the primary VM will be sent to the replica server. By default, the VHDs are sent over the network. Sending very large files over a network such as the Internet isn't always a realistic option, however. As an alternative, you can choose the second option, to export the VHDs to external media (and then physically transport them to the replica server). The final option is to use an existing VM on the replica server as the initial copy. You can choose this option if you have restored an exact copy of the VM and its VHDs on the replica server.

  This page also allows you to configure the initial network transfer to take place at a specified future time. You can use this option to minimize user disruption.

NOTE BANDWIDTH

Typically, the initial transfer of the VHD is far more bandwidth-intensive than the updates sent through replication are. After the initial copies of the VHDs are sent, only the changes (deltas) to these VHDs are sent during replication, which occurs every 5 to 15 minutes.

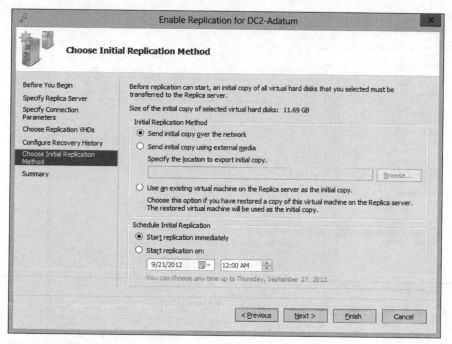

FIGURE 3-36 Determining how to send the base copy of the VHDs attached to a primary VM

Configuring failover TCP/IP settings

After you enable replication on a VM, you might need to specify the TCP/IP settings that will apply to the replica VM after failover. By default, the replica VM will inherit the same IPv4 and IPv6 configuration as the primary VM. In many cases, however, the replica VM will need a different IP configuration to communicate in its environment.

To assign a different IP configuration to the replica VM, in Hyper-V Manager on the replica server, right-click the replica VM and select Settings from the shortcut menu. In the Settings dialog box, expand Network Adapter in the left column and then select Failover TCP/IP, as shown in Figure 3-37. In the right pane, assign the new IP configuration as appropriate.

Then, on the primary server, assign the original IP configuration in the same settings area. Otherwise, the replica settings will persist if you fail back to the original location. (Remember this last point for the exam.)

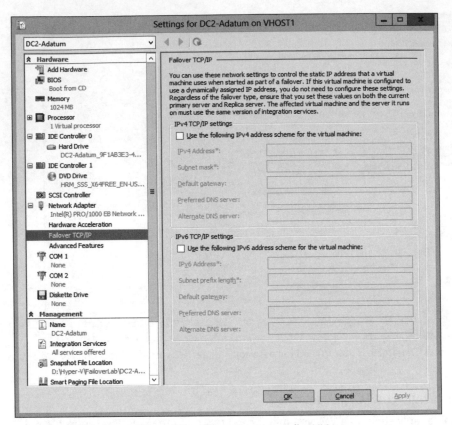

FIGURE 3-37 Assigning a different IP configuration to a replica VM

Resynchronizing the primary and replica VMs

After you complete the Enable Replication wizard, you can modify the replication settings for a VM in the Settings dialog box for that VM. Replication settings appear in the Management category in the menu on the left, as shown in Figure 3-38.

One configuration setting appears here that does not appear in the Enable Replication wizard: Resynchronization. Resynchronization is a highly resource-intensive operation that is performed occasionally between a primary and replica VM. By default, resynchronization can occur at any time. You have the option, however, to restrict resynchronizations to selected off-peak hours. Alternatively, you can opt to perform resynchronization manually.

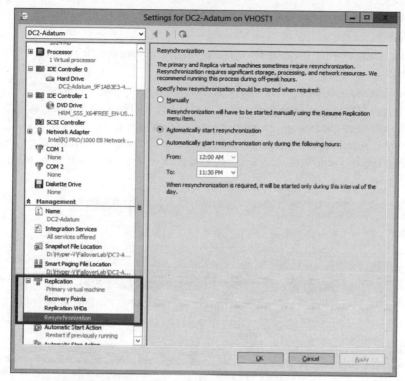

FIGURE 3-38 Replication settings for a VM

Performing Hyper-V Replica failover

You can perform three types of failovers with Hyper-V Replica after it is configured: planned failovers, unplanned failovers, and test failovers. It's somewhat likely you'll see an exam question in which you need to understand the difference among them and when they are used.

Planned failover

A *planned failover* is the only failover you initiate from the primary server. You use this method whenever you can manually shut down the primary VM, and the primary and replica servers can still communicate.

A planned failover is the preferred failover type because no data is lost. In fact, you cannot even use this option to fail over to the latest recovery point or to any earlier recovery point. With a planned failover, only an exact copy of the current primary VM and its VHDs can be failed over to the replica server.

A planned failover is a good option in the following situations:

- You want to perform host maintenance on the primary server and temporarily want to run the VM from the replica.

- Your primary site is anticipating a possible power outage and you want to move the VM to the replica site.

- You are expecting a weather emergency, such as a flood, and you want to ensure business continuity.

- Your compliance requirements mandate that you regularly run your workloads for certain periods of time from the replica site.

To perform a planned failover, you begin by *shutting down the primary VM*. You then right-click the VM in Hyper-V Manager, click Replication, and then click Planned Failover, as shown in Figure 3-39. The latest updates are then sent to the replica server, the VM is failed over, and the replica VM is automatically started on the remote server. At the end of this operation, the replication relationship is reversed, so what was the replica server becomes the primary server, and vice versa.

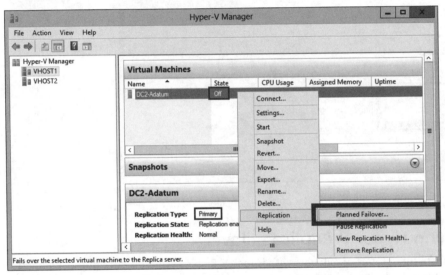

FIGURE 3-39 Performing a planned failover from the primary server

Unplanned failover

This type of failover is called an *unplanned failover* in the Windows Server 2012 and Windows Server 2012 R2 documentation, but in the actual interface, it's called just "failover." On the 70-412 exam, you might see it referred to either way.

An unplanned failover is performed at the replica server. You perform this failover type when the primary VM fails suddenly and cannot be brought back online. An unplanned failover is a good option in the following situations:

- Your primary site experiences an unexpected power outage or a natural disaster.

- Your primary site or VM has had a virus attack, and you want to restore your business quickly with minimal data loss by restoring your replica VM to the most recent recovery point before the attack.

To perform an unplanned failover, in Hyper-V Manager on the replica server, right-click the replica VM, click Replication, and then click Failover, as shown in Figure 3-40.

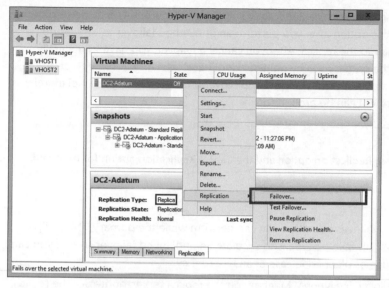

FIGURE 3-40 Performing an unplanned failover on the replica server

When you perform an unplanned failover, you have to choose a recovery point, as shown earlier in Figure 3-34. The VM is then started on the replica server.

After the replica VM is started, the replica relationship with the primary VM is broken, and replication stops. If at some later point you can bring the original primary VM online, you can resume replication by reversing the replication relationship. After you perform this operation, the local replica server becomes the new primary, and the remote primary becomes the new replica. To reverse replication in this way, right-click the VM on the replica server, click Replication, and then click Reverse Replication, as shown in Figure 3-41. This step starts the Reverse Replication Wizard, which allows you to reenter the settings for the replica.

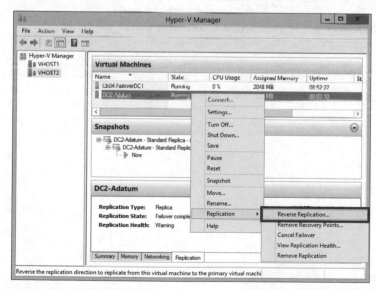

FIGURE 3-41 Reversing replication

Another option you can see on the Replication submenu in Figure 3-41 is Cancel Failover. You can safely choose this option after you perform an unplanned failover as long as no changes have been made to the replica. After you cancel a failover, you have to manually resume replication on the primary VM by right-clicking it and selecting Resume Replication. Cancelling a failover is a good idea if you quickly discover after performing an unplanned failover that the primary VM can be brought online.

EXAM TIP

Remember the Reverse Replication option and the Cancel Replication option for the exam.

Test failover

A *test failover* is the only failover operation you can perform while the primary VM is still running. The purpose of this failover type is to simulate an unplanned failover so that you can ensure that it will function as planned in case of an emergency.

To perform a test failover, in Hyper-V Manager on the replica server, right-click the replica VM, click Replication, and then click Test Failover. You then have to select a recovery point, just as you do with an unplanned failover. Next, a local, disposable copy of the replica VM is created on the replica server. The new copy of the VM appears in Hyper-V Manager in a stopped state with the tag "- Test." For example, a test failover of a VM named "MyVM1" would result in a new VM called "MyVM1 - Test". You can then start the new VM manually to see if it works as expected.

By default, the virtual network adapters of the test VM are disconnected from all virtual switches. If desired, you can preattach the adapter(s) of the test VM to a virtual switch of your choice. To do so, open the settings of the base replica VM, expand Network Adapter, and then click Test Failover, as shown in Figure 3-42. Make sure you choose a virtual switch that will not create any conflicts in a production network.

After you examine the functioning of the test VM, you can safely delete it in Hyper-V Manager.

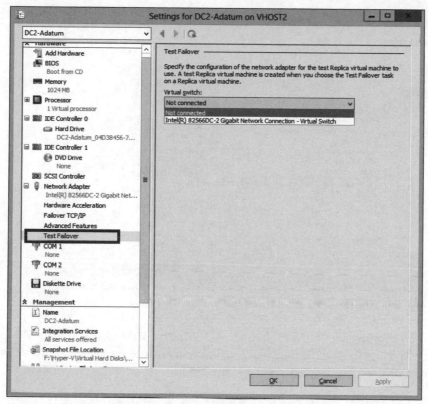

FIGURE 3-42 Preattaching the network adapter of a failover test VM to a virtual switch

Using Hyper-V Replica in a failover cluster

The configuration steps previously described apply to VMs that are not hosted in a failover cluster. However, you might want to provide an offsite replica VM for a clustered VM. In this scenario, you would provide two levels of fault tolerance. The failover cluster is used to provide local fault tolerance, for example, if a physical node fails within a functioning data center. The offsite replica VM, on the other hand, could be used to recover only from site-level failures, for example, in case of a power outage, weather emergency, or natural disaster.

The steps to configure a replica VM for a clustered VM differ slightly from the normal configuration, but they aren't complicated. The first difference is that you begin by opening Failover Cluster Manager, not Hyper-V Manager. In Failover Cluster Manager, you then have to add a failover cluster role named *Hyper-V Replica Broker* to the cluster.

To add the Hyper-V Replica Broker role, right-click the Roles node in Failover Cluster Manager and select Configure Role. This step opens the High Availability Wizard. In the High Availability Wizard, select Hyper-V Replica Broker, as shown in Figure 3-43.

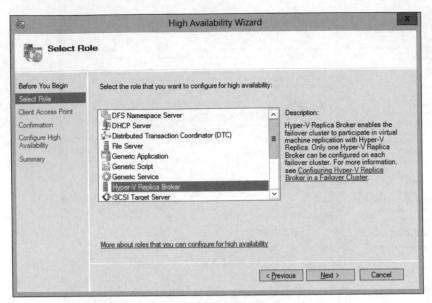

FIGURE 3-43 Adding the Hyper-V Replica Broker role to a failover cluster

When you choose this role, the High Availability Wizard will then ask you to provide a NetBIOS name and IP address to be used as the connection point to the cluster (called a *Client Access Point*, or *CAP*). This step is shown in Figure 3-44.

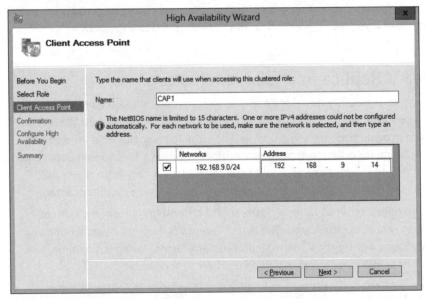

FIGURE 3-44 Providing a name and address for the Client Access Point

Next, you configure the equivalent of the server replication settings shown earlier in Figure 3-28. To do so, right-click the Hyper-V Replica Broker node in Failover Cluster Manager and select Replication Settings from the shortcut menu, as shown in Figure 3-45. The difference between the settings here and the settings in Figure 3-28 is that in this case, the settings apply to the entire cluster as a whole.

FIGURE 3-45 Configuring replication settings for the cluster

On the remote Replica server, you configure replication as you normally would, by configuring Hyper-V Settings in Hyper-V Manager as described in the earlier section named "Configuring Hyper-V physical host servers." However, if you want the remote Replica also to be a multi-node failover cluster, then you would need to configure that remote failover cluster through Failover Cluster Manager (by adding and configuring the Hyper-V Replica Broker role).

After you configure the host server settings, you can configure replication on the VM in Failover Cluster Manager just as you would in Hyper-V Manager. Right-click the clustered VM, click Replication, and then click Enable Replication, as shown in Figure 3-46.

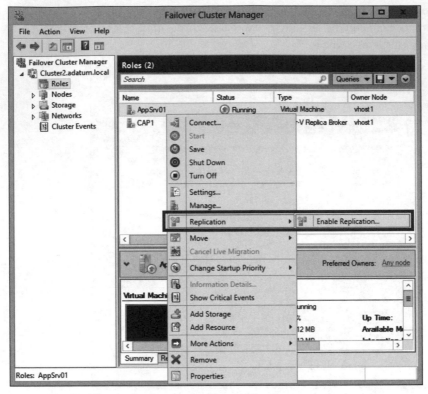

FIGURE 3-46 Enabling replication on a clustered VM

This step opens the same Enable Replication wizard that you see when you configure replication on a nonclustered VM. The remaining configuration steps are therefore identical.

For the 70-412 exam, there's a good chance you'll be asked about basic concepts related to configuring replication on clustered VMs. First, remember that you use Failover Cluster Manager to configure replication for a clustered VM at the primary site but still use Hyper-V Manager at the Replica site (if the Replica VM isn't also clustered). Also, remember that in Failover Cluster Manager at the primary site, you need to add the Hyper-V Replica Broker role to the failover cluster, and that this role is used to configure Hyper-V Replica "server" settings for the cluster. Finally, you also need to remember that when you configure Hyper-V Replica in a failover cluster, the CAP name and address are used as the server name and address.

Configuring Hyper-V Replica Extended Replication

Extended Replication is a feature available in Windows Server 2012 R2 that allows you to extend replication beyond the host and replica server to a third site. For example, you may have configured Hyper-V replica so that a VM hosted in the Melbourne datacenter is automatically replicated to a computer running Windows Server 2012 R2 with the Hyper-V role installed in the Sydney datacenter. With Hyper-V Extended Replication, you could then configure replication so that the replica in the Sydney datacenter is replicated on to an additional computer running Windows Server 2012 R2 with the Hyper-V role installed that is located in the Canberra datacenter.

> **MORE INFO** **HYPER-V EXTENDED REPLICATION**
>
> To learn more about Hyper-V Extended Replication, visit *http://blogs.technet.com/b/ virtualization/archive/2013/12/10/hyper-v-replica-extend-replication.aspx*

Using Global Update Manager

When the state of a cluster is changes, for example when a node is taken offline, all of the other nodes in the cluster must acknowledge the change before the cluster will commit the change to the cluster database. *Global Update Manager* is the component that is responsible for managing cluster database updates. Windows Server 2012 R2 allows you to configure Global Update Manager settings through the (Get-Cluster).DatabaseReadWriteMode Windows PowerShell command. Using this command, you can configure the following options:

- **0 = All (write) And Local (Read)** This is the default setting in Windows Server 2012 R2 for all cluster workloads except Hyper-V. It requires that all cluster nodes acknowledge the update before the change is committed to the database. Database reads occur on the local node.

- **1 = Majority (Read And Write)** This is the default setting for Windows Server 2012 R2 Hyper-V failover clusters. Requires that only a majority of nodes acknowledge the update before the change is committed to the database. Database read involves comparing the most recent timestamp from the majority of available nodes and using the most recent data.

- **2 = Majority (Write) And Local (Read)** This mode also requires the majority of cluster nodes acknowledge the update before committing the change to the database. The difference is that database read occurs on the local node, which means that the data may be stale.

Microsoft recommends that you not use mode 1 or 2 when you need to ensure that the cluster database is consistent, such as when using AlwaysOn availability groups with Microsoft SQL Server 2012 or Database Availability Groups with Microsoft Exchange Server 2010 or 2013.

MORE INFO GLOBAL UPDATE MANAGER

To learn more about the changes to Global Update Manager in Windows Server 2012 R2, visit *http://technet.microsoft.com/en-us/library/dn265972.aspx#BKMK_GUM*.

Recovering multi-site failover clusters

In some cases it can be necessary to force a cluster restart during a multi-site cluster failure. For example, you have a seven-node cluster, with four nodes in the first site and three nodes in the second site. A network outage disrupts inter-site communication. In this situation, the first site with the four nodes would remain operational and the cluster nodes in the second site would shut down because they would be unable to achieve quorum. However, what if the network outage happens to only impact external network communication to the first site and that the second site—the one with the cluster nodes that shut down—remains accessible to clients at other locations and to clients on the Internet? In that scenario, you'd force-start the cluster nodes in the second site using the cluster.exe command with the /fq switch. When you do this, everything will work fine until you restore network connectivity back to the first site, where the original four nodes still believe they have quorum. Then you have two collections of nodes which both believe they hold quorum. This scenario is termed a *partitioned cluster*, *split cluster*, or *"split brain"* cluster.

With Windows Server 2012 clusters, once you restored connectivity, you'd need to manually restart partitioned nodes in the first site using the cluster.exe command with the /pq switch. Windows Server 2012 R2 includes improvements that allow partitioned clusters to automatically reconcile when they detect "split brain" configuration. With Windows Server 2012 R2, the nodes that you started with the /fq switch are deemed authoritative and other cluster nodes will automatically restart using the /pq switch without requiring manual intervention.

MORE INFO MULTI-SITE FAILOVER CLUSTERS

To learn more about multi-site failover clusters, visit *http://technet.microsoft.com/en-gb/video/Hh133452*.

Thought experiment
Designing fault tolerance at Adatum

In the following thought experiment, apply what you've learned about this objective to predict what steps you need to take. You can find answers to these questions in the "Answers" section at the end of this chapter.

You are a network administrator for Adatum.com, an organization with head-quarters in San Francisco and a branch office in Montreal. You are designing fault tolerance and business continuity for a new application server and VM that will be named AppVM1. AppVM1 will be hosted in the San Francisco office.

You want to meet the following goals:

- You want to prevent any disruption of service and data loss in case an individual server fails unexpectedly.

- You want to be able to resume service with minimal data loss in case a catastrophe such as an earthquake brings the main office offline for an extended period.

- You always want to retain daily backups from the previous two weeks.

With these goals in mind, answer the following questions:

1. Which features in Windows Server 2012 can enable you to meet the first goal?

2. How might you design fault tolerance so that you can meet the first goal even after a catastrophe brings the main office offline for an extended period?

3. Describe two ways you might design fault tolerance for AppVM1 so that you can continue to meet the third goal even through a catastrophe that brings the main office offline for an extended period.

Objective summary

- Hyper-V Replica is a new feature of Windows Server 2012 that creates an offline copy (replica) of a running VM and its storage. This replica can exist anywhere in the world. The online original (called the primary VM) sends the replica updates of any changes every 5 to 15 minutes. In case the primary VM fails, you can fail over to the replica and bring it online.

- To configure Hyper-V Replica, you first configure authentication and authorization settings for both physical host servers, called the primary server and replica server. Then, in Hyper-V Manager on the primary server, run the Enable Replication Wizard for the desired VM.

- By default, you can fail over only to the most recent recovery point, which is normally no more than 5 to 15 minutes old. However, you can choose to store additional, older recovery points that allow you to return to point-in-time snapshots of the primary VM.

- A planned failover is performed on the primary server after you shut down the primary VM. A planned failover brings the replica VM online with no loss of data. You can perform an unplanned failover on the replica server if the primary server fails without warning. With an unplanned failover, the replica VM recovers a copy of the primary VM that is normally no more than 5 to 15 minutes old. Finally, you can also perform a test failover while the primary VM is still running. A test failover brings a copy of the replica VM online in a state that is disconnected from the network.

- If you want to configure Hyper-V Replica for a VM that is hosted in a failover cluster, you need to add the Hyper-V Replica Broker role to the cluster. You also need to provide a CAP name and address for the cluster that will act as the server name.

- Global Update Manager is the component that is responsible for managing cluster database updates.

Objective review

Answer the following questions to test your knowledge of the information in this objective. You can find the answers to these questions and explanations of why each answer choice is correct or incorrect in the "Answers" section at the end of the chapter.

1. You are configuring Hyper-V Replica on a VM that is hosting Microsoft Exchange. You want to help ensure that if you fail over to the replica VM, the application data will remain in a consistent state.

   What should you do? (Choose all that apply.)

   A. Configure the replica server to save additional recovery points.

   B. Configure the primary server to replicate incremental VSS copies.

   C. Configure a resynchronization schedule for the primary and replica VM.

   D. Configure Hyper-V Replica Broker.

2. You have configured Hyper-V Replica for a VM named AppSrv1, which is hosted on a primary server named VMhost1 in Cleveland. The replica server is named RepHost1 and is located in Denver.

   An unexpected power outage suddenly brings the entire Cleveland site offline. You perform a failover at the Denver site and start the replica VM on RepHost1. Power is returned to the Cleveland site after several hours, but only after changes have been made to AppSrv1.

   You are able to bring VMhost1 back online and now want to return AppSrv1 to its original host. Which step should you take next?

   A. Perform an unplanned failover.

   B. Choose the option to cancel the failover.

   C. Perform a planned failover.

   D. Choose the option to reverse replication.

3. Within your organization, a clustered VM named SQL1 is hosting SQL Server. The failover cluster hosting SQL1 is named Cluster1 and includes three nodes, named Node1, Node2, and Node3. Node1 is the preferred owner of the SQL1 VM. All three nodes are located in the same data center.

   You want to configure an offsite replica of SQL1 to protect the VM in case the entire failover cluster is brought down because of a power outage or other emergency.

   You deploy a physical server named RepSrv2 at a remote site. You want to configure RepSrv2 as the replica server. You install Windows Server 2012 and then the Hyper-V role on RepSrv2. You then connect the server to the Internet and establish a VPN connection between the two sites.

   Which of the following steps should you take? (Choose two.)

   A. At the primary site, configure Hyper-V Replica Broker and provide a CAP name.

   B. At the replica site, configure Hyper-V Replica Broker and provide a CAP name.

   C. In the replication settings on Cluster1, restrict authorization to the CAP.

   D. In the replication settings on RepSrv2, restrict authorization to the CAP.

Answers

This section contains the solutions to the "Thought experiments" and the "Objective review" questions in this chapter.

Objective 3.1: Thought experiment

1. You need to create a Windows Azure subscription, create a backup vault, and upload a management certificate.

2. The maximum retention period for data backed up to Windows Azure using Windows Azure Backup is 30 days.

3. You need a copy of a management certificate uploaded to the Windows Azure account and you'll need the passphrase used to protect the backed up data.

Objective 3.1: Review

1. **Correct Answer:** C

    A. **Incorrect:** Backup Operators have the right to back up files and directories, restore files and directories, shut down the system, log on locally, and access the computer from the network. You want User1 only to able to back up the system.

    B. **Incorrect:** Power Users do not have the right to back up the system.

    C. **Correct:** By assigning the right to back up files and directories to User1, you can avoid assigning any other unnecessary privileges to the account.

    D. **Incorrect:** The question does not state that User1 needs to be able to restore the system.

2. **Correct Answer:** A

    A. **Correct:** VSSAdmin is the command-line tool used to manage shadow copies (snapshots) of disks.

    B. **Incorrect:** Shadow is a command used to follow another user's session in Remote Desktop Services.

    C. **Incorrect:** The Get-VMSnapshot cmdlet is used on a Hyper-V host to list all of the available snapshots of a VM.

    D. **Incorrect:** Wbadmin is the command-line utility for Windows Server Backup. You can't use this utility to create a snapshot (shadow copy) of a disk.

3. **Correct Answer:** B

   A. **Incorrect:** Changing the bandwidth assigned to the work hours will not help you achieve your goal of having the backup operation complete before the work day begins at 8 AM.

   B. **Correct:** The bandwidth setting assigned to non-work hours is restricted to 1023.0 Kbps, which is much lower than the default setting of 1023 Mbps. This low setting could be unnecessarily limiting the bandwidth allowed at night. If you raise this value, the backup operation could proceed much more quickly (assuming more bandwidth is available).

   C. **Incorrect:** Adjusting the work hours could potentially cause disruption for workers, and it will not help you meet your goal of completing the backup operation before 9 A.M.

   D. **Incorrect:** The workdays are not currently affecting the backup because the backup is being performed outside of work hours. If you include Wednesday as a workday, you would actually apply bandwidth throttling to the first hour of the backup operation, and slow the procedure down for that hour.

4. **Correct Answer:** C

   A. **Incorrect:** This step would exclude the C:\Windows\Temp folder and its subfolders from the backup set, but it would not meet your goal of allowing the backup to be performed weekly. This folder is too small to reduce the size of the backup in any significant way.

   B. **Incorrect:** This step would exclude the C:\Windows\Temp folder but not its subfolders from the backup set, but it would not meet your goal of allowing the backup to be performed weekly. Too little data is stored in this folder to reduce the size of the backup in any significant way.

   C. **Correct:** This setting would allow the previous week's backup to be deleted in order to make space for the current week's backup. The size of the backup from the previous week is approximately 220 GB, and your storage quota is 300 GB. Consequently, you need to be able to remove the previous week's backup to make room for the current week's backup.

   D. **Incorrect:** This setting would not fix your problem. It would require all backups to be kept at least 30 days on Microsoft servers. If there is insufficient space to allow a new backup, as is the case in this scenario, the new backup will fail.

5. **Correct Answer:** A

   A. **Correct:** You don't need to modify the default settings. The bandwidth of the backup operation will be throttled to 256 Kbps beginning at 9AM every weekday.

   B. **Incorrect:** You don't want to increase the bandwidth settings assigned to work hours because this would increase the impact on network performance for users during work hours.

   C. **Incorrect:** Increasing the bandwidth setting assigned to non-work hours would not help you achieve your goal of minimizing impact on users if the backup operation proceeds into the work day.

   D. **Incorrect:** You don't need to adjust workdays because the current selection reflects the Monday - Friday schedule of the organization.

Objective 3.2: Thought experiment

1. You enable the Boot Logging option to track which services and drivers are loaded as a way of determining which was the last loaded before the system freezes.

2. The boot log is written to the file ntbtlog.txt and this file is located in the Windows folder.

3. You use Last Known Configuration to start the computer using the configuration that was in place the last time a successful sign-on occurred.

Objective 3.2: Review

1. **Correct Answers:** B, D

   A. **Incorrect:** Bootrec is used to repair the boot sector, the master boot record, and the BCD store. It cannot be used to configure a server to start in Safe Mode.

   B. **Correct:** You can use the Bcdedit /Set SafeBoot Minimal command to ensure that a computer running Windows Server 2012 will boot into Safe Mode the next time it starts.

   C. **Incorrect:** Startrep is used to before a startup repair of the local system. It cannot be used to configure a server to start in Safe Mode.

   D. **Correct:** You can use Msconfig in the GUI to configure a system to boot into Safe Mode the next time it starts. To do this, click the Boot menu, click Safe Boot, and then ensure that Minimal is selected.

2. **Correct Answer:** C

   A. **Incorrect:** Safe mode will never allow the device driver to load, so it will not allow testing of the new device driver.

   B. **Incorrect:** Last Known Good Configuration will revert to a version of the registry that did not include the driver that you need to test. You need to be able to test the driver.

   C. **Correct:** The problem is most likely caused by the fact that Windows Server 2012 does not load unsigned kernel mode drivers. To proceed with testing, you need to choose Disable Driver Signature Enforcement.

   D. **Incorrect:** This option will disable the defense against certain types of malware, but it will not allow you to load an unsigned driver.

3. **Correct Answer:** B

   A. **Incorrect:** This option is not available because Windows is not loaded on the disk array.

   B. **Correct.** You need to boot from the Windows installation media and then perform a System Image Recovery. This procedure will allow you to restore the system to its former state as quickly as possible.

   C. **Incorrect:** This option is not available because Windows is not loaded on the disk array.

   D. **Incorrect:** This option would to install a completely new deployment of Windows. You don't want a new deployment. You want to recover the old installation as quickly as possible.

Objective 3.3: Thought experiment

1. Only failover clustering can prevent any disruption of service and data loss in case of an individual server failure.

2. You can configure Hyper-V Replica on failover clusters in both the San Francisco and Montreal offices. The failover cluster in the San Francisco office can act as the primary server and the failover cluster in the Montreal office can act as the replica server.

3. One option is to use a cloud backup service such as Windows Azure Backup to back up AppVM1 daily and specify a retention range of 15 days. Another option is to perform daily backups of AppVM1 to local file storage on a file server that is itself a virtual machine. You can then configure this file server as a primary VM with a replica VM in the replica site (Montreal). In case of site-level failure at the primary site, the replica VMs of AppVM1 and the file server at the replica site will continue to operate as before with no loss of backup data.

Objective 3.3: Review

1. **Correct Answers:** A, B

    A. **Correct:** You need to enable the option to save additional recovery points. This step allows you to configure some of these additional recovery points as incremental VSS copies, which are application-consistent.

    B. **Correct:** Incremental VSS copies are snapshots that are application-consistent for VSS-aware applications like Microsoft Exchange.

    C. **Incorrect:** Resynchronization does not affect the consistency of applications within recovery point snapshots.

    D. **Incorrect:** Hyper-V Replica Broker is used for failover clustering, not for application consistency.

2. **Correct Answer:** D

    A. **Incorrect:** You have already performed an unplanned failover. You cannot perform failover to the other site until replication is re-established between the two servers.

    B. **Incorrect:** It's too late to cancel the failover because changes have already been made to AppSrv1.

    C. **Incorrect:** You cannot perform a planned or unplanned failover to the other site until replication is re-established.

    D. **Correct:** Choosing the option to reverse replication starts the Reverse Replication wizard. This wizard lets you re-establish replication between the two servers, with the local server in Denver acting as the new primary. After you complete this wizard, you can perform a planned failover to return the VM to the site in Cleveland.

3. **Correct Answers:** A, D

    A. **Correct:** You need to configure the Hyper-V Replica Broker role for the failover cluster if you want to add an offsite replica to a clustered VM.

    B. **Incorrect:** To configure Hyper-V Replica Broker at the replica site, you would need to create a failover cluster at the replica site. This step is unnecessary because you want to configure RepSrv2 as the replica server. Your goal is not to create a replica cluster.

    C. **Incorrect:** In the replication settings for Cluster1, you want to restrict authorization to RepSrv2. However, this step is not immediately necessary. It would be required only if the VM were failed over to the replica site and you later wanted to fail back to the original site.

    D. **Correct:** The server-level replication settings allow you to limit which remote servers can act as a primary server to the local replica server. In this case, you need to configure the Client Access Point as the name of the primary server.

CHAPTER 4

Configure network services

The Configure Network Services domain includes three objectives: implement an advanced DHCP solution, implement an advanced DNS solution, and deploy and manage IPAM (IP Address Management). As with other objectives on the 70-412 exam, it's fair to assume that you have passed the 70-410 and 70-411 exams. Passing these exams suggests that you already have a good grounding in understanding the Windows Server 2012 R2 DHCP and DNS server roles. Understanding the topics covered in this domain requires a deeper understanding of DHCP and DNS and will involve using new technologies that you may not have implemented in your own environment. You should supplement the information in this chapter with some hands-on practice so that you can develop an understanding of how you can use these technologies to address real-world scenarios and solve problems in an advanced server environment.

Objectives in this chapter:

- Objective 4.1: Implement an advanced DHCP solution
- Objective 4.2: Implement an advanced DNS solution
- Objective 4.3: Deploy and manage IPAM

Objective 4.1: Implement an advanced DHCP solution

Setting up a basic DHCP solution is straightforward. Authorize the server, configure an IP address pool, configure a few options such as the DNS server address, and throw in a reservation or two. An "advanced" DHCP solution requires you to go further and might involve configuring features such as superscopes, multicast scopes, DHCPv6, high availability, name protection, and DNS registration. For the exam, you need to know what these advanced features do and when to deploy them to solve specific problems in a complex network environment.

Creating and configuring superscopes and multicast scopes

The majority of the scopes that you configure on a DHCP server are going to cover traditional IP address ranges. Occasionally, it will be necessary to configure a superscope to collect scopes together or to configure a multicast scope to address the needs of a specific application. In this section, you'll learn about both scope types and the sorts of problems that they can help you solve.

DHCP superscopes

DHCP superscopes are useful when you have more DHCP clients on a network segment than your DHCP scopes can handle individually. For example, let's say you inherit a network segment assigned the 192.168.1.0/24 address range, with a DHCP scope range of 192.168.1.21 - 192.168.1.254, and the first 20 addresses reserved for static assignments. As the number of DHCP clients on this segment grows and approaches the upper limit of 234, you might see clients failing to obtain an address because no leases are available when needed. When the number of clients surpasses 234, it will become impossible for all clients to have an address at the same time. You need more addresses, for the network, but the scope as currently configured is exhausted.

DHCP superscopes provide a solution to this problem. A superscope allows you to create a second, spillover scope that will be used to provide addresses when the first scope no longer has any addresses available to lease out to clients. For example, in the previous scenario, you can create a second scope in the 192.168.2.0/24 range and roughly double the number of leasable addresses on the network segment.

Superscopes are necessary because if DHCP server has only one network interface, it can only provide addresses from DHCP scope to clients on a specific network segment. If you just created an additional DHCP scope, only the scope corresponding to the DHCP server's primary address will be used. The superscope unifies two or more scopes into one scope so that more than one scope can provide address leases to clients if necessary. You can also use superscopes to add non-contiguous ranges together, so if you are using 192.168.2.0/24 on another segment already, you could add 192.168.3.0/24 to 192.168.1.0/24 when creating a superscope.

There's one slight complication about using two scopes that we're glossing over here. If you've used up all the addresses in a first logical subnet (for example, 192.168.1.0/24), then any new scope you add to the same network segment will, of course, be in its own logical subnet, distinct from the first. The second logical subnet will therefore only be able to communicate with the first subnet through a router; also, the second subnet will require its own corresponding default gateway address, such as 192.168.2.1. (It's recommended that you use a second network interface on the router to enable this routing between logical segments, but some routers, including the Routing and Remote Access service in Windows Server 2012 and Windows Server 2012 R2, let you assign the two addresses to the same network interface.)

> **NOTE MIGRATING CLIENTS WITH A SUPERSCOPE**
>
> Another reason to use a superscope might be if you need to migrate clients gradually into a new IP numbering scheme. To do this, you can create an exclusion range covering the entire first scope, so that when clients renew leases, they will automatically receive leases in the new scope. When no more addresses in the old subnet are leased out, you can retire the old subnet.

To create a superscope, first create all the scopes that you want to include in the superscope. Then, in the DHCP console navigation pane, right-click the IPv4 node and select New Superscope from the shortcut menu. You then specify which scopes you want to add to the superscope, as shown in Figure 4-1.

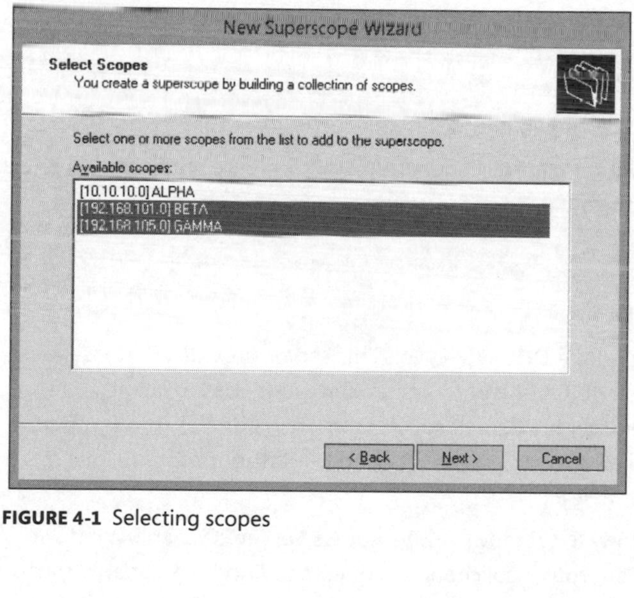

FIGURE 4-1 Selecting scopes

Multicast scopes

Certain applications support multicast, which uses a specific segment of the IPv4 address space to allow IP hosts to communicate with groups of other hosts efficiently. With multicast, applications send data to one of these special IPv4 multicast addresses and all of the clients (and only the clients) that have subscribed to that address receive the data. An example of an application that can use multicast is Windows Deployment Services (WDS).

The protocol by which clients request and automatically obtain a multicast address is not DHCP but Multicast Address Dynamic Client Allocation Protocol (MADCAP). Despite this technical difference, MADCAP is handled by the DHCP Server service in Windows Server and it's configured in the DHCP console. As with DHCP for unicast, MADCAP isn't required for multicast. You can also configure multicast addresses manually on individual clients.

Configuring MADCAP on a DHCP server amounts to creating a multicast scope, which is easy. In the DHCP console navigation pane, right-click the IPv4 node, and then select New Multicast Scope from the shortcut menu. You will be prompted to name the scope and give it an address range within the larger multicast range of 224.0.0.0 to 239.255.255.255 (224.0.0.0/3). The specifics of the range you'll need to configure depend on the application and your environment, but keep in mind that unlike unicast addresses, you don't need assign one multicast address per client. However, each multicast client will additionally need a unique, unicast address.

Implementing DHCPv6

The Windows Server DHCP role includes a DHCPv6 server. This server provides DHCP services for IPv6 hosts. While you can use a DHCPv6 server to assign IPv6 addresses to clients, you cannot use DHCPv6 to provide clients with a default router (gateway) address through DHCP options. IPv6 addresses obtained through DHCPv6 aren't routable without some further configuration performed outside of DHCP.

When computers running Windows 8, Windows 8.1, Windows Server 2012 and Windows Server 2012 R2 start up, they send out router solicitation requests to find IPv6-capable routers. An IPv6 router responds to these requests and informs clients of its IPv6 address. An IPv6 router can also periodically send out router advertisements containing its address or additional configuration information.

For example, you can automatically provide IPv6 hosts on a subnet with a default router address in IPv6 by configuring the local router to advertise its default route. If you are using a server running Windows Server 2012 or Windows Server 2012 R2 as your IPv6 router, you can perform this configuration step by using the following Windows PowerShell command:

```
Set-NetIPInterface -InterfaceAlias InterfaceName -AddressFamily IPv6 -Advertising
Enabled -AdvertiseDefaultRoute Enabled
```

Or you can use the following Netsh command if the server acting as an IPv6 router is running Windows Server 2008, Windows Server 2008 R2, Windows Server 2012, or Windows Server 2012 R2:

```
Netsh Interface IPv6 Set Interface InterfaceNameOrIndex Advertise=Enabled
AdvertiseDefaultRoute=Enabled
```

The commands above provide clients with a default router address in IPv6 as long as forwarding is also enabled on the router's interface, which it is by default in Windows Server 2012 and Windows Server 2012 R2. If forwarding becomes disabled, you can enable it with one of the following commands:

```
Set-NetIPInterface -InterfaceAlias InterfaceName -AddressFamily IPv6 -Forwarding Enabled
```

```
Netsh Interface IPv6 Set Interface InterfaceNameOrIndex Forwarding=Enabled
```

DHCPv6 is arguably not the simplest way to assign routable IPv6 addresses. If you configure an IPv6 router to publish the network prefix assigned to an interface, you can make neighboring IPv6 clients self-configure with an IPv6 address that is based on that network prefix. This mechanism is called *stateless address autoconfiguration (SLAAC)* and is distinct from the non-routable link-local address beginning with "fe80::", which IPv6 hosts always assign to themselves.

If you are using a server running Windows Server 2012 or Windows Server 2012 R2 as your IPv6 router, you can configure local IPv6 hosts to self-configure with an IPv6 address based on the network prefix of the router's locally facing interface. To do so, on the router, first enable advertising on the interface as described in the previous sidebar "Configuring IPv6 hosts with a default router," and then type the following Windows PowerShell command, where *NetworkPrefix* is the IPv6 network ID:

```
Set-NetRoute -DestinationPrefix NetworkPrefix::/64 -InterfaceAlias InterfaceName
-AddressFamily IPv6 -Publish Yes
```

Or, you can use the following Netsh command if the server acting as an IPv6 router is running Windows Server 2008 or later:

```
Netsh Interface IPv6 Set Route NetworkPrefix::/64 Interface=InterfaceNameOrIndex
Publish=Yes
```

These two commands use the number 64 for the length in bits of the IPv6 network prefix, which is typical. If you are using another network prefix length, use that length instead of "64."

Even though you can use SLAAC and router advertisements to configure IPv6 hosts with a routable IPv6 configuration, DHCPv6 still has a few advantages that make it useful. One advantage is that, unlike SLAAC, DHCPv6 provides a record of which hosts are assigned which address leases. In addition, with DHCPv6 it is easy to automatically assign options other than the default router, such as the address of a local DNS server. A final advantage of DHCPv6 is that you can use exclusions in each DHCPv6 scope to limit the host addresses to a user-friendly, manageable range. For example, if the network prefix for a subnet with fewer than 256 nodes is 2001:a:b:c::/64, you can use DHCPv6 exclusions to limit addresses assigned to hosts to the range 2001:a:b:c::1 to 2001:a:b:c::ff. Without these exclusions, IPv6 addresses obtained through either DHCPv6 or SLAAC are assigned randomly within the available address space, resulting in unwieldy sequences such as 2001:a:b:c:79da:927c:48d2:cff1.

Understanding Windows clients and stateful addressing

By default, Windows Vista, Windows 7, Windows 8, and Windows 8.1 clients all accept both DHCPv6 addresses and options from a local DHCPv6 server. Another way of saying this is that these clients are *stateful* by default. Stateful addressing in Windows clients is managed by the following two IPv6 protocol flags, configured locally on each machine or set by a neighboring IPv6 router:

- **Managed address configuration flag (M-flag)**   This flag, when set, indicates that clients should obtain an IPv6 address through DHCPv6, in addition to any addresses they obtain using SLAAC.
- **Other address configuration flag (O-flag)**   This flag, when set, indicates that clients should use DHCPv6 to obtain additional configuration options, such as the IPv6 address of a DNS server.

The state of these flags as configured at the local IPv6 router overwrites any local IPv6 setting. The flags are enabled by default in Windows Server 2012 and Windows Server 2012 R2, so if you are using a server running either operating system as your IPv6 router, any neighboring IPv6-enabled clients will automatically be configured as stateful by default. Conversely, if these properties become disabled on this router, Windows clients can be disabled for stateful addressing. If necessary, you can re-enable these flags by using the following Windows PowerShell command:

```
Set-NetIPInterface -InterfaceAlias InterfaceName -ManagedAddressConfiguration Enabled
-OtherStatefulConfiguration Enabled
```

Or you can use the following Netsh command:

```
Netsh Interface IPv6 Set Interface InterfaceNameOrIndex ManagedAddress=Enabled
OtherStateful=Enabled
```

Configuring DHCPv6

Configuring DHCPv6 simply requires you to assign a static IPv6 address to the DHCP server and then configure a DHCPv6 scope. The IPv6 address you assign to the DHCP server must share the same network prefix as the one you define for the scope (assuming the scope is serving the local subnet).

To configure a DHCPv6 scope, perform the following steps:

1. In the DHCP console, right-click the IPv6 node and then click New Scope.

2. On the Scope Name page, choose a name and description for the scope.

3. On the Scope Prefix page, configure a scope prefix and preference.

    The IPv6 address prefix is the most important setting in the DHCPv6 scope. It defines the first half (64 bits) of each IPv6 address assigned from the scope and is analogous to the network ID in an IPv4 scope.

    The preference value informs DHCPv6 clients which server to use if multiple DHCPv6 servers are available. The higher the value, the higher the priority. Figure 4-2 shows the prefix and preference settings.

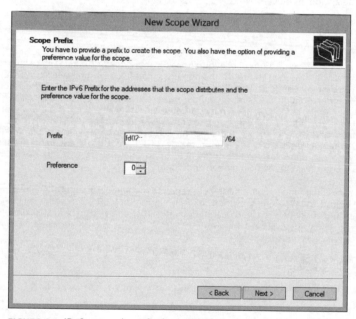

FIGURE 4-2 IPv6 network prefix for a DHCPv6 scope

4. On the Add Exclusions page, define any exclusion ranges for IPv6 addresses you don't want to be assigned to clients through DHCP.

5. On the Scope Lease page, configure the Preferred and Valid lifetime properties.

6. Activate the scope to enable it.

Configuring high availability for DHCP

DHCP is a critical network service. If the DHCP server is unavailable for any length of time, clients will be unable to get valid IP addresses to communicate on the network. It was difficult to make DHCP highly available in versions of the Window Server operating system prior to Windows Server 2012. Windows Server 2012 and Windows Server 2012 R2 support DHCP failover, a process through which you can either configure DHCP servers as a load-balanced pair or configure a second DHCP server to lease addresses from a properly configured scope if the DHCP server that usually manages leases from that scope goes offline.

DHCP failover

DHCP failover enables two DHCP servers to provide IP addresses and optional configurations to the same subnets or scopes. The benefit of this method is that when failover occurs, the second server is aware of existing lease information and is able to renew leases that were originally issued by the partner server.

Table 4-1 lists the two methods through which you can configure DHCP failover.

TABLE 4-1 Network Load Balancing cmdlets in Windows Server 2012

Mode	Characteristics
Hot Standby	In this mode, one server is the primary server and the other is the secondary server. The primary server actively assigns IP configurations for the scope or subnet. The secondary DHCP server only assumes this role if the primary server becomes unavailable. A DHCP server can simultaneously act as the primary for one scope or subnet and be the secondary for another. Administrators must configure a percentage of the scope addresses to be assigned to the standby server. These addresses are supplied during the Maximum Client Lead Time (MCLT) interval if the primary server is down. The default MCLT value is 5 percent of the scope. The secondary server takes control of the whole IP range after the MCLT interval has passed. Hot Standby mode is best suited to deployments in which a disaster recovery site is located at a different location. That way the DHCP server will not service clients unless there is a main server outage.
Load Sharing	This is the default mode. In this mode both servers simultaneously supply IP configuration to clients. The server that responds to IP configuration requests depends on how the administrator configures the load distribution ratio. The default ratio is 50:50.

> **MORE INFO** **DHCP FAILOVER**
>
> To learn more about DHCP failover, visit *http://technet.microsoft.com/en-us/library/hh831385.aspx*.

Configuring DHCP split scopes

Creating split scopes—usually with one server hosting 80 percent of the scope addresses and a second hosting the remaining 20 percent—is the traditional method of providing highly available DHCP. If your organizations DHCP servers are running a version of Windows Server released prior to Windows Server 2012, this is probably how you are implementing highly available DHCP.

The Split Scope Wizard, included with Windows Server operating systems since Windows Server 2008 R2, allows you configure two DHCP servers with identical configurations that split an address range. To accomplish this goal, you prepare the first DHCP server with the full address range and all desired options and settings. Then you add the DHCP server role to a second server but don't configure any scopes. You then select a scope on the first folder and run the DHCP Split-Scope Configuration Wizard. The wizard asks you to specify the second DHCP server and then it lets you distribute the addresses within the range as you choose, with a default of an 80/20 split, as shown in Figure 4-3.

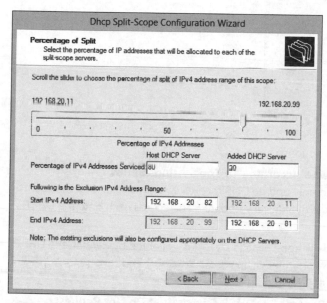

FIGURE 4-3 DHCP Split-Scope Configuration Wizard

Configuring DNS registration

When a DHCP server leases an address to a client, it can also perform registration of that computer's address in DNS. DNS registration ensures that the addresses configured in the DNS zone match the IP addresses leased by the DHCP server. You can configure DNS registration at the server level or at the individual scope level on the DNS tab of either the IPv4, IPv6 or individual scope properties dialog box. Figure 4-4 shows configuring DNS registration for an IPv4 scope named ALPHA.

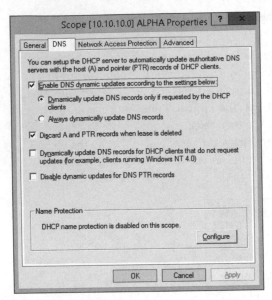

FIGURE 4-4 DNS registration

You can configure the following options:

- **Enable DNS Dynamic Updates According To The Settings Below**   Allows you to configure the DHCP server to only update DNS records when requested by the client (the default value) or to always dynamically update DNS records each time the DHCP server leases an address.

- **Discard A And PTR Records When Lease Is Deleted**   Enabled by default, the DHCP server instructs the DNS server to remove any associated host and reverse lookup records when a DHCP lease expires and is deleted.

- **Dynamically Update DNS Records For DHCP Clients That Do Not Request Updates**   Ensures that DNS records are always updated when the DHCP server leases an address. This functions in a manner similar to the Always dynamically update DNS records option.

- **Disable Dynamic Updates for DNS PTR Records**   Configures the DHCP server to update host (A) records, but does not update records in a reverse lookup zone. This option is useful for organizations that haven't configured reverse lookup zones where attempts to register PTR records cause errors in the event log.

Configuring DHCP Name Protection

DHCP Name Protection allows you to protect the names that DHCP registers in DNS on behalf of DHCP clients from being overwritten by devices running non-Microsoft systems that may have the same name. DHCP name protection also protects the names from being overwritten by systems that use static addresses that conflict with DHCP-assigned addresses when DHCP is not configured for conflict detection. For example, a UNIX-based system named Client1 could potentially overwrite the DNS address that was assigned and registered by DHCP on behalf of a Windows-based system also named Client1.

DHCP Name Protection uses a resource record known as a Dynamic Host Configuration Identifier (DHCID) to track which host originally requested a specific name. The DHCP server provides the DHCID record, which is stored in DNS. If a DHCP server receives a request by a host with an existing name for an IP address, the DHCP server refers to the DHCID in DNS to verify that the host that is requesting the name is the original host that assigned the name. If the host requesting the name isn't the same as the original host, the DNS resource record is not updated.

The DHCP Server role supports name protection for both IPv4 and IPv6. You can configure DHCP Name Protection at the server level and the scope level. Implementation at the server level only applies to newly created scopes.

To enable DHCP Name Protection for an IPv4 or IPv6 node:

1. Open the DHCP console.

2. Right-click the IPv4 or IPv6 node and then open the Properties dialog box.

3. On the DNS tab, click Configure.

4. On the Name Protection dialog box select the Enable Name Protection check box as shown in Figure 4-5.

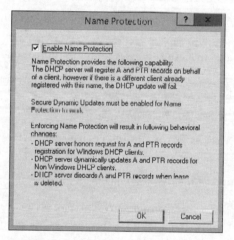

FIGURE 4-5 Enabling name protection

To enable DHCP Name Protection for a scope:

1. Open the DHCP Microsoft Management Console (MMC).

2. Expand the IPv4 or IPv6 node, right-click the scope, and then open the Properties dialog box.

3. On the DNS tab, click Configure and then select the Enable Name Protection check box.

Thought experiment

Configuring DHCP at Wingtip Toys

In the following thought experiment, apply what you've learned about this objective to predict what steps you need to take. You can find answers to these questions in the "Answers" section at the end of this chapter.

Wingtip Toys has three sites, one in Melbourne, one in Canberra, and the other in Sydney. Each location has an office building. The Melbourne building has approximately 700 hosts, the Canberra building 500 hosts, and the Sydney building approximately 1500 hosts. Each location has a single DHCP server running the Windows Server 2008 R2 operating system.

All IP addresses in use at Wingtip Toys are IPv4 addresses in the 192.168.0.0/16 IP address range. Subnets at Wingtip Toys are 24 bits long. Each scope leases addresses from a single subnet. The Melbourne location has 3 DHCP scopes, the Sydney location has 7 DHCP scopes and the Canberra location has 2 DHCP scopes.

You have the following objectives:

- IP address allocation should still occur when the WAN link is down.
- IP address allocation should still occur in the event that a single server fails
- During normal operation, no single DHCP server should be responsible for leasing all the addresses in a single scope.
- A DHCP server in each site should be able to lease addresses from the entire scope without reconfiguration if necessary.
- In the next 6 months, 200 clients will be added at the Melbourne site.

With the preceding information in mind, answer the following questions.

1. What is the minimum number of DHCP servers do you need to deploy at each site to accomplish your goals?

2. What operating system should you upgrade the DHCP servers to?

3. What method should you use to ensure that DHCP is highly available?

4. How many scopes will be necessary at the Melbourne site in six months time assuming the existing subnet length is used for any new scopes?

Objective summary

- Superscopes allow you to combine existing DHCP scopes. When the available addresses in the first scope are exhausted, addresses will be provided from the additional scopes in the superscope.

- Multicast scopes allow hosts to be allocated with multicast IP addresses in the 224.0.0.0 to 239.255.255.255 IP address range.

- DHCPv6 allows you to provision DHCP clients with IPv6 addresses

- DHCP servers can be configured in paired relationships. These relationships can be configured to function as failover from one server or another, or can be configured so that the DHCP servers are load balanced.

- Name registration allows a DHCP server to update a DNS server with the name details of a DHCP client. You can configure name registration at either the server or the scope level.

- DHCP Name Protection protects names registered in DNS by DHCP clients from being overwritten by hosts running non-Microsoft operating systems.

Objective review

Answer the following questions to test your knowledge of the information in this objective. You can find the answers to these questions and explanations of why each answer choice is correct or incorrect in the "Answers" section at the end of the chapter.

1. You work at Contoso, which has a number of office buildings at an outer-suburban industrial park. The buildings use the following IP address ranges:

   - Building One: 192.168.15.0/24

   - Building Two: 192.168.16.0/24

   - Building Three: 192.168.17.0/24

   - Building Four: 192.168.18.0/24

   The IP address range 192.168.0.0/24 through 192.168.14.0/24 are used at other branch office locations, as are the IP address ranges 192.168.24.0/24 through 192.168.254.0/24. You have a DHCP server running the Windows Server 2012 R2 operating system that hosts four scopes. There is one scope for each building. Building One has recently been renovated and three additional floors have been added. There will be an additional 100 computers deployed in Building One. Unfortunately the DHCP scope used for Building One is already 95 percent utilized. What steps could you take to resolve this situation without reassigning address ranges from other buildings? (Choose three answers. Each answer forms part of the complete solution.)

   A. Create a new scope for the IP address range 192.168.19.0/24.

   B. Create a new superscope that includes the IP address ranges 192.168.15.0/24 and 192.168.19.0/24.

   C. Create a new superscope that includes the IP address ranges 192.168.15.0/24 and 192.168.16.0/24

   D. Configure the router in Building One to support an additional address range.

2. Which of the following techniques can you use to provide high availability for a DHCP scope? (Choose all that apply.)

   A. Split scopes

   B. Multicast scopes

   C. DHCP Failover

   D. DHCP Name Protection

3. Which type of scope would you configure if you needed to lease IP addresses in the following range: 224.0.0.0 to 239.255.255.255?

   A. Split scope

   B. Superscope

   C. Multicast scope

   D. DHCPv6 scope

4. Your organization has not configured a reverse lookup zone in DNS and management does not believe one must be configured in the future. Errors are occurring because DHCP clients are attempting to register records in the reverse lookup zone. Which of the following settings would you change on the DHCP server to stop these errors from occurring?

   A. Discard A And PTR records When Lease Is Deleted

   B. Dynamically Update DNS Records For DHCP Clients That Do Not Request Updates.

   C. Disable Dynamic Updates For DNS PTR Records

   D. Enable DHCP Name Protection

Objective 4.2: Implement an advanced DNS solution

As an experienced server administrator, you will already be familiar with the core components of DNS, from configuring different types of zones to creating different record types. To meet the knowledge requirements for this objective, you need to have a deeper understanding of what you can accomplish with DNS on Windows Server 2012 and Windows Server 2012 R2 and when to leverage features such as DNSSEC, DNS Socket Pool, delegated administration, recursion, and cache locking.

This objective covers how to:

- Implement DNSSEC
- Configure DNS Socket Pool
- Configure DNS cache locking
- Configure DNS logging
- Configure delegated administration
- Configure recursion
- Configure netmask ordering
- Configure a GlobalNames zone
- Analyze zone level statistics

Implementing DNSSEC

DNSSEC allows you to provide clients with a way of checking the integrity of the results returned when they perform a query against a DNS server. DNSSEC works by using digital certificates to cryptographically sign information stored in DNS zones. When a DNS client performs a query against a record in a zone that has been configured for DNSSEC, the DNS server that hosts the zone will provide the client with both the information about the requested record and a digital signature that allows the client to validate that the information returned is authentic.

Implementing DNSSEC creates the following cryptographic keys:

- **Trust anchor** This is a special public key that is associated with a DNS zone. The trust anchor is used to verify the DNSKEY record. When you implement DNSSEC on Active Directory Integrated Zones, the trust anchor replicates to all DNS servers hosted on domain controllers in the Active Directory forest.
- **Key Signing Key (KSK)** This key signs all DNSKEY records. This key is created on the computer that hosts the DNSSEC Key Master role. The DNSSEC Key Master is generally the computer that hosts the DNS server on which DNSSEC is first implemented in the Active Directory forest. In Windows Server 2012 R2, the Key Master role can be configured for file-backed multi-master zones and the DNSSEC master key can be stored on a cryptographic next-generation (CNG) compliant offline storage module.
- **Zone Signing Key (ZSK)** This key is used to sign zone data, including individual host records. The DNSSEC Key Master generates the ZSK.

When you sign a DNS zone, a number of special resource records are created. These include:

- **Resource Record Signature (RRSIG) record** One of these is associated with each individual zone record. Stored in the DNS zone. DNS server will return RRSIG record with the queried record when queried.

- **DNSKEY record**   This is a special DNS record that allows clients to verify the authenticity of RRSIG records.
- **Next Secure (NSEC/NSEC3) record**   This is a special record that verifies that a queried record does not exist. For example, if a client queries dragon.contoso.com and there is no dragon record in the contoso.com zone and this zone is configured with DNSSEC, the DNS server hosting the contoso.com zone will return a NSEC record.

Once you have implemented DNSSEC, you can configure Group Policy to ensure that clients will accept records only from a specific zone if those records are verified with an RRSIG record. You accomplish this using the Name Resolution Policy Table (NRPT), which is located in a standard Group Policy Object.

> **MORE INFO** **DNSSEC**
>
> To learn more about DNSSEC, visit *http://technet.microsoft.com/en-us/library/jj200221.aspx*.

Configuring DNS Socket Pool

DNS Socket Pool minimizes the chances of successful cache-tampering and DNS spoofing attacks by randomizing the source port used to issue DNS queries to remote DNS servers. To successfully perform a DNS spoofing attack, an attacker needs to know the port that was used for the query and the transaction ID issued with the query. The transaction ID is randomized by default. Randomizing the source port reduces the likelihood of a DNS spoofing attack being successful. A DNS server running on a server running on the Windows Server 2012 R2 operating system has a socket pool of 2,500 by default. Increasing the size of the socket pool allows the DNS server to increase the source port randomization. It's also possible to decrease the size of the socket pool to 0, in which case the DNS server uses a single socket for remote DNS query operations. You can modify the DNS Socket Pool size using the dnscmd.exe command line utility. For example, to set the socket pool size to 6,000, issue the following command from an elevated command prompt on the computer that hosts the DNS server role:

```
Dnscmd /config /socketpoolsize 6000
```

> **MORE INFO** **DNS SOCKET POOL**
>
> To learn more about DNS Socket Pool, visit *http://technet.microsoft.com/en-us/library/ee683907.aspx*.

Configuring DNS cache locking

By configuring DNS cache locking, you can control if and when records stored in the DNS server cache can be overwritten. When a DNS server resolves a query for a client, it will store the results of that query in the cache for the length of time specified by the records Time To

Live (TTL) value. This allows the DNS server to respond quickly to subsequent requests for this address without having to contact the authoritative DNS server that hosts the appropriate record. One type of attack against DNS servers involves polluting the cache with false records by overwriting existing cached records. DNS cache locking allows you to block records in the cache from being changed for the length of the record's TTL value. DNS servers running on the Windows Server 2008 R2 and later operating systems have a cache-locking value set to 100 percent of the DNS record's TTL value. You can modify this using the Set-DNSServer-Cache Windows PowerShell cmdlet to a different value. For example, to set the cache-locking value to 75 percent of a record's TTL value, issue the following command from an elevated Windows PowerShell prompt:

```
Set-DNSServerCache -LockingPercent 75
```

> **MORE INFO** DNS CACHE LOCKING
>
> To learn more about DNS cache locking, visit *http://technet.microsoft.com/en-us/library/ ee683892.aspx*.

Configuring DNS logging

The DNS server log is available through the Applications And Services Logs folder on the server that hosts the DNS server role. The events that are recorded in this long depend on the configuration of the DNS server. You can configure which events are logged on the Event Logging tab of the DNS server properties, as shown in Figure 4-6.

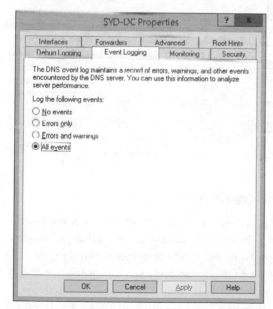

FIGURE 4-6 Event Logging tab

When configured to record all events, the DNS event log will store information about the following:

- Changes to the state of the DNS server service, such as when the service starts or stops
- When a DNS zone is loaded or signed
- Changes to the configuration of the DNS server
- DNS warning events and error events, such as when a DHCP server attempts to update a PTR record and no reverse lookup zone exists

You can configure detailed logging of DNS server operations by configuring debug logging. This differs from the usual event logging in that it provides much more data and that data is written to a text based log rather than a Windows event log visible in event viewer. By using debug logging, you can log incoming and outgoing packets as well as packet contents. You configure debug logging on the Debug Logging tab of the DNS server properties dialog box shown in Figure 4-7.

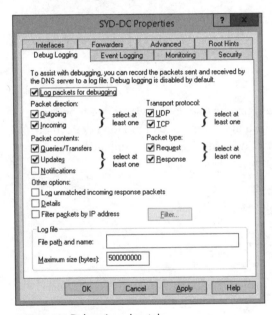

FIGURE 4-7 Debug Logging tab

Configuring delegated administration

In small and medium sized organizations, one person is usually responsible for managing and maintaining all aspects of DNS server operations. In very large organizations, different people may be responsible for managing different aspects of DNS server operations. Through delegation, you can allow a person to perform DNS administration tasks without giving him the ability to perform other tasks. He might even be unable to directly sign on to the DNS server and instead must use the Remote Server Administration Tools to perform DNS administration tasks.

By default, users who are members of the Enterprise Admins group are able to perform any DNS administration task on a server that has the DNS server role installed on it in the forest. Members of the Domain Admins group are able to perform any DNS administration task on any server that has the DNS server role installed on it within a domain. If you want to allow a user to perform DNS administration tasks without adding them to either of these highly privileged groups, you can add the user's account to the DnsAdmins domain local group. Members of the DnsAdmins domain local group are able to perform DNS administration tasks only. The default permissions assigned to the DnsAdmins group are shown on the Security tab of the DNS server properties dialog box, shown in Figure 4-8. You can use this dialog box to add and assign permissions to additional security principals.

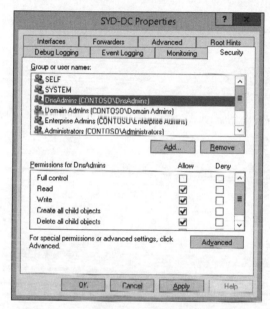

FIGURE 4-8 Security tab with DnsAdmins selected

You can also assign permissions at the zone level. For example, you might want to allow a user named Chris to add DNS records on the australia.margiestravel.com DNS zone, but not want to allow Chris permissions to any other zone. In this scenario you'd assign Chris permissions at the zone level, but not add his user account to the DnsAdmins, Domain Admins, or Enterprise Admins groups.

Configuring recursion

When a client queries a Windows Server DNS server, the default behavior of the DNS server, if the record isn't stored in a zone hosted on the DNS server, is to go and query other DNS servers and then to pass the results of that query back to the client. This is feature is called DNS recursion. You can disable recursion on the Advanced tab of the DNS server properties dialog box as shown in Figure 4-9. The main reason you might consider disabling recursion is to stop denial-of-service attacks against your organization's public facing DNS servers. One method of attacking an organization is to send large numbers of queries to DNS servers, slowing them to the point where they become unresponsive. The drawback of disabling recursion on a DNS server is that it also disables DNS forwarding.

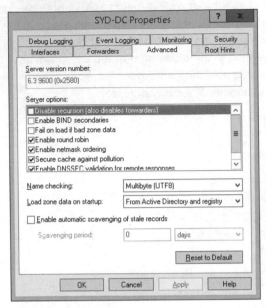

FIGURE 4-9 Advanced tab

MORE INFO DNS RECURSION

To learn more about DNS recursion, visit *http://technet.microsoft.com/en-us/library/ cc771738.aspx.*

Configuring netmask ordering

Netmask ordering is a feature of DNS that ensures that the DNS server returns the host record on the requesting client's subnet if such a record exists. For example, imagine that the following host records existed on a network that used 24-bit subnet masks for WSUS servers at each site:

- 192.168.10.105 wsus.adatum.com
- 192.168.20.105 wsus.adatum.com
- 192.168.30.105 wsus.adatum.com

If you enable netmask ordering and a client with the IP address 192.168.20.50 performs a lookup of wsus.contoso.com, the DNS server will always return the record 192.168.20.105 because this record is on the same subnet as the client when a 24-bit subnet mask is used. When netmask ordering is not enabled, the DNS server returns records in a round-robin fashion.

If the requesting client is not on the same network as any of the host records, the DNS server also returns records in a round-robin fashion. Netmask ordering is useful for services such as Windows Server Update Services (WSUS), where you might have servers hosting that role at each branch office. Netmask ordering is enabled by default on Windows Server 2012 R2 DNS servers.

Configuring a GlobalNames zone

GlobalNames zones provide single-label name resolution. Single-label name resolution allows single names to be translated to IP addresses—for example, using the name *wsus* rather than the fully qualified domain name (FQDN) of wsus.contoso.com. GlobalNames zones provide organizations with the ability to replace WINS servers, which have been used in previous versions of the Windows Server operating system to provide single-label name resolution. You use alias (CNAME) records when populating a GlobalNames zone, which maps the single-label name to an existing FQDN.

GlobalNames zones provide single label-name resolution for both IPv4 and IPv6 addressing. The drawback of GlobalNames zones is that you must populate the zone manually by creating CNAME records.

> **MORE INFO** **GLOBALNAMES ZONES**
>
> To learn more about GlobalNames zones, visit *http://technet.microsoft.com/en-us/library/cc731744.aspx*.

Analyzing zone-level statistics

In addition to viewing information in log files, DNS servers record statistical information about queries and other DNS server operations. You can use the Get-DnsServerStatistics cmdlet to view statistics of a DNS server, including using the cmdlet to view the following statistics:

- Cache statistics
- Database statistics
- DNSSEC statistics
- Directory services statistics
- Error statistics
- Master statistics

- Memory statistics
- NetBios statistics
- Packet statistics
- Private statistics
- Query statistics
- Record statistics
- Recursion statistics
- Secondary statistics
- Security statistics
- Timeout statistics
- Time statistics
- Update statistics
- WINS statistics
- Zone Query statistics
- Zone Transfer statistics
- Zone Update statistics

To view the zone-level statistics of a specific DNS zone, use the –ZoneName parameter. For example, to view the zone-level statistics of the contoso.com DNS zone, issue the following command from an elevated Windows PowerShell prompt:

```
Get-DnsServerStatistics –ZoneName contoso.com
```

> **MORE INFO** DNS STATISTICS
>
> To learn more about DNS statistics, visit *http://technet.microsoft.com/en-us/library/dn305898.aspx*.

Thought experiment

Configuring advanced DNS at Tailspin Toys

In the following thought experiment, apply what you've learned about this objective to predict what steps you need to take. You can find answers to these questions in the "Answers" section at the end of this chapter.

Recently the internal DNS servers at tailspin toys were compromised. The attackers managed to cause problems that lead to the DNS servers returning incorrect information to clients that queried the servers. You have recently upgraded the DNS servers so that all servers are now hosted on computers running the Windows Server 2012 R2 operating system. All servers that host the DNS server role are also domain controllers.

With the preceding information in mind, answer the following questions.

1. Which feature would you configure to ensure that all DNS records in the tailspin-toys.com zone were cryptographically signed?

2. Which group policy item would you configure to ensure that clients at Tailspin Toys only accepted cryptographically verified records from the tailspintoys.com zone?

3. Which DNS feature would you configure to ensure that records stored in the DNS server cache couldn't be overwritten until 75 percent of the TTL associated with the record had expired?

4. Which domain local group would you add a user account to if you wanted them to be able to add new host records to any zone hosted on the Tailspin Toys DNS servers without giving them unnecessary administrative privileges?

Objective summary

- DNSSEC uses certificates and digital signatures to allow clients to verify the integrity and authenticity of DNS records.
- The Name Resolution Policy Table (NRPT) allows you to specify whether a client requires specific zones to be digitally signed through DNSSEC
- The DNS event log records DNS service events such as zone loading, service status, and errors.
- The DNS debugging log allows you to create a text based log to record incoming and outgoing DNS traffic.
- The DNS socket pool allows you to configure how port randomization works with DNS requests.

- DNS Cache Locking allows you to ensure that records in the DNS servers cache can't be overwritten until a specific amount of the records Time To Live (TTL) has elapsed.
- When DNS recursion is enabled, the DNS server resolves the DNS query on behalf of the client.

Objective review

Answer the following questions to test your knowledge of the information in this objective. You can find the answers to these questions and explanations of why each answer choice is correct or incorrect in the "Answers" section at the end of the chapter.

1. Which of the following should be configured when you wanted to change the number of ports available when a DNS server makes a query to another DNS server on behalf of a client?

   A. Netmask ordering

   B. Socket pool

   C. Cache locking

   D. DNSSEC

2. Which of the following Windows PowerShell cmdlets are used to view DNS zone statistics?

   A. Get-DNSServerForwarder

   B. Get-DNSServerSigningKey

   C. Get-DNSServerStatistics

   D. Get-DNSServerZone

3. Which of the following resource records is associated with a host record in a zone and allows a DNS client to verify the authenticity of the host record?

   A. NSEC

   B. PTR

   C. RRSIG

   D. CNAME

4. Which of the following resource records is returned when a zone protected by DNSSEC does not contain the record queried by the client?

   A. NSEC

   B. PTR

   C. RRSIG

   D. CNAME

Objective 4.3: Deploy and manage IPAM

Once configured, an IPAM (IP Address Management) server automatically collects information from your organization's DHCP and DNS servers. You can then use the IPAM interface to manage those servers centrally. In this lesson you'll learn what you can use IPAM to accomplish, how to configure IPAM, and the ways in which you can use IPAM to manage IP addresses in your organization.

> **This objective covers how to:**
> - Understand IPAM
> - Install and configure IPAM
> - Manage address space
> - Configure IPAM database storage

Understanding IPAM

IPAM lets you centrally view, manage, and configure the IP address space in your organization. With IPAM, you can look at all your address blocks and ranges, find free IP addresses, manage DHCP scopes across multiple servers, create DHCP reservations and DNS host records, and even search for address assignments by device name, location, or other descriptive tag.

IPAM works by first discovering your infrastructure servers and then importing from them all available IP address data. You then manually add whatever additional data you need to complete the picture of your organization's IP address assignments. Once you have this information in place, you can track updates to your IP address space.

To better understand the purpose and functionality of IPAM and these many aspects, it's helpful to view IPAM as a means to solve the following kinds of administrative issues:

- How can I track my organization's address space and know the addresses that are either in use or available across different locations?
- How can I find a free static IP address for a new device and register it in DNS?
- How can I learn which DHCP scopes in my organization are full or close to being full?
- How can I efficiently change a DHCP option across dozens of scopes residing on multiple servers?
- How can I find an unused address range within our organization's address space to dedicate to a new subnet?
- How can I determine which public and private address ranges are used by my organization?

- How can I determine which portion of the address space used by the organization is dynamically assigned, and which part is statically assigned?
- How can I search for and locate an IP address or set of addresses by name, device, location, or another descriptive tag?

IPAM has the following limitations:

1. IPAM can import data only from Windows servers running Windows Sever 2008 and later which are members of the same Active Directory forest.

2. IPAM does not support management and configuration of non-Microsoft network elements.

3. IPAM does not check for IP address consistency with routers and switches.

4. A single IPAM server can support up to 150 DHCP servers for a total of 6,000 scopes, and 500 DNS servers for a total of 150 zones.

5. Address utilization trends and reclaiming support are provided only for IPv4.

6. IPAM does not support auditing of IPv6 stateless address auto configuration on an unmanaged machine to track the user.

Installing and configuring IPAM

To install the IPAM feature in Windows Server 2012 or Windows Server 2012 R2, you can use the Add Roles And Features Wizard or the following Windows PowerShell command:

```
Install-WindowsFeature IPAM -IncludeManagementTools
```

Once IPAM installed, you configure and manage the feature through the IPAM client in Server Manager, as shown in Figure 4-7, or by using Windows PowerShell cmdlets from the IpamServer module. (There is no other graphical IPAM console.)

 EXAM TIP

You can install just the IPAM client tool without installing the server component. To accomplish this task by using the Add Roles And Features Wizard, select IPAM in the wizard, choose to install the prerequisite features of IPAM, clear the selection of IPAM you have just selected, and then complete the wizard. *The IPAM client doesn't appear by default in Server Manager, however.* To make the IPAM client appear, you need to add the remote IPAM server to Server Manager by using the Add Other Servers To Manage option (shown in Figure 4-10).

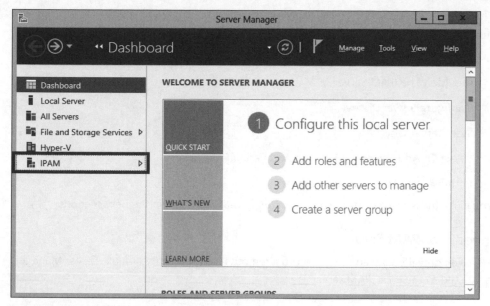

FIGURE 4-10 IPAM node

When you click IPAM in the navigation pane of Server Manager, the navigation pane narrows and the details pane reveals the Overview page, as shown in Figure 4-11.

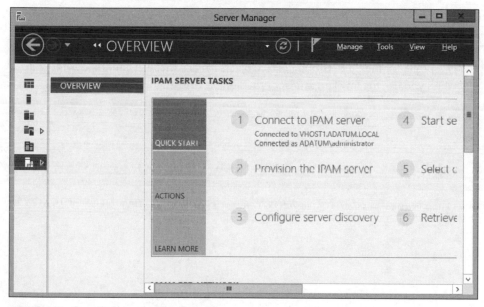

FIGURE 4-11 Overview page preconfiguration

The Overview page presents the following six links that help guide you through configuration:

1. Connect To IPAM Server

2. Provision The IPAM Server

3. Configure Server Discovery

4. Start Server Discovery

5. Select Or Add Servers To Manage And Verify IPAM Access

6. Retrieve Data From Managed Servers

You'll use these same steps to cover the configuration process in the next sections.

Connect To IPAM Server

Use this link only if you need to connect to a remote IPAM server. By default, Server Manager is connected to the local IPAM server.

Provision The IPAM Server

Clicking this link starts the Provision IPAM Wizard. Provisioning the IPAM server is the term used to prepare the IPAM server by performing steps such as automatically creating the IPAM database, creating IPAM security groups, and configuring access to IPAM tasks and folders.

You also use this wizard to determine how you want to configure the infrastructure servers that IPAM will manage. The two choices are to configure the infrastructure servers manually or to do so through Group Policy, as shown in Figure 4-12. If you choose to use Group Policy, you specify a prefix for the three Group Policy Objects (GPOs) that will later be created automatically when you use the Invoke-IpamGpoProvisioning cmdlet.

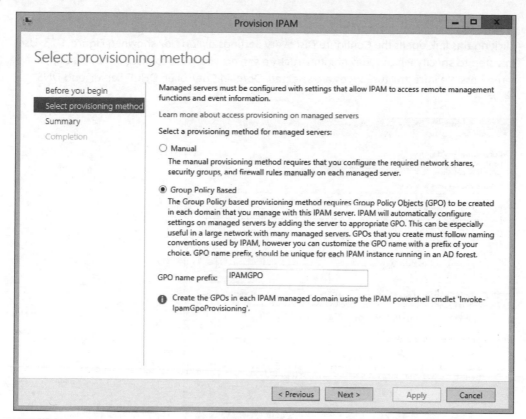

FIGURE 4-12 Choosing Group Policy Based configuration with a GPO name prefix

You wouldn't select Manual here unless there were some unusual factor that made the Group Policy Based option impossible or ineffective. Despite this limited real-world applicability of the Manual option, configuring IPAM manually is one of the tasks officially mentioned in the Deploy and manage IPAM objective. (The process of manual configuration is discussed in the section "Select Or Add Servers To Manage" later.)

EXAM TIP

You can't change the provisioning method after you complete the Provision IPAM Wizard. To change from manual provisioning to Group Policy based provisioning or the other way around, you have to uninstall and reinstall IPAM.

Configure Server Discovery

Clicking this link opens the Configure Discovery Settings dialog box shown in Figure 4-13. Use this step to specify which types of infrastructure servers you want to discover. By default, all three possible infrastructure types are selected: Domain Controller, DHCP Server, and DNS Server.

FIGURE 4-13 Selecting infrastructure server types to discover

Start Server Discovery

This link begins the process of discovering infrastructure servers in your environment. To determine when the process is complete, you can click the notification flag in Server Manager and then click Task Details. The process is complete when the IPAM ServerDiscovery task displays a status of Complete, as shown in Figure 4-14.

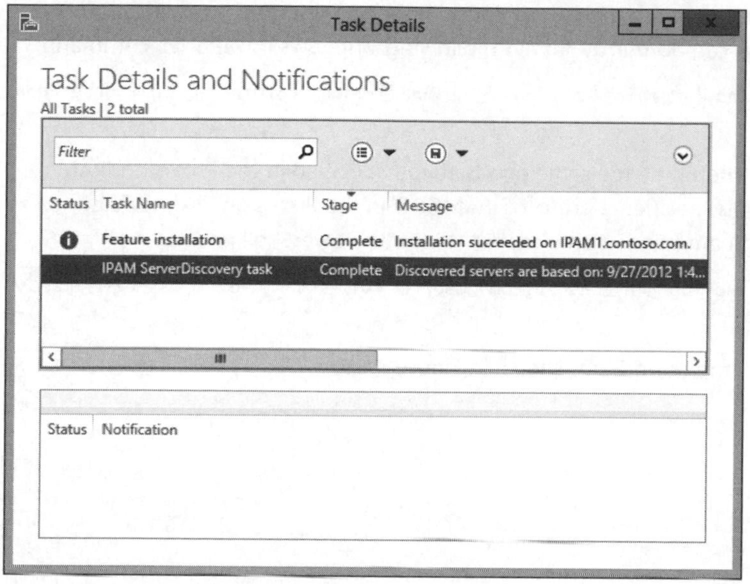

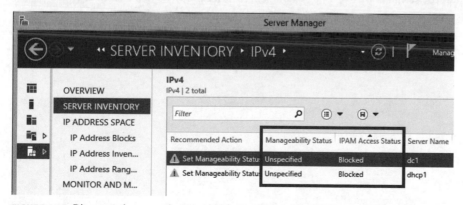

FIGURE 4-14 Server discovery complete

Select Or Add Servers To Manage And Verify IPAM Access

Clicking this link displays the SERVER INVENTORY page in the IPAM client of Server Manager. This page shows the servers that have been discovered by the server discovery task in the previous step. At first, the discovered servers display a Manageability Status of Unspecified and an IPAM Access Status of Blocked, as shown in Figure 4-15. This status simply means you still need to configure the servers for IPAM management. To perform this step, you need to run a Windows PowerShell command and then designate the desired servers as managed. (You need to perform this step if you have chosen the Group Policy Based option on the Select Provisioning Method page shown in Figure 4-12. If you have chosen the Manual option, the entire IPAM configuration process is different. For instructions on manual configuration, see the sidebar "Manual configuration of managed servers" later in this chapter.)

FIGURE 4-15 Discovered servers that need to be configured for IPAM management

To configure the servers through the Group Policy Based provisioning method, you need to create IPAM GPOs. You can do this by running following Windows PowerShell command:

```
Invoke-IpamGpoProvisioning [-Domain] <String> [-GpoPrefixName] <String> [-IpamServerFqdn
<String> ]
```

The GPO prefix name should be the same one that you specified in the Provision IPAM Wizard. For example, if you specified a prefix of IPAMGPO in the Provision IPAM Wizard, you could enter the following command at an elevated Windows PowerShell prompt:

```
Invoke-IpamGpoProvisioning –Domain contoso.com –GpoPrefixName IPAMGPO –IpamServerFqdn
ipam1.contoso.com
```

This command creates the three GPOs shown in Figure 4-16.

FIGURE 4-16 GPOs created for IPAM

These three new GPOs apply only to servers that you designate as managed, but no servers are designated as managed by default. (Remember this last point for the exam because it could easily serve as the basis for a test question.) To change the manageability status of servers, right-click each server you want to manage on the SERVER INVENTORY page and then click Edit Server. In the Add Or Edit Server dialog box that opens, in the Manageability Status drop-down list, select Managed (as shown in Figure 4-17) and then click OK.

> **NOTE IPAM PROVISIONING GROUP**
>
> The IPAM provisioning process creates a domain security group named IPAMUG. This group is used to grant permissions on managed servers.

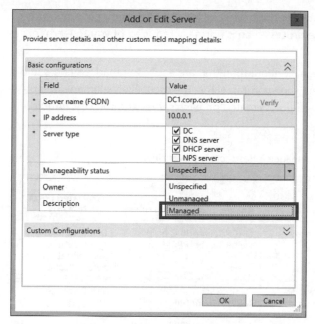

FIGURE 4-17 Setting a server's manageability status to Managed

Finally, you need to force an update of Group Policy on all the servers you have designated as managed. You can do this, of course, either by running Gpupdate /force on each of these servers, by restarting them, or by invoking Gpupdate centrally through Group Policy Management or the Invoke-Gpupdate cmdlet.

Next, click the refresh icon in Server Manager In the menu bar next to the notification flag. (Alternatively, you can right-click your servers on the SERVER INVENTORY page and select the Refresh Server Access Status option.) After you refresh the server status, the Manageability Status of the servers will appear as Managed and the IPAM Access Status will appear as Unblocked on the SERVER INVENTORY page, as shown in Figure 4-18. If the status is not immediately updated, wait several minutes and refresh the server status again.

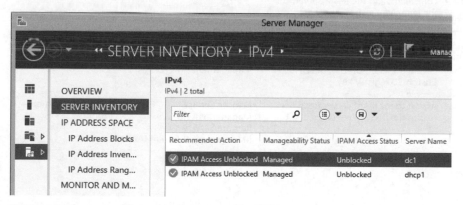

FIGURE 4-18 Servers configured to be managed by IPAM

Configuring IPAM manually from start to finish without the use of Group Policy involves a far more elaborate and cumbersome process than is normally required of you to learn for Microsoft certification exams.

However, there are aspects of manual configuration that are easily summarized and could plausibly appear on the exam; these are shown in Table 4-2. The most likely elements to appear in an exam question are the firewall ports created on each server and the DHCPAudit share on the managed DHCP server.

TABLE 4-2 Manual configuration steps for managed infrastructure servers in IPAM

On this managed server...	Perform this configuration step	Enable these firewall rules	Associated IPAM functionality
DHCP	Add the IPAM server to the local DHCP Users security group	DHCP Server (RPC-In) DHCP Server (RPCSS-In)	DHCP address space, settings, and utilization data collection
	Assign to the IPAM server Read access in the DHCP Server service access control list (ACL)	Remote Service Management (RPC) Remote Service Management (RPC-EPMAP)	DHCP Service monitoring
	Add the IPAM server to the local Event Log Readers security group	Remote Event Log Management (RPC) Remote Event Log Management (RPC-EPMAP)	DHCP configuration event monitoring
	Create a network share named DHCPAudit for %windir%\system32\dhcp and assign read access to the IPAM server on this share	File and Printer Sharing (NB-Session-In) File and Printer Sharing (SMB-In)	DHCP lease event collection for IP address tracking
DNS	For DNS servers that are also domain controllers, assign to the IPAM server Read access in the domain-wide DNS ACL* OR For DNS servers that are not domain controllers, add the IPAM server to the local Administrators group	DNS Service RPC DNS Service RPC Endpoint Mapper	DNS zone configuration collection
	Add the IPAM server to the local Event Log Readers security group Assign to the IPAM server Read access in the ACL stored in the DNS CustomSD registry key	Remote Event Log Management (RPC) Remote Event Log Management (RPC-EPMAP)	DNS zone event collection for DNS zone monitoring
	Assign to the IPAM server Read access in the DNS Server service ACL	Remote Service Management (RPC) Remote Service Management (RPC-EPMAP)	DNS service monitoring

On this managed server...	Perform this configuration step	Enable these firewall rules	Associated IPAM functionality
DC/NPS	Add the IPAM server to the local Event Log Readers security group	Remote Event Log Management (RPC) Remote Event Log Management (RPC-EPMAP)	Logon event collection for IP address tracking
IPAM (local server)	Add the local Network Service to the local Event Log Readers security group	N/A	IPAM configuration event monitoring

EXAM TIP

The IPAM server needs to be able to read the event logs on the DHCP, DNS, DC, and NPS servers. For this reason, it needs to be added to the local Event Log Readers security group on all of these servers.

Retrieve Data From Managed Servers

The final step in configuring IPAM is to load data from your managed servers into the IPAM database. To do so, on the Overview page, click Retrieve Data From Managed Servers. Then click the notification flag and wait for all tasks to complete.

Alternatively, you can select and right-click the managed servers on the SERVER INVENTORY page and then select Retrieve All Server Data from the shortcut menu, as shown in Figure 4-19.

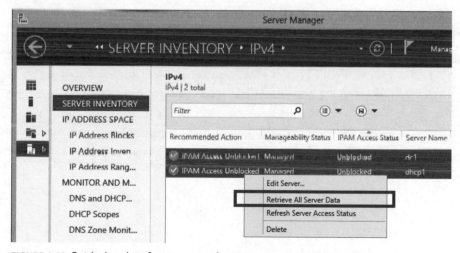

FIGURE 4-19 Retrieving data from managed servers

Managing address space

The most basic function of IPAM is to let you view, monitor, and manage the IP address space in your organization. With IPAM, you can search and sort IP blocks, ranges, and individual addresses based on built-in fields or user-defined custom fields. You can also track IP address utilization within scopes or display utilization trends.

Adding your IP address space to the IPAM database

You can browse and search your organization's address space in the IPAM client in Server Manager, but only after you add this data to the IPAM database. In IPAM, the IP address space is organized according to blocks, ranges, and addresses. Blocks represent the largest sections of IP address space used by a company, such as 10.0.0.0/8. Ranges are portions of blocks that typically correspond to DHCP scopes. IP addresses exist within ranges.

How are these elements added to IPAM? IPAM discovers DHCP scopes automatically and it automatically imports the corresponding address ranges into the IPAM database. However, IPAM doesn't import blocks or addresses into its database automatically. You have to add them manually or import them from a comma-delimited file. (You can also export addresses to a file in comma-delimited format.) In addition, you might want to create additional ranges that have not been discovered by IPAM. For example, these address ranges might correspond to space reserved for statically assigned addresses or the ranges might be used by DHCP servers that are not members of the local Active Directory forest.

To add an IP address block, range, or address to the IPAM database, click IP Address Blocks in the IPAM navigation menu, and then, from the Tasks menu, select Add IP Address Block, Add IP Address Range, or Add IP Address, as shown in Figure 4-20.

> ### *REAL WORLD* IP ADDRESS TRACKING
>
> Although IPAM doesn't automatically import addresses associated with DHCP leases into the IPAM database, you can use the EVENT CATALOG page and the IP Address Tracking tool to search the DHCP server log directly for DHCP leases by client name or address.

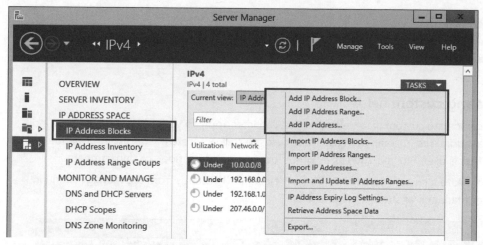

FIGURE 4-20 Adding a block, range, or address to the IPAM database

After this step, you can view the elements you have added by selecting the appropriate category (IP Address Ranges, IP Addresses, or IP Address Blocks) in the Current View drop-down list, as shown in Figure 4-21.

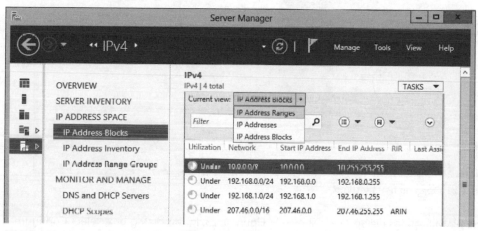

FIGURE 4-21 Viewing added ranges, addresses, or blocks

Creating custom fields

You can create custom data fields that you can later apply to your blocks, ranges, and individual addresses. You can then use these fields to sort or locate IP address information in a way that is useful to you, such as by office location, building, floor, or department.

To create a custom field for IPAM, first select IPAM Settings from the Manage menu in Server Manager, as shown in Figure 4-22.

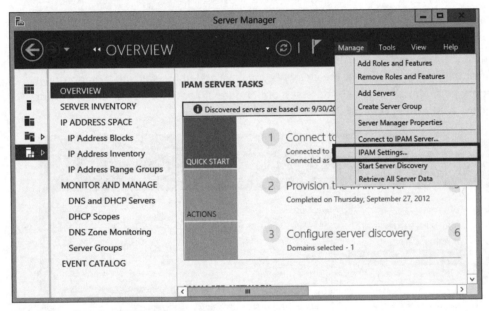

FIGURE 4-22 Opening IPAM settings

The IPAM Settings dialog box is shown in Figure 4-23. In this dialog box, select Configure Custom Fields.

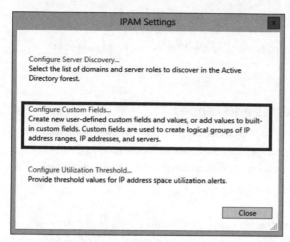

FIGURE 4-23 Configuring custom fields

This step opens the Configure Custom Fields dialog box, shown in Figure 4-24. Use this dialog box to create custom field names (such as Building) and then possible values for that value (such as Headquarters, Sales, Operations, and Data Center).

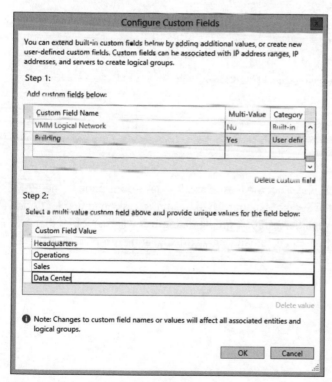

FIGURE 4-24 Configuring custom fields

EXAM TIP

Remember that you can use custom fields to categorize the IP addresses and ranges in your IPAM database.

Applying a custom field to addresses and ranges

To add a custom field to an IP address range or IP address, right-click the element and select the option to edit it. (You can edit multiple ranges or addresses simultaneously.) Then click Custom Configuration in the associated dialog box and provide the desired field and value.

Creating IP address range groups

An IP address range group is a view of IP addresses or ranges sorted by stacked categories, as shown in Figure 4-25. In this figure, an IP address range group named Building/Floor has been created. When you select this IP address range group, you can view or search ranges and address by building name and then by floor name.

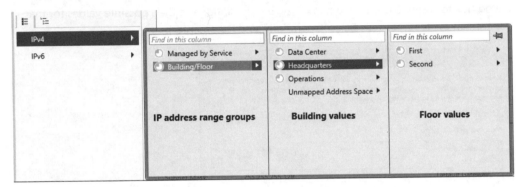

FIGURE 4-25 An IP address range group

To create an IP address range group, select the IP Address Range Groups page in the IPAM navigation pane in the IPAM client in Server Manager. Then, from the Tasks menu, select Add IP Address Range Group, as shown in Figure 4-26. A simple dialog box will then open that allows you to specify parent and child values for your new address range group.

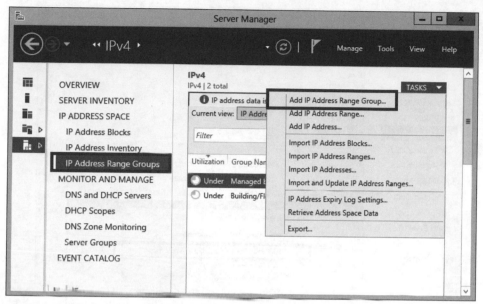

FIGURE 4-26 Adding an IP address range group

EXAM TIP

Expect to see a question about IP address range groups on the 70-412 exam.

Finding and allocating an address from a range

Finding an unused address to allocate to a device is a common task for a network administrator. IPAM lets you perform this task within a chosen IP address range and it verifies for you that the IP address is unused.

To perform this function, select the IP Address Blocks page in the IPAM client in Server Manager and verify that IP Address Ranges is selected in Current View. Then right-click the desired IP Address range and select Find And Allocate Available IP Addresses, as shown in Figure 4-27.

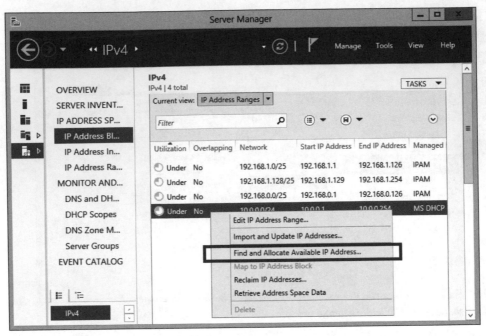

FIGURE 4-27 Finding an available IP address

Viewing and configuring IP utilization thresholds

When you select the IP Address Blocks page, the first column in the list of blocks or ranges displayed is Utilization, as shown in Figure 4-28. This value lets you know how much of a displayed address block or range is already assigned to devices. By default, if fewer than 20 percent of the addresses defined in the range are in use, the status reads Under. If more than 80 percent of the addresses are in use, the status reads Over. Optimal utilization is shown when the IP address usage is between 20 percent and 80 percent.

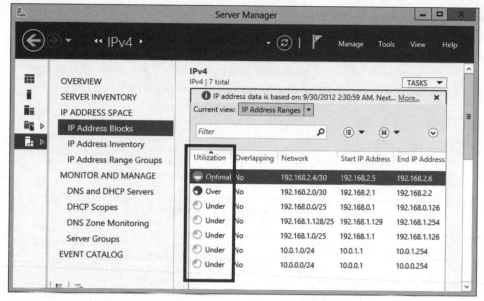

FIGURE 4-28 Utilization rates of IP address ranges

You have the option of altering these 20 percent and 80 percent parameters that separate Under, Optimal, and Over status messages. To do so, in Server Manager, select IPAM Settings from the Manage menu and then select the Configure Utilization Threshold option in the IPAM Settings dialog box. (You can see these options in Figures 4-19 and 4-20 earlier in this chapter.) In the Configure IP Address Utilization Threshold dialog box that opens, shown in Figure 4-29, adjust the percentage for Under Utilized or Over Utilized, as desired.

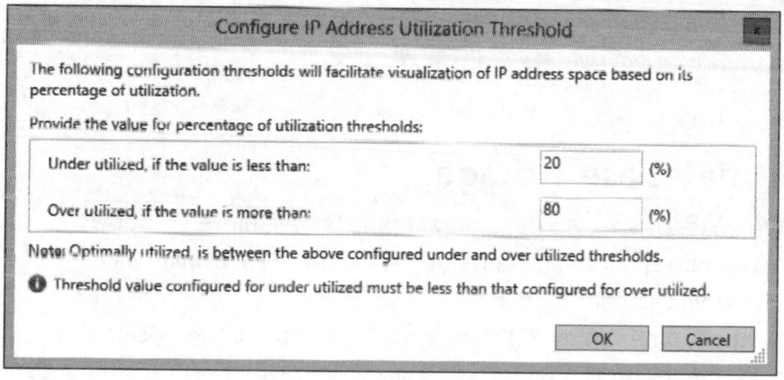

FIGURE 4-29 Changing the over-utilization and underutilization thresholds

Delegating IPAM administration

IPAM uses role-based access control to allow you to delegate the ability for users to perform specific operations, such as manage IP addresses, without providing the ability to perform all tasks. These roles are associated with local security groups on the IPAM server. You delegate a role by adding a user account or group to the appropriate security group (see Table 4-3).

TABLE 4-3 Local security groups created on the IPAM server

Role	Description
DNS record administrator	Is able to manage DNS resource records through IPAM
IP address record administrator	Is able to manage IP addresses, but cannot manage IP address spaces, ranges, blocks, or subnets
IPAM administrator	Is able to manage all settings and objects in IPAM
IPAM ASM administrator	Is able to manage all IP addresses, address spaces, ranges, blocks, and subnets
IPAM DHCP administrator	Is able to manage DHCP servers configured through IPAM
IPAM DHCP reservations administrator	Is able to mange DHCP reservations through IPAM
IPAM DHCP scope administrator	Is able to manage DHCP scopes through IPAM
IPAM MSM administrator	Is able to manage DHCP and DNS servers through IPAM

> **MORE INFO** **IPAM**
>
> To learn more about IPAM, refer to the IPAM Step-by-Step Guide at *http://technet. microsoft.com/en-us/library/hh831622.aspx* or the IPAM Test Lab Guide at *http:// www.microsoft.com/en-us/download/details.aspx?id=29020*.

Configuring IPAM database storage

The initial release of IPAM for Windows Server 2012 only supported using the Windows Internal Database to host IPAM information. The updated version of IPAM available in Windows Server 2012 R2 allows you to configure IPAM to use an instance of SQL Server 2012 or later to host IPAM information. When using SQL Server 2012, you can either locate the IPAM database on the IPAM server or deploy it on a separate server. Microsoft recommends that if you want to use an instance of SQL Server 2012 to host the IPAM database, that instance should host the IPAM database exclusively and not also host additional workloads such as databases for System Center products or line-of-business applications.

Thought experiment

Implementing IPAM at Adatum

In the following thought experiment, apply what you've learned about this objective to predict what steps you need to take. You can find answers to these questions in the "Answers" section at the end of this chapter.

You are a network administrator for Adatum.com, where the network is spread out over four buildings on a single campus near Sydney, Australia, and consists of 1,000 clients and 60 servers, including the following infrastructure servers:

- 12 DHCP servers, including:
    - 8 running Windows Server 2012 R2 (four scopes)
    - 2 running Windows Server 2008 R2 (one scope)
    - 1 running Windows Server 2003 R2 (one scope)
    - 1 running CentOS distribution of Linux (one scope)
- 4 domain controllers that are also DNS servers, including:
    - 2 running Windows Server 2012 R2
    - 2 running Windows Server 2008 R2
- 2 DNS servers running Debian Linux

All clients and servers on the network that are running Windows are also members of the Adatum.com domain. As a network administrator, you want to use the IPAM feature in Windows Server 2012 R2 to manage the company's address space. The 12 DHCP servers are used to support seven /24 IPv4 networks within the 10.0.0.0/16 address block. The first 10 addresses in each scope are configured as exclusions and are reserved for static IP assignments. Twelve public servers are hosted on a /28 IPv4 network obtained from the APNIC regional registry. All 12 of these public addresses are statically assigned.

With this information in mind, answer the following questions.

1. How many of the infrastructure servers are not compatible with IPAM?

2. Assuming you want to add all of the organization's public and private addresses to the IPAM database, how many IP address blocks should you add? How many IP address ranges must be added manually?

3. Server Manager displays the public IP address range utilization as "Over." Your organization isn't intending to assign any more public IP addresses to servers. What step can you take to allow your IP ranges to use 90 percent of the available addresses before displaying the "Over" status?

4. You want to assign a static IP address to a new device in the logical subnet that contains the DHCP server running Windows Server 2012 R2. What is the most efficient way to discover an unused address in this range?

Objective summary

- IPAM is a new feature that lets you centrally manage the IP addressing information in your organization. IPAM works only with Microsoft servers in a domain environment.
- To configure IPAM, you run the Provision IPAM Wizard, start a process to discover your infrastructure servers automatically, mark chosen servers as managed, and then run a special cmdlet (Invoke-IpamGpoProvisioning) to create GPOs that automatically configure required settings on those servers.
- DHCP scopes discovered on the network are automatically imported into the IPAM database as IP address ranges. To these IP address ranges you can add larger IP address blocks and individual IP addresses.
- IPAM includes many features for IP address management. These features allow you to describe data in a way that helps you sort and find information about your address space. They also help you keep track of the addresses used in available ranges and update DHCP and DNS servers directly.
- You can delegate aspects of IPAM administration to different users by assigning these users to any of five IPAM security groups.

Objective review

Answer the following questions to test your knowledge of the information in this objective. You can find the answers to these questions and explanations of why each answer choice is correct or incorrect in the "Answers" section at the end of the chapter.

1. You have installed the IPAM feature on a server named IPAM1 that is a member of the Contoso.com domain. You want to configure the IPAM server to retrieve data from all DHCP servers, DNS servers, and domain controllers in the domain.

   You choose the option to use the Group Policy–based provisioning method to discover the servers and you select all three server roles to discover. You start server discovery and all of the DHCP servers, DNS servers, and domain controllers in the domain are discovered. However, they appear in the Server Manager with an IPAM Access Status of Blocked.

   You want the IPAM Access Status of the discovered infrastructure servers to appear as Unblocked. What should you do? (Choose all that apply.)

   A. Run the Invoke-IpamGpoProvisioning cmdlet.

   B. Mark the servers as managed.

   C. Add the IPAM server to the local Event Log Readers security group.

   D. Refresh Group Policy on the discovered servers.

2. You work as a network administrator for Fabrikam.com, a company with 2,500 employees and offices in New York, London, Paris, and Munich. Each office site includes its own Active Directory Domain Services domain within the Fabrikam.com forest.

    As an administrator, you occasionally need to know the IP address ranges used in various parts of your organization. You want to be able to browse the IP address ranges assigned to each city.

    You install IPAM on a server running Windows Server 2012 R2 named IPAM2 in your local office. You then configure IPAM; you perform server discovery of the DHCP servers, DNS servers, and domain controllers in your organization; and, finally, you retrieve addressing data from these servers.

    Your goal is to be able to use Server Manager to browse the IP address ranges assigned to each city. Which of the following steps do you need to take? (Choose all that apply.)

    A. Configure a custom field.

    B. Create an IP address range group.

    C. Assign custom values to IP address ranges.

    D. Edit the Description field in IP address ranges.

3. You have installed the IPAM feature on a server named IPAM3 that is a member of the Litwareinc.com domain. You want to allow a certain user named Pam to manage DHCP servers but not DNS servers through IPAM.

    You don't want to assign any additional rights to Pam. Which role should you assign to Pam?

    A. DNS record administrators

    B. IPAM MSM administrators

    C. IPAM ASM administrators

    D. IPAM DHCP administrators

4. You have installed the IPAM feature on a server named IPAM2 that is a member of the margiestravel.com domain. You want to allow a certain user named Chris to manage IP addresses, but he shouldn't be able to manage IP address spaces, ranges, blocks, or subnets. Which IPAM role should you assign Chris?

    A. IP address record administrator

    B. IPAM ASM administrator

    C. IPAM DHCP reservations administrator

    D. IPAM DHCP scope administrator

Answers

This section contains the solutions to the "Thought experiments" and the "Objective review" questions in this chapter.

Objective 4.1: Thought experiment

1. You need to deploy 2 DHCP servers at each site to meet the goals of ensuring IP address allocation when the WAN link is down and when a single server fails.

2. The DHCP servers should be upgraded to Windows Server 2012 or Windows Server 2012 R2 because these operating systems support DHCP failover.

3. You should use DHCP failover with the load-balanced method. This meets the goal of ensuring that no single DHCP server is responsible for leasing all the addresses in a single scope.

4. Melbourne will have a total of 900 hosts. It presently has 700 hosts and three scopes. Each scope supports up to 254 hosts. It will need an additional scope, leading to a total of four scopes.

Objective 4.1: Review

1. **Correct Answers:** A, B, D

   A. **Correct:** An additional scope is required.

   B. **Correct:** This will allow the new computers to receive addresses from either the 192.168.15.0/24 or 192.168.19.0/24 ranges.

   C. **Incorrect:** You would only take this step if you were going to reassign the addresses in Building Two.

   D. **Correct:** When using superscopes, you need to configure any routers to support the new as well as the existing IP address range.

2. **Correct Answers:** A, C

   A. **Correct:** Split scopes separate a scope across two servers.

   B. **Incorrect:** Multicast scopes provide hosts with multicast addresses.

   C. **Correct:** DHCP failover provides high availability for a DHCP scope through either load balancing the scope across two servers or having the scope fail over to a new server in the event that the original one is offline.

   D. **Incorrect:** DHCP name protection ensures that names registered with DNS through DHCP are not overwritten by clients running non-Microsoft operating systems.

3. **Correct Answer:** C

   A. **Incorrect:** You configure a split scope when you want to split a single scope across multiple DHCP servers.

   B. **Incorrect:** You use a superscope when you want to extend an existing scope by adding an additional scope.

   C. **Correct:** You use Multicast scopes to lease IP addresses in the range 224.0.0.0 to 239.255.255.255.

   D. **Incorrect:** You use DHCPv6 scopes for IPv6 addresses.

4. **Correct Answer:** C

   A. **Incorrect:** Configuring this setting deletes A and PTR records when the lease is deleted; it does not stop PTR records from being created or updated.

   B. **Incorrect:** This setting allows clients that do not request dynamic updates to have updates to DNS processed.

   C. **Correct:** You want to stop the creation of and updating of PTR records. Configuring this setting will accomplish this goal.

   D. **Incorrect:** This setting stops non-Microsoft clients from registering names in DNS that already exist.

Objective 4.2: Thought experiment

1. You would implement the DNSSEC feature to ensure that all DNS records in the tailspintoys.com zone were cryptographically signed.

2. You would configure the NRPT through Group Policy to ensure that clients would only accept cryptographically signed records from the tailspintoys.com zone.

3. You would configure DNS cache locking to ensure that the records stored in the DNS server cache couldn't be overwritten until 75 percent of the TTL associated with the record had expired.

4. You would add the user accounts to the DnsAdmins domain local group to accomplish this goal.

Objective 4.2: Review

1. **Correct Answer:** B

   A. **Incorrect:** Netmask ordering allows a DNS server to return a record that exists on the client's subnet if multiple records exist and one of those records indicates that the queried host resides on the client's subnet.

   B. **Correct:** You configure the socket pool when you want to change the number of ports available when a DNS server makes a query to another DNS server on behalf of a client.

   C. **Incorrect:** Cache locking determines how long a record remains in the DNS server cache before it can be overwritten.

   D. **Incorrect:** DNSSEC allows DNS records to be cryptographically signed so that clients can verify their authenticity.

2. **Correct Answer:** C

   A. **Incorrect:** This cmdlet gets information about DNS forwarder configuration.

   B. **Incorrect:** This cmdlet retrieves information about DNS server signing keys.

   C. **Correct:** Use the Get-DNSServerStatistics cmdlet to retrieve DNS server zone statistics.

   D. **Incorrect:** This cmdlet gets details of the zones hosted by the DNS server. It does not retrieve DNS server zone statistics.

3. **Correct Answer:** C

   A. **Incorrect:** NSEC records are returned when a host record does not exist in a DNSSEC secured zone.

   B. **Incorrect:** PTR records are used in reverse lookup zones to point to host records.

   C. **Correct:** Each record in a DNSSEC secured DNS zone has an associated RRSIG record that allows a DNS client to verify the authenticity of the record.

   D. **Incorrect:** A CNAME record, also known as an alias record, points at a host record and allows for an alternate name to be associated with the host record.

4. **Correct Answer:** A

   A. **Correct:** NSEC records are returned when a host record does not exist in a DNSSEC secured zone.

   B. **Incorrect:** PTR records are used in reverse lookup zones to point to host records.

   C. **Incorrect:** Each record in a DNSSEC secured DNS zone has an associated RRSIG record that allows a DNS client to verify the authenticity of the record.

   D. **Incorrect:** A CNAME record, also known as an alias record, points at a host record and allows for an alternate name to be associated with the host record.

Objective 4.3: Thought experiment

1. Four—one running Windows Server 2003 R2 and three running Linux.

2. You should add two IP address blocks—one for the 10.0.0.0/16 private address block and one for the public /28 address block. You need to add three IP address ranges manually, one for the public address range, one for the scope hosted on the Windows Server 2003 R2 server, and one for the scope hosted on the CentOS Linux server. (The others are imported automatically.)

3. Change the Over Utilized utilization threshold in IPAM Settings to 90 percent.

4. Use the Find And Allocate Available IP Addresses function in IPAM.

Objective 4.3: Review

1. **Correct Answers:** A, B, D

    A. **Correct:** Use the Invoke-IpamGpoProvisioning cmdlet to create the GPOs needed to configure discovered servers for IPAM management.

    B. **Correct:** The GPOs created by running the Invoke-IpamGpoProvisioning cmdlet apply only to servers you mark as Managed in IPAM.

    C. **Incorrect:** This setting needs to be configured on the domain controller you want to manage in IPAM, but it is automatically configured by the GPO created by the Invoke-IpamGpoProvisioning cmdlet. You therefore don't need to take this step.

    D. **Correct:** After running the Invoke-IpamGpoProvisioning cmdlet, you need to refresh Group Policy on the discovered infrastructure servers so that the settings in the newly created GPOs are applied to these servers.

2. **Correct Answers:** A, B, C

    A. **Correct:** You need to configure a custom field that includes the values New York, London, Paris, or Munich. You can create a new custom field for these values and name it City or you can use an existing custom field such as Location and add the four cities as new custom values.]

    B. **Correct:** An IP address range group allows you to sort and browse your IP address ranges by any field you choose.

    C. **Correct:** You need to tag each IP address range with the City (or Location) value of New York, London, Paris, or Munich.

    D. **Incorrect:** You cannot browse IP addresses based on the values included in the Description tag. To accomplish that, you need an IP address range group.

3. **Correct Answer:** D

   A. **Incorrect:** The DNS record administrator is able to manage DNS resource records through IPAM.

   B. **Incorrect:** While the IPAM MSM administrator role allows managing of DHCP servers, it also allows management of DNS servers.

   C. **Incorrect:** The IPAM ASM administrator role allows management of address space, not DHCP servers.

   D. **Correct:** The IPAM DHCP administrator role allows users assigned the role the ability to manage DHCP servers through IPAM.

4. **Correct Answer:** A

   A. **Correct:** The P address record administrator role will allow Chris to manage IP address spaces without giving him permission to manage IP ranges, blocks, or subnets.

   B. **Incorrect:** The IPAM ASM administrator role allows a user to manage IP addresses, address spaces, ranges, blocks, and subnets.

   C. **Incorrect:** The IPAM DHCP reservations administrator role allows a user to create DHCP reservations.

   D. **Incorrect:** The IPAM DHCP scope administrator role allows a user to manage DHCP scopes.

CHAPTER 5

Configure the Active Directory infrastructure

The is domain relates to configuring and managing an advanced Active Directory infrastructure, going beyond simple topics covered in earlier exams into topics relevant to administrators managing larger environments. Topics in this domain include forest, trust and site configuration as well as managing Active Directory replication. Understanding the topics covered in this domain requires a deep understanding of technologies that you may not have implemented in your own environment. You should supplement the information in this chapter with some hands on practice so that you can develop an understanding of how you can use these technologies to address real-world scenarios and solve problems in an advanced server environment.

Objectives in this chapter:

- Objective 5.1. Configure a forest or a domain
- Objective 5.2: Configure trusts
- Objective 5.3: Configure sites
- Objective 5.4: Manage Active Directory and SYSVOL replication

Objective 5.1: Configure a forest or a domain

The 70-412 exam questions deal with larger environments than those covered in previous exams. Specifically, you'll be asked questions about the configuration and maintenance of multi-domain Active Directory forests as well as managing environments with multiple forests. You'll need to understand when you can introduce domain controllers running Windows Server 2012 or Windows Server 2012 R2 to an existing domain and the strategies that you should pursue when upgrading an existing domain so that all domain controllers are running the Windows Server 2012 or Windows Server 2012 R2 operating system.

Implementing multi-domain Active Directory environments

Each Windows Server 2012 R2 functional level domain supports the creation of around 2.15 billion relative identifiers (RIDs) and domain controller is able to create around 2.15 billion objects. These numbers are theoretical approximations and these limits haven't been reached in a real world production Active Directory environments. When you consider these figures you'll understand that the primary reason for creating a multi-domain Active Directory forest won't be because the current domain can't support the creation of any more objects.

While considerations around replication are one reason, primarily organizations implement multi-domain forests because of issues beyond the strictly technical, including, but not limited to, the following conditions:

- **Historical naming structure**   Many organizations have a domain structure inherited from when their organization first adopted Active Directory. It might be that there are multiple domains in an environment where Windows Server 2012 R2 is used to host domain controllers because no one got around to altering the structure that was in place when Windows 2000 domain controllers were first introduced.

- **Organizational and political reasons**   Many organizations are conglomerates where separate companies share a single administrative and management group. For example, a university in a Commonwealth country might use a structure where each faculty has a separate domain that is a member of the same forest, with users in the Faculty of Arts signing on to the Arts domain and users in the Faculty of Science signing on to the Science domain.

- **Security considerations**   Domains allow the implementation of authentication and authorization boundaries, allowing one set of administrators to manage users and computers from one part of the organization without allowing those same administrators to manage users and computers from another part of the organization. While you can implement a solution to accomplish the same objectives using delegation of privileges, you may have to comply with legislation that is worded in such a way that it's easier to meet those compliance obligations by segmenting users and computers across separate domains in the same forest.

Even though a single domain forest might appear to be the most appropriate technical solution, it might not be the most appropriate organizational or political solution. Although questions around organizational politics aren't likely to turn up on the 70-412 exam, they will arise when you go to apply the knowledge tested on the exam in the real world.

When considering the creation of a multi-domain forest, you have the choice between using one or more domain trees. A domain tree is a collection of domains that share a common root domain name in a parent/child relationship. For example, adatum.com, queensland. adatum.com, victoria.adatum.com, melbourne.victoria.adatum.com, and tasmania.adatum. com could all be domains that are members of the same domain tree. All domains in this tree share the adatum.com suffix. The parent/child relationship between domains in this tree is indicated by the addition to the domain name namespace. In this example, queensland. adatum.com, victoria.adatum.com, and tasmania.adatum.com are all child domains of the adatum.com domain and the melbourne.victoria.adatum.com domain is a child domain of the victoria.adatum.com domain. The depth of the any one branch of a domain tree is limited by a domain having fully qualified domain name length, including periods, of 64 characters.

An Active Directory forest supports multiple domain trees, meaning that you could have Adatum.com as the root domain and a domain tree under Adatum.com, but that you could also have additional domain trees that use separate name spaces that also are child domains of Adatum.com. For example, it's possible to have contoso.com and fabrikam.com as child domains of Adatum.com. You might use this configuration for conglomerates, where multiple separate public facing business entities are actually all managed centrally.

The advantage of being able to support non-continuous namespaces in a single forest is that all domains in a forest automatically trust one another. This means that in the example where contoso.com and fabrikam.com are child domains of adatum.com, you can assign permissions to objects in the Adatum.com and fabrikam.com domains to a user who signs on to the contoso.com domain.

Implementing multi-forest Active Directory environments

In some circumstances, an organization may require two (or more) completely separate Active Directory environments. For example, you can only deploy one Microsoft Exchange organization in an Active Directory forest. Organization is the Microsoft Exchange term for a common deployment consisting of one or more servers running Microsoft Exchange. It, for political or regulatory reasons, you needed to have two entirely separate Microsoft Exchange organizations for the institution you work for, then you'd need two entirely separate Active Directory forests. If you need to support multiple Active Directory schemas, you'll need multiple Active Directory forests because each forest can have only a single schema.

You can configure trust relationships between domains in different forests or configure entire forest trusts when you need to support multiple Active Directory forests for a single organization. Multi-forest environments are common during migration and merger scenarios where a period of coexistence is required between the existing structure and the new structure. Some organizations also configure resource forests where resources (such as Microsoft

Exchange) are located in one Active Directory forest and user accounts are hosted in one or more separate Active Directory forests. Trust relationships are covered later in this chapter.

EXAM TIP

When looking at questions related to single or multi-forest Active Directory deployments, remember that in a single forest deployment, trust relationships between domains are configured automatically. In multi-forest deployments, trusts must be established manually.

Configuring interoperability with previous versions of Active Directory

When are deploying servers running the Windows Server 2012 R2 operating system, you aren't necessarily going to instantly upgrade all your organization's domain controllers to run Windows Server 2012 R2. In the majority of cases, organizations upgrade their domain controllers some time after they have deployed their first computers running Windows Server 2012 R2.

You can add Windows Server 2012 R2 domain controllers to an existing Active Directory deployment as long as the existing domain functional level is set to Windows Server 2003 or higher. While you can add domain controllers running Windows Server 2012 R2 to a domain running at the Windows Server 2003 functional level, remember that the Active Directory functionality that Windows Server 2012 R2 domain controllers allow won't become fully available until you upgrade the domain functional level to Windows Server 2012 R2. The minimum domain functional level is dependent on the least recent version of the operating system running on any domain controller in the domain. If a domain has 20 domain controllers running on the Windows Server 2012 R2 operating system and one running Windows Server 2003 operating system, the domain functional level will be limited to Windows Server 2003 until that domain controller is no longer present. The forest functional level is dependent on the minimum domain functional level in a forest. You can't raise the forest functional level until all of the domains have had their functional levels raised.

The new features available at the Windows Server 2012 and Windows Server 2012 R2 domain functional levels are as follows:

- Key Distribution Center (KDC) support for claims, compound authentication, and Kerberos armoring.
- The ability to use Group Managed Service Accounts, which allows a single managed service account to be used on multiple computers.
- Domain Controller side protections for Protected Users, which allows you to limit the types of authentication and delegation specific users can use or be configured for (Windows Server 2012 R2 only).

- Authentication Policies, which allows you to limit which hosts an account can sign-on from as well as control authentication conditions for services running as an account (Windows Server 2012 R2 only).
- Authentication Policy Silos, which allow you to classify accounts for specific authentication policies or authentication isolation (Windows Server 2012 R2 only).

> **MORE INFO** **DOMAIN FUNCTIONAL LEVELS**
>
> To learn more about the different functionality available at each domain functional level, visit *http://technet.microsoft.com/library/understanding-active-directory-functional-levels%28v=WS.10%29.aspx.*

Upgrading existing domains and forests

You can take several paths to upgrading an existing domains and forests to run at the Windows Server 2012 or Windows Server 2012 R2 functional levels. The path you take depends on the resources that you have available. You can:

- Perform an operating system upgrade of existing domain controllers so that they are running Windows Server 2012 or Windows Server 2012 R2. This strategy is limited to organizations that have domain controllers running the x64 version of Windows Server 2008 or later. If your organization's domain controllers are running the Windows Server 2003 operating system or an x86 version of Windows Server 2008, you won't be able to implement this strategy.
- Introduce new domain controllers running Windows Server 2012 or Windows Server 2012 R2 into the existing domain, transfer Flexible Single Master Operations (FSMO) roles to these new domain controllers from existing domain controllers, and then decommission the domain controllers running the previous version of the Windows Server operating system. Once these domain controllers have been decommissioned, you can raise the domain and forest functional level to Windows Server 2012 or Windows Server 2012 R2. This is generally the most straightforward method of upgrading an existing domain running earlier domain controllers. It has the advantage of retaining all existing objects and settings.

Unlike previous upgrades where it was necessary to run the adprep.exe utility to prepare the existing Active Directory environment, promoting a domain controller running the Windows Server 2012 or Windows Server 2012 R2 operating systems automatically upgrades the existing environment's schema. This will occur as long as the account used to promote the Windows Server 2012 or Windows Server 2012 R2 domain controller is a member of the Schema Admins, Domain Admins, and Enterprise Admins group. You should promote the first computer running Windows Server 2012 or Windows Server 2012 R2 to a domain controller in the same site as the computer that hosts the Schema Master FSMO role.

Configuring multiple user principal name (UPN) suffixes

Usually, users sign on to a computer by providing their username and password. The domain information is provided automatically based on the domain membership of the computer onto which they are signing. In organizations where there are multiple domains, it is more common for users to sign on using a user principal name (UPN). A UPN looks like an email address and in organizations that have deployed Microsoft Exchange may actually be the user's email address. The advantage of a UPN in a multiple-domain environment is that it's easy for the user to remember and they don't have to worry about remembering the domain name when they sign in. By default, all users are configured to use the UPN suffix that is the name of the forest root domain. For example, if Chris has an account in the victoria.margie-stravel.com domain, which is a child of the margiestravel.com domain, his UPN would be chris@margiestravel.com. When your organization is configured to synchronize with Windows Azure Active Directory, such as when your organization uses Windows Intune or Office 365, you can configure the service so that users can sign on to cloud resources using their local UPN. In some cases, you might want to allow users to use a UPN that is separate from your root domain name. For example, if Chris was a member of an organization that had been configured with a forest root domain named margiestravel.local, his default UPN would be chris@margiestravel.local. By configuring margiestravel.com as an alternative UPN suffix, Chris can instead sign on using chris@margiestravel.com as his UPN.

You can configure new UPN suffixes using the Active Directory Domains And Trusts console shown in Figure 5-1.

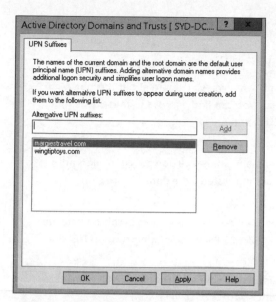

FIGURE 5-1 Configuring UPN suffixes

MORE INFO **UPN SUFFIXES**

To learn more about configuring UPN suffixes, visit *http://technet.microsoft.com/en-us/ library/cc772007.aspx*

EXAM TIP

Remember which console that you use to configure additional UPN suffixes.

Thought experiment

Upgrading the forest at Adatum

In the following thought experiment, apply what you've learned about this objective to predict what steps you need to take. You can find answers to these questions in the "Answers" section at the end of this chapter.

You are the systems administrator at Adatum. You are in the process of planning the upgrade of an existing forest that has 5 domains so that all domain controllers are running the Windows Server 2012 R2 operating system. The domains are configured in the following manner:

- The root domain is named Adatum.local. All domain controllers in this domain are running the Windows Server 2003 with Service Pack 2 operating system. This domain holds the forest level FSMO roles.

- The Adelaide.adatum.local and Brisbane.adatum.local domains have all domain controllers running Windows 2000 Server with Service Pack 4

- The Melbourne.adatum.local and Sydney.adatum.local domains have all domain controllers running the Windows Server 2003 with Service Pack 2 operating system.

You have the following objectives:

- Upgrade every domain in the forest so that all domain controllers are running the Windows Server 2012 R2 operating system.

- Ensure that users can sign on with the username@adatum.com UPN.

With the preceding information in mind, answer the following questions.

1. Which domains must you upgrade before you can install a domain controller running Windows Server 2012 R2?

2. In which domain should you first introduce a domain controller running the Windows Server 2012 R2 operating system?

3. What step must you take to allow users to sign on with the appropriate UPN?

Objective summary

- A forest can contain multiple domains. Domain trees share a namespace. A forest can have multiple domain trees.

- An organization needs multiple forests if it requires separate schemas.

- No Active Directory domain name can exceed 64 characters including periods.

- A domain must be running at the Windows Server 2003 functional level before you can introduce domain controllers running Windows Server 2012 or Windows Server 2012 R2.
- The default UPN is the domain name of the forest root domain.
- Alternate UPN suffixes allow users to sign on with different UPN names.

Objective review

Answer the following questions to test your knowledge of the information in this objective. You can find the answers to these questions and explanations of why each answer choice is correct or incorrect in the "Answers" section at the end of the chapter.

1. Which of the following is the minimum domain functional level required before you can promote a member server running Windows Server 2012 R2 so that it functions as a domain controller?

   A. Windows Server 2003

   B. Windows Server 2008

   C. Windows Server 2008 R2

   D. Windows Server 2012

2. You are considering adding a child domain to the dandenong.melbourne.victoria. australia.contoso.com domain tree. Which of the following represents the maximum length in characters, including periods, of an Active Directory domain name?

   A. 64 characters

   B. 128 characters

   C. 256 characters

   D. 512 characters

3. You are about to promote a server running the Windows Server 2012 R2 operating system to domain controller. The domain is currently running at the Windows Server 2008 domain functional level. Your account is a member of the Domain Admins group. Which additional groups should your account be a member of to ensure that the environment is appropriately configured for this domain controller running Windows Server 2012 R2? (Choose two. Each answer forms part of a complete solution.)

   A. Schema Admins

   B. Enterprise Admins

   C. Account Operators

   D. Server Operators

4. The root domain of the Adatum forest is Adatum.local. The contoso.com domain tree is part of the Adatum forest. Don has an account in the australia.contoso.com domain and is signing on to a computer that is a member of the computers.adatum.local domain. No additional UPNs have been configured. Which UPN suffix will Don use to sign on to this computer?

   A. @adatum.com

   B. @adatum.local

   C. @computers.adatum.local

   D. @australia.contoso.com

Objective 5.2: Configure trusts

Trusts define the security relationship between domains and forests. When a trust exists, users with an account in one domain can be assigned permissions to resources in a separate domain. By default, all domains in a forest are configured to trust each other.

> **This objective covers how to:**
> - Configure external, forest, shortcut, and realm trusts
> - Configure trust authentication
> - Configure Security IDentifier (SID) filtering
> - Configure name suffix routing

Understanding trust concepts

To understand trust, you need to understand two terms: trusting domain and trusted domain. The *trusting domain* contains the resources to which you want to allow access. The *trusted domain* hosts the security principals to which you want to grant access. For example, you want to grant users in the tailspintoys.remote domain access to resources in the fabrikam.local domain. In this scenario, the trusted domain will be tailspintoys.remote and the trusting domain will be fabrikam.local. You also need to understand the concept of trust transitivity. Trust transitivity allows a trust to extend beyond the original trusting domain. When you configure a trust, you also determine whether the trust is transitive. For example, while you might trust the administrators of the tailspintoys.remote domain, do you trust the administrators of child domains such as childdomain.tailspintoys.remote?

When you create a trust, you specify the trust direction as shown in Figure 5-2. You can select a two-way trust, a one-way incoming trust, or a one-way outgoing trust. The two-way trust is also known as a *bidirectional trust*. When you configure a bidirectional trust, both sides of the trust act as both trusting and trusted domains (or forests). When you configure a one-way incoming trust, the local domain is the trusting domain and the remote domain is the trusted domain. When you configure a one-way outgoing trust, the local domain is the trusted domain and the remote domain is the trusting domain.

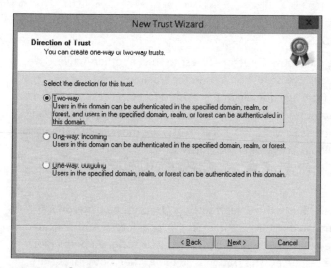

FIGURE 5-2 Configuring the Direction Of Trust page

MORE INFO UNDERSTANDING TRUSTS

To learn more about trusts, visit *http://technet.microsoft.com/en-us/library/cc731335.aspx.*

Configuring external trusts and realm trusts

External trusts allow you to configure a trust where a domain in one forest trusts a domain in a separate forest without any other domains in either forest being included in that relationship. For example, if you wanted to allow users from the Melbourne.adatum.com domain in the Adatum forest to access resources in the Auckland.contoso.com domain in the Contoso forest without allowing any other domains in the Adatum or Contoso forests to participate in the relationship, you would configure an external trust.

You can use an external trust to configure a trust relationship between a Windows Server 2012 domain and a domain running unsupported Windows Server operating systems (such as Windows 2000, which does not support forest trusts). Although unlikely to be mentioned on an exam, there are still organizations running these unsupported operating systems in the real world. Realm trusts are used when you want to create a trust relationship between a non-Windows Kerberos realm, such as one running in a Linux environment, and an Active Directory Domain Services domain.

> **MORE INFO**   **EXTERNAL TRUSTS**
>
> To learn more about external trusts, visit *http://technet.microsoft.com/en-us/library/cc732859.aspx*. For more about realm trusts, visit *http://technet.microsoft.com/en-us/library/cc731297.aspx*.

Configuring forest trusts

Forest trusts allow you to configure one Active Directory forest to trust another Active Directory forest. Forest trusts are transitive, so all domains in the trusting forest can be accessible to any security principal from any domain in the trusted forest. Forest trusts can be uni-directional or bi-directional. Forest trusts require each forest to be configured at a minimum forest functional level of Windows Server 2003. Forest trusts are most likely to be used when a single organization has multiple Active Directory forests.

When you configure a forest trust, you can configure one of the following authentication scopes:

- **Forest-wide authentication**   This is the default setting. Users in the trusted forest are automatically authenticated for all resources in the local forest. Authenticated doesn't mean that they have access; these users still need to be assigned permissions before they can access these resources. This option is suitable when both forests are owned by the same organization, such as in a merger or acquisition.

- **Selective authentication**   When configured, users from the trusted forest will not be automatically authenticated. This allows you to configure the specific servers and domains within the trusting forest that you want to make available to users in the trusted forest. This option is suitable when each forest belongs to a separate entity. To allow a user or group from a trusted forest to access a resource in a trusting forest, configure the Allowed To Authenticate permission on that resource for the user or group from the trusting forest.

You configure the authentication scope on the Authentication tab of the trust's properties, as shown in Figure 5-3.

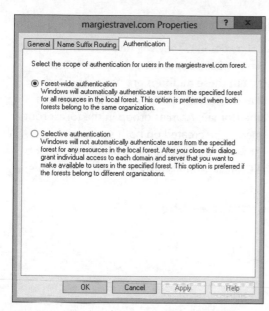

FIGURE 5-3 Configuring forest-wide authentication

Configuring shortcut trusts

You configure a *shortcut trust* when you want to speed up authentication between two domains in the same forest that are on separate branches of the same domain tree or separate domain trees entirely. For example, Chris's user account is located in the Brunswick. melbourne.victoria.margiestravel.com domain. Chris wants to access resources in the cairns. queensland.margiestravel.com domain. Normally the authentication traffic would need to pass all the way up to the margiestravel.com root domain before being passed back down to the destination domain. In this scenario, you could configure a shortcut trust so that authentication traffic from the Brunswick.melbourne.victoria.margiestravel.com domain passed directly to the cairns.queensland.margiestravel.com domain without needing to traverse the intervening domains. You configure shortcut trusts using the Active Directory Domains And Trusts console. Shortcut trusts can be uni-directional or bi-directional.

EXAM TIP

Remember that shortcut trusts allow you to speed up authentication in forests that have large numbers of domains.

Configuring trust authentication

Trusts use the Kerberos V5 authentication protocol by default. They will revert to using NTLM only if Kerberos V5 is not supported. Windows Server 2003 supports both Digest authentication and Schannel authentication across trusts, but these methods are not supported for authenticating trusts in Windows Server 2012 and Windows Server 2012 R2. Creating a forest trust requires that a user be a member of the Domain Admins group in the forest root domain or the Enterprise Admins group. Trusts need to be created on both sides, so these permissions are also required in the partner forest. To create an external trust, a user must be a member of the Enterprise Admins group or the Domain Admins group in the domain where the external trust is being configured.

Configuring trusts requires that the following ports be available:

- Port 387 UDP and TCP, used by LDAP
- Port 445 TCP, used by Microsoft SMB
- Port 88 UDP, used by Kerberos
- Port 135 TCP, used for trust endpoint resolution

> **MORE INFO**   **TRUST AUTHENTICATION**
>
> To learn more about trust authentication, visit *http://technet.microsoft.com/en-us/library/cc773178%28v=ws.10%29.aspx.*

Configuring Security IDentifier (SID) filtering

SID (Security IDentifier) filtering is a security measure that blocks users in a trusted forest or domain from being able to elevate their privileges in a trusting domain if their account has an SID from the trusted domain that is the same as the SID of a privileged account in the trusting domain. SID filtering works by discarding any SID that does not include the domain SID of the trusting domain. SID filtering is enabled by default on domain controllers running Windows Server 2012 and Windows Server 2012 R2. You can disable SID filtering using the netdom trust command with the /enablesidhistory:Yes option. You can reenable SID filtering using the netdom trust command with the /enablesidhistory:No option. Unless there is a specific organizational reason to disable SID filtering, you should leave it in the default enabled state.

> **MORE INFO**   **SID FILTERING**
>
> To learn more about SID filtering, visit *http://technet.microsoft.com/en-us/library/cc794801%28v=ws.10%29.aspx.*

Configuring name suffix routing

You use name suffix routing to configure how authentication requests are routed when you have configured a forest trust. When you create the trust, all unique name suffixes will be routed. By configuring name suffix routing, you can allow or disallow specific UPN suffixes. For example, you might want to allow users from the trusted forest to use the contoso.com and wingtiptoys.com UPN suffixes, whilst blocking the contoso.internal UPN suffix, as shown in Figure 5-4. You configure name suffix routing on the Name Suffix Routing tab of the trust properties in the Active Directory Domains And Trusts console.

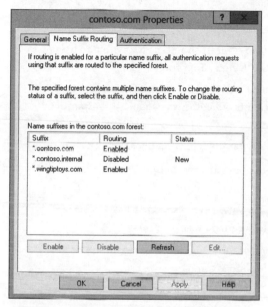

FIGURE 5-4 Configuring name suffix routing

> **MORE INFO   NAME SUFFIX ROUTING**
>
> To learn more about name suffix routing, visit *http://technet.microsoft.com/en-us/library/cc731648.aspx*.

Thought experiment
Resolving trust issues at Tailspin Toys

In the following thought experiment, apply what you've learned about this objective to predict what steps you need to take. You can find answers to these questions in the "Answers" section at the end of this chapter.

You are the systems administrator at Tailspin Toys. Tailspin Toys has recently acquired Wingtip Toys and Margie's Travel.

You have the following objectives:

- Resources in any domain in the Tailspin Toys forest should be accessible to users whose accounts are in any domain in the Wingtip Toys forest.
- Resources in the sales.margiestravel.com domain of the margiestravel.com forest should be available to users whose accounts are in the management.tailspintoys. com domain of the Tailspin Toys forest.

With the preceding information in mind, answer the following questions.

1. Which type of trust should you configure between the Tailspin Toys and the Wingtip Toys forest?

2. Which type of trust should you configure between the sales.margiestravel.com domain and the management.tailspintoys.com domain?

3. When configuring this trust, which domain should be the trusting domain: sales. margiestravel.com or management.tailspintoys.com?

Objective summary

- Trusts can be uni-directional or bi-directional. A one-way outgoing trust allows security principals in the remote domain to access resources in the local domain.
- External trusts allow trusts between separate domains in different forests without having all domains in one forest trust all domains in the other.
- Forest trusts allow all domains in one forest to trust all domains in the other.
- Selective authentication allows you to configure a forest trust so that only certain users and groups in the trusted domain can authenticate.
- Shortcut trusts allow you to speed authentication in forests with a large number of domains.
- Name suffix routing allows you to configure which users can authenticate based on the UPN suffix used.

Objective review

Answer the following questions to test your knowledge of the information in this objective. You can find the answers to these questions and explanations of why each answer choice is correct or incorrect in the "Answers" section at the end of the chapter.

1. You have configured a forest trust relationship between the Adatum forest and the Contoso forest. You want to ensure that users from the Contoso forest can authenticate only when needing to access resources in the Adatum forest using the username@secure.contoso.com UPN rather than any other UPN that is available for them. Which of the following should you use to accomplish this goal?

   A. SID filtering

   B. Name suffix routing

   C. Shortcut trust

   D. External trust

2. There are 42 domains in the tailspintoys.com forest. Users in the Melbourne.victoria. australia.tailspintoys.com find the process of authenticating to resources in the Copenhagen.denmark.europe.tailspintoys.com domain to be much too slow. Which of the following steps can you take to speed up authentication between these domains?

   A. Create a forest trust.

   B. Create an external trust.

   C. Create a shortcut trust.

   D. Configure name suffix routing.

3. Your organization is deploying a second Active Directory forest because a substantial number of users need to access a resource that requires significant changes to the Active Directory schema, which are not compatible with your current forest's schema. You want users in your forest to be able to access any resource in any domain in the new forest. Which of the following should you do to accomplish this goal?

   A. Configure a forest trust.

   B. Configure an external trust.

   C. Create a shortcut trust.

   D. Configure name suffix routing.

4. You want to configure a security relationship by which users in the Melbourne domain of the Adatum.com forest are able to access resources in the Sydney domain of the Contoso forest. Users do not require access to resources in any other domains in either forest. Which of the following should you configure to accomplish this goal?

   A. Configure a forest trust.

   B. Configure an external trust.

   C. Create a shortcut trust.

   D. Configure name suffix routing.

Objective 5.3: Configure sites

When properly configured, sites allow Active Directory clients to locate the closest instance of a particular resource. For example, site information is used to ensure that a user signing on to a computer in the Melbourne, Australia branch office isn't authenticated by a domain controller in the London, England head office.

This objective covers how to:

■ Configure sites and subnets, including managing site coverge

■ Create and configure site links

■ Manage registration of SRV records

■ Move domain controllers between sites

Configuring sites and subnets

An Active Directory site represents a location where hosts share a fast local network connection. This might be a building or a collection of buildings in close geographic proximity. A site can be one or more TCP/IP subnets. You use sites to optimize replication between locations connected by WAN links and to ensure that clients at one location preference resources at that location. For example, if your organization had Distributed File System (DFS) shares at each branch office, properly configured sites would ensure that a user would connect to the DFS share in her branch office rather than a DFS share in a remote branch office.

You associate sites with an IP address range. Sites work with both IPv4 and IPv6 addresses. A computer determines which site it is located in by comparing its IP address with the ranges defined for each site. When you install Active Directory, a default site named Default-First-Site-Name is created. You can (and should) rename this site and use a consistent naming scheme for any additional sites that you create. You manage sites using the Active Directory Sites And Services console. Figure 5-5 shows this console where the default first site has been renamed and additional sites have been created using a naming scheme based on three-character capital city/major city airport codes.

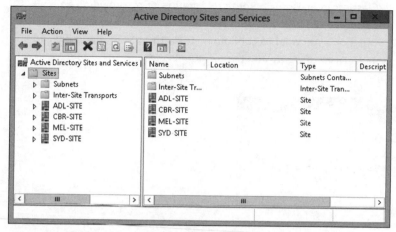

FIGURE 5-5 The Active Directory Sites And Services console

Ensure that you create a separate site for each organizational location. If you don't, it can cause replication problems. Many other products, including Exchange Server 2013 and System Center 2012 R2 Configuration Manager, use Active Directory site information when providing services to client computers. Replication will be covered in more detail later in this chapter.

You can create new sites using the Active Directory Sites And Services console. When you create a new site, you specify a name for the site and choose a site link. When creating a site for the first time, you can select DEFAULTIPSITELINK, as shown in Figure 5-6. Once you've configured site links, you can go back and modify the site link settings.

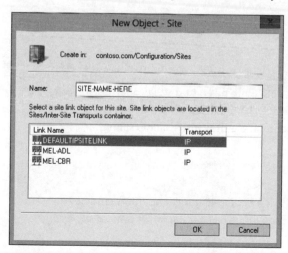

FIGURE 5-6 Creating a new site

After creating the site, you create a subnet and associate it with the site. You do this from the Active Directory Sites And Subnets console as shown in Figure 5-7. You can create the subnet using IPv4 CIDR (Classless Inter-Domain Routing) notation or by providing an IPv6 subnet prefix. Remember that you can have multiple subnets associated with a site, so if there is more than one IPv4 subnet, or if you want to configure sites with both IPv4 and IPv6 addressing information, you just need to create additional subnets and then associate them with the site.

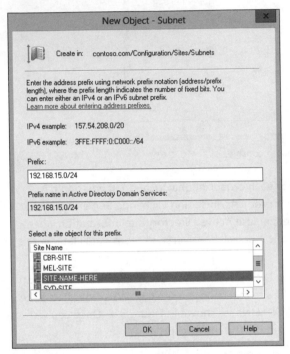

FIGURE 5-7 The New Object – Subnet dialog box

EXAM TIP

You don't change the subnets associated with a site by editing site properties. Instead you edit subnet properties to change site association. Remember that you can associate multiple subnets with a single site, but not multiple sites with a single subnet.

MORE INFO SITES OVERVIEW

Even though the following TechNet article is a bit dated, it includes information pertinent to understanding Active Directory sites: *http://technet.microsoft.com/en-us/library/cc782048%28v=ws.10%29.aspx.*

Creating and configuring site links

You use site links to specify how separate Active Directory sites connect to each other. When you connect sites to the same site link, you are specifying that those sites are able to replicate with each other directly. You create new IP site links using the Active Directory Sites And Services console. When you create a site link, you specify the sites that will use the link. Figure 5-8 shows a site link that represents the connection between the Melbourne (MEL-SITE) site and the Hobart (HBA-SITE) site.

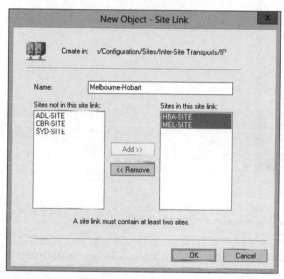

FIGURE 5-8 Creating a site link

You manage the cost and replication schedule for a site link by editing the site link properties after you have created it. The default cost of a site link is 100. Site links that you configure with lower costs will be preferred for replication over site links that have a higher cost. By default, replication occurs every 180 minutes throughout the day. You can modify when replication occurs by configuring the replication schedule. For example, you can configure the replication schedule so that replication occurs only after hours. Figure 5-9 shows the site link cost and replication interval for the MEL-ADL site link.

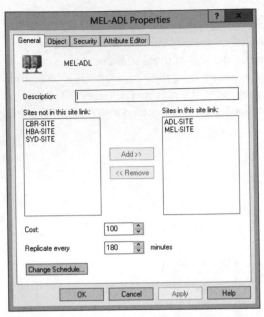

FIGURE 5-9 Site link cost and replication schedule

MORE INFO   SITE LINKS

To learn more about site links, visit *http://technet.microsoft.com/en-us/library/cc960573. aspx*.

Site link bridges allow you to create transitive links between site links. You only need to create site link bridges if you have cleared the Bridge All Site Links check box for the transport protocol in use. Figure 5-10 shows this check box cleared for the IP protocol. You should only create site link bridges if your network is not fully routed.

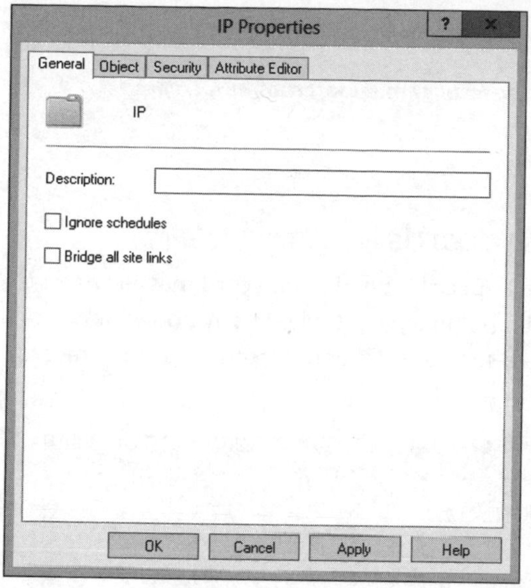

FIGURE 5-10 Configuring protocol properties

When you create a site link bridge, you specify two site links to bridge, as shown in Figure 5-11. Each site link in the bridge must have a site in common with another site in the bridge. For example, when creating a site link using the MEL-ADL and MEL-CBR site links, both site links have the MEL site in common.

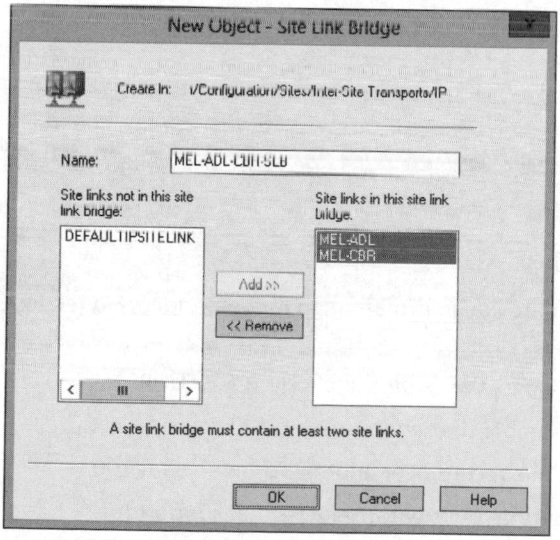

FIGURE 5-11 Creating a site link bridge

MORE INFO   **SITE LINK BRIDGES**

To learn more about site link bridges, visit *http://technet.microsoft.com/en-us/library/cc778718%28v=ws.10%29.aspx.*

Managing registration of SRV records

SRV records, also known as *Locator Records*, are a special type of DNS record that allows clients to locate resources using DNS queries. Each domain controller in a Windows Server 2012 and Windows Server 2012 R2 domain has a separate _kerberos record and _ldap record, as shown in Figure 5-12.

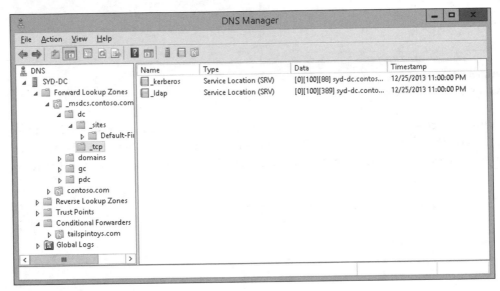

FIGURE 5-12 SRV records

SRV records contain the following information:

- **Service**   Describes the service. Can provide information on Kerberos, ldap, Finger, Ftp, Http, Msdcs, Nntp, Telnet, or Whois services.
- **Protocol**   Specifies the protocol used by the service, typically TCP or UDP.
- **Port Number**   Specifies the port number the service uses.
- **Weight**   Allows you to preference one record over another. The default is 100.
- **Priority**   Allows you to configure service priority for services that support this functionality.

You can configure these settings on the resource record's properties page, as shown in Figure 5-13. Each domain controller's Netlogon service reregisters its SRV records every 60 minutes. You can trigger manual SRV record reregistration by restarting the Netlogon service.

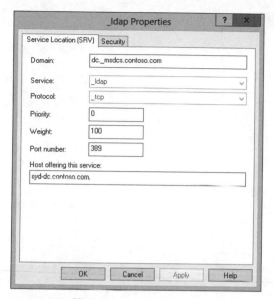

FIGURE 5-13 SRV record properties

EXAM TIP

Remember which service to restart when you want to reregister a domain controller's SRV records.

Moving domain controllers between sites

When you promote a server running the Windows Server 2012 or Windows Server 2012 R2 operating system to be a domain controller, a check occurs to determine which Active Directory site will host the domain controller based on its IP address. If a site corresponding to the computer's IP address hasn't been created, the domain controller will be assigned to the first Active Directory site, which is Default-First-Site-Name unless you've already changed it.

The newly promoted domain controller will remain in the original site even if you create a new site that includes the IP address range of the newly promoted domain controller. In this scenario, you'll need to move the domain controller to the new site using the Active Directory Sites And Services console. You can do this by right-clicking the domain controller in this console and clicking Move. You then select the site that the domain controller will be associated with on the Move Server dialog box, as shown in Figure 5-14.

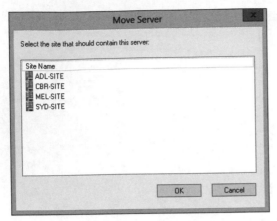

FIGURE 5-14 The Move Server dialog box

Thought experiment
Managing sites and subnets at Contoso

In the following thought experiment, apply what you've learned about this objective to predict what steps you need to take. You can find answers to these questions in the "Answers" section at the end of this chapter.

You are the systems administrator at Contoso. Contoso has four sites: Melbourne, Sydney, Canberra, and Brisbane. Currently there are site links between Melbourne and Canberra, Melbourne and Sydney, Sydney and Brisbane, and Canberra and Brisbane.

You have the following objectives:

- You want to add additional subnets to the Melbourne and Sydney sites.
- Replication traffic between Melbourne and Brisbane should pass through Canberra rather than through Sydney.

With the preceding information in mind, answer the following questions.

1. Describe how to add additional subnets to the Melbourne and Sydney sites.
2. Should the total site link cost between Melbourne and Brisbane through Canberra be greater than or less than the total site link cost between Melbourne and Brisbane through Sydney?

Objective summary

- You configure subnets in the Active Directory Sites And Subnets console to associate IP address range with network locations.
- Sites allow you to connect one or more subnets together to represent hosts that are connected to the same a high-bandwidth network.
- Site links allow you to connect sites.
- Site link bridges allow you to connect site links, but are necessary only when used in environments that are not fully routed.
- SRV records allow clients to locate services using DNS.

Objective review

Answer the following questions to test your knowledge of the information in this objective. You can find the answers to these questions and explanations of why each answer choice is correct or incorrect in the "Answers" section at the end of the chapter.

1. At present, the subnet 192.168.15.0/24 is associated with the Brisbane site. You want to instead associate this subnet with the Melbourne site. Which of the following steps can you take to resolve this problem?

   A. Use the Active Directory Sites And Services console to edit the properties of the 192.168.15.0/24 subnet.

   B. Use the Active Directory Sites And Services console to edit the properties of the Melbourne site.

   C. Use the Active Directory Sites And Services console to edit the properties of the Brisbane site.

   D. Use the Active Directory Domains And Trusts console to edit the properties of the 192.168.15.0/24 subnet.

2. You are configuring secondary links for the connections between the Melbourne and Sydney sites and between the Melbourne and Adelaide sites. The existing Melbourne to Sydney site link is called MEL-SYD-ALPHA and has a site link cost of 100. The existing Melbourne to Adelaide site link is called MEL-ADL-ALPHA and has a site link cost of 100. You want the secondary site links to be used only when the existing site links are unavailable. The new site links are named MEL-SYD-BETA and MEL-ADL-BETA. Which of the following steps should you take to accomplish this goal?

   A. Configure the site link cost for the MEL-SYD-BETA with a value of 110.

   B. Configure the site link cost for the MEL-ADL-BETA with a value of 110.

   C. Configure the site link cost for the MEL-ADL-BETA with a value of 90.

   D. Configure the site link cost for the MEL-SYD-BETA with a value of 90.

3. You have moved several domain controllers out of your organization's head office site to a new secondary datacenter that has its own site. Which of the following consoles should be used to update the site association of these domain controllers?

   A. Active Directory Administrative Center

   B. Active Directory Users and Computers

   C. Active Directory Sites And Services

   D. Active Directory Domains And Trusts

4. Which of the following services would you restart on a domain controller if you wanted to trigger a reregistration of the domain controller's _ldap and _kerberos SRV records?

   A. DNS Server

   B. Server

   C. Workstation

   D. Netlogon

Objective 5.4: Manage Active Directory and SYSVOL replication

Read Only Domain Controllers (RODCs) provide administrators with an option for deploying domain controllers in environments that might not be as secure as a datacenter guarded 24 hours a day, 7 days a week and which requires multiple forms of identification and authentication to access.

You should also periodically check domain controller replication to ensure that each domain controller is communicating reliably with other domain controllers in your environment. Understanding how to deploy and manage RODCs as well as monitor Active Directory replication are topics tested on the 70-412 exam.

> **This objective covers how to:**
>
> - Configure replication to Read-Only Domain Controllers (RODCs)
> - Configure Password Replication Policy (PRP) for RODCs
> - Monitor and manage replication
> - Upgrade SYSVOL replication to Distributed File System Replication (DFSR)

Configuring replication to Read-Only Domain Controllers (RODCs)

RODCs are a special type of domain controller that store only a specific number of user passwords rather than the passwords for all users in the domain. This provides you with the special ability, should the RODC be somehow compromised, of needing to reset only a small number of user account passwords rather than all of the user account passwords in the domain. Because they are designed for environments that are less secure than those where you typically would deploy a domain controller, RODCs only host a read-only copy of the Active Directory database. This means that RODCs cannot directly process updates to the Active Directory database and must instead pass updates on to a "writable" domain controller. You are likely to deploy RODCs in locations that are less secure but which still require a local domain controller to process activities such as user sign-ons.

In the majority of cases, RODCs pull updates to the Active Directory database from writable domain controllers. In the following scenarios, RODCs perform inbound replication using a replicate-single-object (RSO) operation:

- The password of a user who has his account password stored on the RODC is changed.
- A DNS client performs a DNS record update, in which case the client is redirected by the RODC to a domain controller that hosts a writable copy of the target Active Directory Integrated DNS zone.
- The client name, DnsHostName, OsName, OSVersionInfo, supported encryption types, and LastLogonTimeStamp attributes are updated.

These replication scenarios are treated differently because they involve objects that are critical to security. If a user had to wait until the next designated cycle for the password update she organized through the service desk to replicate to her branch office's RODC, she'd be unable to sign on to her computer with that new password.

One of the key aspects to managing an RODC is controlling which user accounts have their passwords replicated to the server. User accounts that are added to the Allowed RODC Password Replication security group have their passwords replicated to the RODC as long as they aren't members of a group that has been configured with the Deny setting in the RODC's Password Replication Policy (PRP). By default, user accounts that are members of the following groups will not have account passwords replicated to any RODC:

- Account operators
- Administrators
- Backup operators
- Denied RODC password replication group
- Server operators

If an account password does not replicate to an RODC, it means that the person associated with that user account cannot use the RODC to authenticate. In these cases, the RODC passes the task of authenticating the user to a writable domain controller. You configure RODC password replication so that the RODC stores only the passwords of users at the site where it is deployed. For example, you configure an RODC so that it stores only the passwords of users who work at the Melbourne site.

Users with sensitive accounts must authenticate against a writable domain controller, which you would deploy in a secure location. Because you deploy RODCs to locations where the security of the domain controller is not assured, you will naturally avoid deploying writable domain controllers in the same location. In the event that the WAN link fails, the majority of users at the site will still be able to sign on to their computers because they will authenticate using the RODC. Only users with sensitive accounts are unable to authenticate when the WAN link to a site that has RODCs fails. This is generally unproblematic because most of the time users with sensitive accounts will be located at central sites with properly secured writable domain controllers and won't be at this type of branch office site anyway.

You configure password replication policy for an RODC on the Password Replication Policy tab of the computer account's properties dialog box, as shown in Figure 5-15. Each RODC has its own password replication policy, which allows you to configure site-specific replication. For example, if you have an RODC in the Melbourne site and an RODC in the Sydney site, you'd configure separate password replication policies because the users who are based in the Melbourne site are going to be different from the users based in the Sydney site. The easiest way to do this is to create a security group for each site, populate it with the accounts of the users located at that site, and then add that security group to the Password Replication Policy of the RODC located at that site.

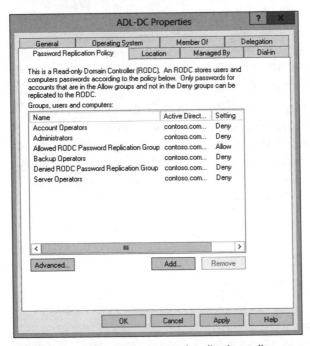

FIGURE 5-15 Configuring a password replication policy

Remember which groups are blocked from having their passwords replicated to an RODC by default.

You can check which user account passwords have replicated to a specific RODC by clicking the Advanced button on the Password Replication Policy tab. This action opens the Advanced Password Replication Policy dialog box. You can also use the Prepopulate Passwords button to replicate the passwords of accounts out to the RODC. The Advanced Password Replication Policy dialog box is shown in Figure 5-16. The Resultant Policy tab of this dialog box allows you to determine if a specific user's password can be replicated to the RODC. You can use this to verify that sensitive user account passwords are not replicated to the RODC.

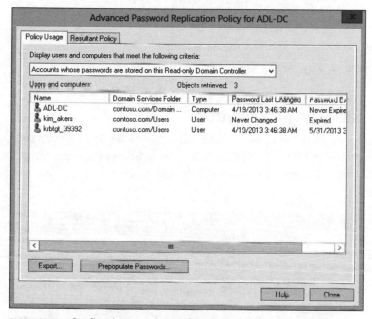

FIGURE 5-16 Configuring an advanced password replication policy

In the event that an RODC is compromised, such as the RODC being stolen or infected with malware that gives you reason to believe that the account database may have been compromised, you can automatically have Active Directory reset the passwords of all accounts that had replicated to the RODC by deleting the RODC computer account. When you take this step, you are prompted by the Deleting Domain Controller dialog box (shown in Figure 5-17), which presents you with the option of resetting all user account passwords and all computer account passwords. You can also export a list of reset accounts so that you can contact the users to explain why their passwords have been reset.

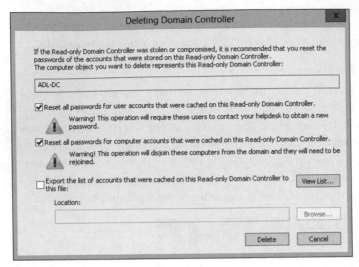

FIGURE 5-17 Deleting a domain controller

Monitoring and managing replication

You can trigger Active Directory replication using the Active Directory Sites And Services console by right-clicking the domain controller's connection object and clicking Replicate Now, as shown in Figure 5-18. Clicking Replicate Now causes the domain controller to replicate with each of its replication partners.

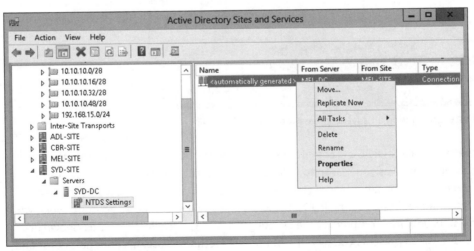

FIGURE 5-18 Triggering replication

You can manage and monitor replication using the repadmin command-line tool. For example, you can use repadmin with the replsummary option to view a summary of a domain controller's replication with its replication partners, as shown in Figure 5-19. This allows you to determine when replication has failed and the largest period between replication events.

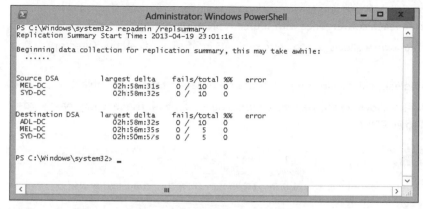

FIGURE 5-19 Output of repadmin /replsummary

When you use repadmin with the /showrepl option on a domain controller, you can view information about inbound replication traffic. This information will include the objects that were replicated and the date stamps associated with that traffic. Figure 5-20 shows the output of this command when run on a domain controller.

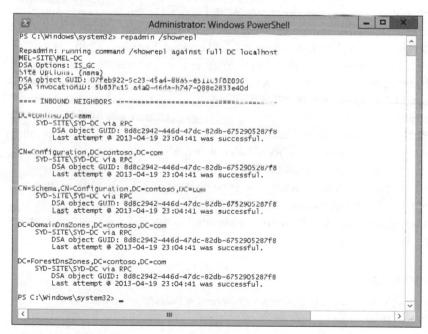

FIGURE 5-20 Output of the repadmin /showrepl command

Using repadmin with the /kcc switch allows you to force the Knowledge Consistency Checker (KCC) to recalculate the inbound replication topology of a domain controller should a situation arise where you didn't want to wait for this to happen normally. Repadmin includes the following additional functionality:

- The /queue switch allows you to view inbound replication requests that must be performed to reach convergence with source replication partners.
- The /replicate switch allows you to force replication of a specific Active Directory partition.
- The /replsingleobj switch allows you to trigger replication for a single object.
- The /prp switch allows you to view which users have had their user account passwords replicated to an RODC.

> **MORE INFO** **REPADMIN.EXE**
>
> To learn more about repadmin.exe, visit *http://technet.microsoft.com/en-us/library/ cc770963%28v=ws.10%29.aspx*.

Upgrading SYSVOL replication to Distributed File System Replication (DFSR)

SYSVOL is a special folder on each domain controller that hosts logon scripts, group policy templates, and other items related to Active Directory. It is located in the %SystemRoot%\ SYSVOL folder on each domain controller and replicates to all domain controllers in the domain. Windows Server 2003 and Windows Server 2003 R2 domain controllers used File Replication Services (FRS) to replicate the SYSVOL folder to other domain controllers. Windows Server 2008 and later operating systems support the use of Distributed File System (DFS) to perform replication of the SYSVOL folder. DFS is substantially more efficient than FRS, however many organizations that upgraded from Windows Server 2003 domain controllers did not upgrade SYSVOL replication from FRS to DFS as this process does not occur automatically. You can upgrade SYSVOL replication from FRS to DFS only if the domain functional level is set to Windows Server 2008 or higher. You use the Dfsrmig.exe utility to perform this upgrade. If your organization deployed Active Directory starting with Windows Server 2008 or later domain controllers, SYSVOL will already use DFS. You can check if FRS is still in use by running Dfsrmig.exe with the /getglobalstate option from an elevated Windows PowerShell prompt on a domain controller.

> **MORE INFO** **DFSRMIG**
>
> To learn more about the Dfsrmig utility, visit *http://technet.microsoft.com/en-au/library/ dd641227%28v=ws.10%29.aspx*.

Thought experiment

Managing RODCs at Tailspin Toys

In the following thought experiment, apply what you've learned about this objective to predict what steps you need to take. You can find answers to these questions in the "Answers" section at the end of this chapter.

You are the systems administrator at Tailspin Toys. After a domain controller at a branch location was compromised by malware recently, you reset all passwords in the domain as a security precaution. As a way of minimizing the impact that such events will have, you are replacing writable domain controllers at each branch office with RODCs

You have the following objectives:

- You want to ensure that each branch office RODC only stores the passwords of users who work in that branch office.

- You want to be able to check which user accounts have passwords stored on specific RODCs.

- You want to develop a procedure to follow in the event that an RODC is compromised.

With the preceding information in mind, answer the following questions.

1. How can you ensure that each branch office RODC only stores passwords of users that work in that branch office?

2. What steps can you take to keep track of the user accounts that have passwords stored on the RODC?

3. What steps should you take in the event that an RODC is compromised?

Objective summary

- RODCs host read-only copies of the Active Directory database.
- Password Replication Policy is unique to each RODC and allows you to specify which user account passwords replicate and are stored on the RODC.
- When you remove an RODC from the domain, you get the option of automatically resetting both computer account passwords and user account passwords stored on the RODC.
- You can use repadmin to manage Active Directory replication.
- The Dfsrmig.exe utility allows you to upgrade a domain that uses FRS for SYSVOL replication so that is uses DFSR.

Objective review

Answer the following questions to test your knowledge of the information in this objective. You can find the answers to these questions and explanations of why each answer choice is correct or incorrect in the "Answers" section at the end of the chapter.

1. Which of the following security groups cannot have their passwords replicated to an RODC by default? (Choose all that apply.)

    A. Backup Operators

    B. Server Operators

    C. Account Operators

    D. Event Log Readers

2. Which of the following utilities can be used to monitor the most recent stage of Active Directory replication?

    A. Dcdiag.exe

    B. Netdiag.exe

    C. Repadmin.exe

    D. Dfsrmig.exe

3. In which of the following scenarios might you need to upgrade SYSVOL replication from FRS to DFSR? (Choose all that apply.)

    A. The first domain controllers installed in the domain were running Windows 2000 Server.

    B. The first domain controllers installed in the domain were running Windows Server 2003.

    C. The first domain controllers installed in the domain were running Windows Server 2008.

    D. The first domain controllers installed in the domain were running Windows Server 2008 R2.

Answers

This section contains the solutions to the "Thought experiments" and the "Objective review" questions in this chapter.

Objective 5.1: Thought experiment

1. You must upgrade the adelaide.adatum.local and brisbane.adatum.local domains to the Windows Server 2003 functional level before you can install a domain controller running Windows Server 2012 R2.

2. You should first introduce a domain controller running the Windows Server 2012 R2 operating system in the Adatum.local domain so that the Schema Master is updated to support Windows Server 2012 R2 domain controllers.

3. You must configure @adatum.com as an alternate UPN suffix.

Objective 5.1: Review

1. **Correct Answer:** A

   A. **Correct:** The Windows Server 2003 functional level supports domain controllers hosted on computers running the Windows Server 2012 R2 operating system.

   B. **Incorrect:** The Windows Server 2003 functional level supports domain controllers hosted on computers running the Windows Server 2012 R2 operating system.

   C. **Incorrect:** The Windows Server 2003 functional level supports domain controllers hosted on computers running the Windows Server 2012 R2 operating system.

   D. **Incorrect:** The Windows Server 2003 functional level supports domain controllers hosted on computers running the Windows Server 2012 R2 operating system.

2. **Correct Answer:** A

   A. **Correct:** The maximum length in characters, including periods, of a domain name is 64 characters.

   B. **Incorrect:** The maximum length in characters, including periods, of a domain name is 64 characters.

   C. **Incorrect:** The maximum length in characters, including periods, of a domain name is 64 characters.

   D. **Incorrect:** The maximum length in characters, including periods, of a domain name is 64 characters.

3. **Correct Answers:** A, B

   A. **Correct:** An account used to promote a server running Windows Server 2012 to function as a Domain Controller must be a member of the Schema Admins and Enterprise Admins groups so that the existing Active Directory schema can be updated.

   B. **Correct:** An account used to promote a server running Windows Server 2012 to function as a Domain Controller must be a member of the Schema Admins and Enterprise Admins groups so that the existing Active Directory schema can be updated.

   C. **Incorrect:** An account used to promote a server running Windows Server 2012 to function as a Domain Controller must be a member of the Schema Admins and Enterprise Admins groups so that the existing Active Directory schema can be updated. Membership of the Account Operators group is not necessary.

   D. **Incorrect:** An account used to promote a server running Windows Server 2012 to function as a Domain Controller must be a member of the Schema Admins and Enterprise Admins groups so that the existing Active Directory schema can be updated. Membership of the Server Operators group is not necessary.

4. **Correct Answer:** B

   A. **Incorrect:** The default UPN suffix for a forest is the forest root domain. Because the forest root domain is Adatum.local, this will be the default UPN suffix.

   B. **Correct:** The default UPN suffix for a forest is the forest root domain. Because the forest root domain is Adatum.local, this will be the default UPN suffix.

   C. **Incorrect:** The default UPN suffix for a forest is the forest root domain. Because the forest root domain is Adatum.local, this will be the default UPN suffix.

   D. **Incorrect:** The default UPN suffix for a forest is the forest root domain. Because the forest root domain is Adatum.local, this will be the default UPN suffix.

Objective 5.2: Thought experiment

1. You should configure a one-way forest trust because resource access is required only in one direction.

2. You should configure a one-way external trust.

3. The sales.margiestravel.com domain should be the trusting domain because accounts from the management.tailspintoys.com domain will be accessing resources in this domain.

Objective 5.2: Review

1. **Correct Answer:** B

    A. **Incorrect:** SID filtering blocks SIDs from foreign domains being associated with accounts from trusted domains or forests.

    B. **Correct:** You can use name suffix routing to manage which UPNs can be used for authentication.

    C. **Incorrect:** You use shortcut trusts to speed authentication in forests that have large numbers of domains.

    D. **Incorrect:** You use external trusts to create non-transitive trust relationships.

2. **Correct Answer:** C

    A. **Incorrect:** The question does not indicate there is a second Active Directory forest.

    B. **Incorrect:** The question does not indicate there is domain in another forest.

    C. **Correct:** Shortcut trusts allow you to speed authentication between domains in the same forest.

    D. **Incorrect:** You use name suffix routing to manage which UPNs can be used for authentication.

3. **Correct Answer:** A

    A. **Correct:** In this scenario, in which you need to provide access to all domains in another forest, configuring a forest trust would best accomplish your goal.

    B. **Incorrect:** You would configure an external trust if users in one domain needed to access resources in a single domain in another forest.

    C. **Incorrect:** You use a shortcut trust to speed up authentication between domains in the same forest.

    D. **Incorrect:** You use name suffix routing to determine which UPN suffixes can be used for authentication in forest trust scenarios.

4. **Correct Answer:** B

    A. **Incorrect:** You configure a forest trust when you want to allow access to multiple domains in another forest.

    B. **Correct:** You would configure an external trust when users in one domain need to access resources in a single domain in another forest.

    C. **Incorrect:** You use a shortcut trust to speed up authentication between domains in the same forest.

    D. **Incorrect:** You use name suffix routing to determine which UPN suffixes can be used for authentication in forest trust scenarios.

Objective 5.3: Thought experiment

1. To add additional subnets to the Melbourne and Sydney sites, you would use the Active Directory Sites and Services console to create each new subnet. When creating each subnet, associate them with the appropriate site.

2. It should be less than; you want replication traffic between these sites to run through Canberra rather than Sydney.

Objective 5.3: Review

1. **Correct Answer:** A

   A. **Correct:** You edit the properties of a subnet to change its site association.

   B. **Incorrect:** You cannot change the subnets associated with a site by editing the site properties.

   C. **Incorrect:** You cannot change the subnets associated with a site by editing the site properties.

   D. **Incorrect:** You cannot use the Active Directory Domains And Trusts console to edit the properties of an Active Directory subnet.

2. **Correct Answers:** A, B

   A. **Correct:** You should set a higher site link cost to ensure that the secondary site link is used only when the primary site link is not available.

   B. **Correct:** You should set a higher site link cost to ensure that the secondary site link is used only when the primary site link is not available.

   C. **Incorrect:** You should set a higher site link cost to ensure that the secondary site link is used only when the primary site link is not available.

   D. **Incorrect:** You should set a higher site link cost to ensure that the secondary site link is used only when the primary site link is not available.

3. **Correct Answer:** C

   A. **Incorrect:** You cannot use the Active Directory Administrative Center to update domain controller site association.

   B. **Incorrect:** You cannot use the Active Directory Users And Computers to update domain controller site association.

   C. **Correct:** You use the Active Directory Sites And Services console to change domain controller site association.

   D. **Incorrect:** You cannot use the Active Directory Domains And Trusts console to manage domain controller site association.

4. **Correct Answer:** D

   A. **Incorrect:** Restarting the DNS Server service will not trigger a reregistration of the domain controller's _ldap and _kerberos SRV records.

   B. **Incorrect:** Restarting the Server service will not trigger a reregistration of the domain controller's _ldap and _kerberos SRV records.

   C. **Incorrect:** Restarting the Workstation service will not trigger a reregistration of the domain controller's _ldap and _kerberos SRV records.

   D. **Correct:** Restarting the Netlogon service will trigger a reregistration of the domain controller's _ldap and _kerberos SRV records.

Objective 5.4: Thought experiment

1. Create a special seurity group that contains the user accounts of users at each branch office. Configure each RODC's Password Replication Policy to only replicate the passwords of members of the associated branch office security group.

2. You can view the user accounts that have had passwords replicated to the RODC by viewing the RODC's computer account properties in Active Directory. You can also view the accounts replicated to the RODC using the repadmin utility.

3. You should delete the RODC's computer account. When you do this, you'll be prompted to reset all of the user and computer accounts stored on the RODC.

Objective 5.4: Review

1. **Correct Answers:** A, B, C

   A. **Correct:** Members of the Backup Operators group cannot have their passwords replicated to an RODC by default.

   B. **Correct:** Members of the Server Operators group cannot have their passwords replicated to an RODC by default.

   C. **Correct:** Members of the Account Operators group cannot have their passwords replicated to an RODC by default.

   D. **Incorrect:** Members of the Event Log Readers group can have their passwords replicated to an RODC by default.

2. **Correct Answer:** C

   A. **Incorrect:** Dcdiag.exe allows you to check domain controller functionality, but it does not allow you to monitor Active Directory replication.

   B. **Incorrect:** Netdiag.exe is a network diagnostics tool available in previous versions of the Windows Server operating system. It is not included in Windows Server 2012 or Windows Server 2012 R2 and cannot be used to monitor Active Directory replication.

   C. **Correct:** You can use the repadmin.exe utility to monitor Active Directory replication.

   D. **Incorrect:** You use Dfsrmig.exe to upgrade SYSVOL replication from FRS to DFSR.

3. **Correct Answers:** A, B

   A. **Correct:** Domains where the domain controllers were initially running Windows 2000 server may still use FRS for SYSVOL replication.

   B. **Correct:** Domains where the domain controllers were initially running Windows Server 2003 may still use FRS for SYSVOL replication.

   C. **Incorrect:** Domains where the first domain controllers were running Windows Server 2008 or later operating systems use DFSR for replication.

   D. **Incorrect:** Domains where the first domain controllers were running Windows Server 2008 or later operating systems use DFSR for replication.

CHAPTER 6

Configure access and information protection solutions

The Configure Access and Information Protection Solutions domain relates to configuring and managing Active Directory Federation Services (AD FS), Active Directory Certificate Services (AD CS), and Active Directory Rights Management Services (AD RMS). Understanding the topics covered in this domain requires a deep understanding of new technologies that you might not have implemented in your own environment. You should supplement the information in this chapter with some hands-on practice so that you can develop an understanding of how you can use these technologies to address real-world scenarios and solve problems in an advanced server environment.

Objectives in this chapter:

- Objective 6.1: Implement Active Directory Federation Services (AD FS)
- Objective 6.2: Install and configure Active Directory Certificate Services (AD CS)
- Objective 6.3: Manage certificates
- Objective 6.4: Install and configure Active Directory Rights Management Services (AD RMS)

Objective 6.1: Implement Active Directory Federation Services (AD FS)

Active Directory Federation Services (AD FS) allows you to configure federated relationships between your organization and a partner organization. Federated relationships are most often used when a traditional Active Directory trust relationship is not appropriate. They are also increasingly used when configuring single sign-on between an on-premises Active Directory deployment and a Windows Azure Active Directory instance, allowing a single account to be used with Exchange Online, SharePoint Online, and Windows Intune. AD FS is also required if you want to implement the new Workplace Join feature of Windows Server 2012 R2.

This objective covers how to:

- Install AD FS
- Implement claims-based authentication including relying-party trusts
- Configure authentication policies
- Configure Workplace Join
- Configure multi-factor authentication

Installing AD FS

AD FS is a role that you can install on computers running Windows Server 2012 R2. An AD FS federation servermanages requests involving identity claims. When deploying AD FS, you need to deploy at least one federation server in a forest. You can only deploy the Federation Server role on a computer that is domain-joined.

The Web Application Proxy role is a role service available as part of the Remote Access role. You deploy a server hosting the Web Application Proxy on a perimeter network. This server then relays connections from hosts on the unprotected network to the Federation Server on a protected network. In Windows Server 2012 and earlier, this function was performed by a role known as the Federation Server Proxy. In addition to the functionality provided by the Federation Server Proxy, the Web Application Proxy also provides reverse proxy functionality for web applications on the protected network.

Before deploying AD FS, ensure the following:

- Client computers must be able to communicate with the Federation Server or web application proxy using HTTPS.
- The Federation Server and Web Application Proxy must be able to communicate with one another using HTTPS.

> **MORE INFO   AD FS DEPLOYMENT**
>
> To learn more about AD FS deployment, visit *http://technet.microsoft.com/en-us/library/ dn486820.aspx*.

Implementing claims-based authentication

Claims-based authentication functions based on claims made about a user. For example, "allow access to this particular web application if this user is described as a contractor by the partner organization." AD FS builds tokens that contain claim data by using the following:

- **Claim**   The description of an object based on the object's attributes.

- **Claim rules**   Specifies how a federation server will interpret a claim. For example, treating a user's email address as a valid claim, treating security group membership as a valid claim, or treating an employment status attribute as a valid claim.
- **Attribute store**   This hosts the values used by claims. In most scenarios, Active Directory functions as the attribute store.

Configuring relying party trusts

A *relying-party server* is a server in an Active Directory forest that hosts the resources that a user in a partner organization wants to access. Relying-party servers accept and validate claims that are stored in the token issued by the federation server functioning as a claims provider. The claims provider is a federation server located in the forest that hosts the user account of the user that wants access.

You configure a relying-party trust on the federation server that functions as the claims provider. Figure 6-1 shows the configuring of a relying-party trust on a claims-provider server where the relying-party server is named adl-dc.wingtiptoys.internal.

EXAM TIP

A relying-party trust means that a specific claims-provider trusts a specific relying party.

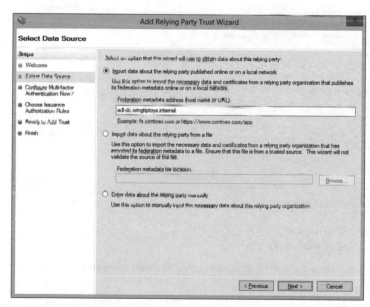

FIGURE 6-1 The Add Relying Party Trust Wizard

MORE INFO   CREATING RELYING-PARTY TRUSTS

To learn more about creating relying-party trusts, visit *http://technet.microsoft.com/en-us/library/dn486828.aspx*

Configuring claims-provider trusts

Claims providers are federation servers that issue claims to users in the form of digitally encrypted and signed tokens. If a user needs a token, the claims-provider federation server interacts with Active Directory in the user's forest to verify that the user has authenticated and then builds the claim based on attributes in the attribute store (usually Active Directory). The attributes that are included in the claim will be dependent on the attributes required by the partner organization.

EXAM TIP

A claims-provider trust means that a relying-party trusts a specific claims provider.

Claims-provider trusts are configured on the federation server that functions as the relying party. Figure 6-2 shows the creation of a claims-provider trust on a relying-party server where the address of the claims provider that will be trusted is cbr-dc.contoso.com.

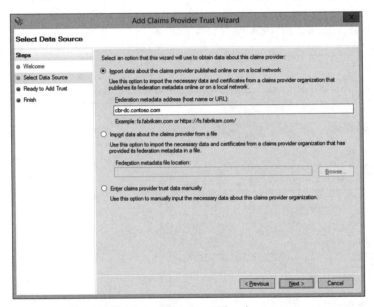

FIGURE 6-2 The Add Claims Provider Trust Wizard

MORE INFO **CREATING CLAIMS-PROVIDER TRUSTS**

To learn more about creating claims-provider trusts, visit *http://technet.microsoft.com/en-us/library/dn486771.aspx*.

Configuring authentication policies

Authentication policies allow you to control how AD FS performs authentication. You can configure the global authentication policy, as shown in Figure 6-3, or configure authentication on a relying-party trust. You configure authentication on a relying-party trust when you want to configure different authentication settings for a specific application or for a specific partner organization.

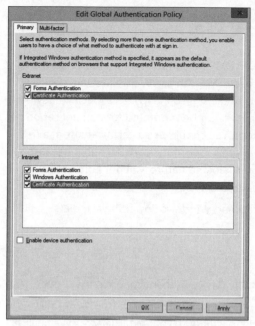

FIGURE 6-3   Configuring the global authentication policy

The authentication methods supported by AD FS are as follows:

- **Forms Authentication**   Credentials are entered on a webpage. This type of authentication is available for Intranet and Extranet clients.

- **Windows Authentication**   Credentials are passed directly to AD FS when using Internet Explorer or users must provide their credentials in a pop-up dialog box. This type of authentication is available only to Intranet clients.

- **Certificate Authentication**   This form of authentication requires the user to already be provisioned with a certificate, either by installing it on the device or by providing it on a smart card. This type of authentication is available for Intranet and Extranet clients.

When you select multiple authentication methods, any of the possible authentication methods can be used.

> **MORE INFO**   **CONFIGURING AUTHENTICATION POLICIES**
>
> To learn more about authentication, visit *http://technet.microsoft.com/en-us/library/dn486781.aspx*.

Configuring Workplace Join

Workplace Join is a feature available only with Windows Server 2012 R2 that you can use to allow non-domain joined computers or devices to access organizational resources in a secure manner. When a non-domain joined computer or device performs Workplace Join registration, a special object representing the computer or device is created in AD DS. This special object has attributes that describe the device, which you can use to mediate access to organizational resources.

Workplace Join is supported for devices running iOS and computers running Windows 8.1. Only applications that are claims-aware and use AD FS can use Workplace Join device registration information. Workplace Join supports single sign-on (SSO). This means that when a user authenticates to access one application, she will not be prompted for authentication credentials when accessing subsequent applications. You should use a certificate from a trusted third-party certification authority with AD FS when supporting Workplace Join because the devices that are connecting, by their non-domain joined nature, will not automatically trust certificates issued by an internal certificate authority.

You enable Workplace Join by running the following Windows PowerShell cmdlets:

```
Initialize-ADFSDeviceRegistration
```

```
Enable-ADFSDeviceRegistration
```

Once you have run these cmdlets, you can enable device authentication in the Global Authentication Policy, as shown in Figure 6-4.

Users authenticate using their UPNs. You'll need to configure your externally resolvable DNS zone with a record that maps enterpriseregistration.upndomainname.com (where upndomainname.com is the UPN suffix) and map this to the IP address of either the AD FS server or the Web Application Proxy server that you've configured to support Workplace Join. You'll also need to ensure that the web server certificate installed on this server includes the name enterpriseregistration.upndomainname.com (where upndomainname.com is the UPN suffix).

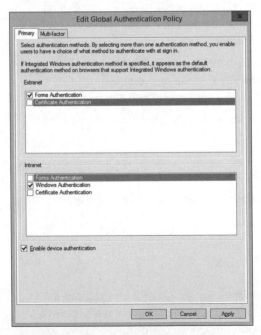

FIGURE 6-4 Enabling device authentication

MORE INFO   **WORKPLACE JOIN WALKTHRU**

To learn more about configuring Workplace Join, visit *http://technet.microsoft.com/en-us/library/dn280938.aspx*.

Configuring multi-factor authentication

Multi-factor authentication allows you to require two separate methods of authentication, such as a username and password as well as a certificate or authenticator application running on a mobile device. You configure multi-factor authentication either globally, as shown in Figure 6-5, or on a per-relying-party trust basis.

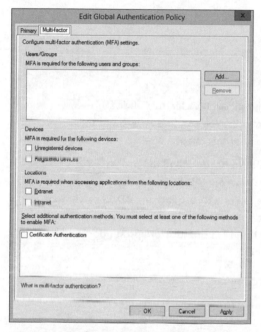

FIGURE 6-5 Configuring multi-factor authentication

One method of providing multi-factor authentication is to use Microsoft's Windows Azure Multi-Factor Authentication service. You can integrate this service with AD FS to support the following types of multi-factor authentication:

- **Phone Call**   An automated phone call is made to the user. The user provides this data when authenticating.
- **Text Message**   The user is sent a text message to a registered mobile phone. The user inputs the information contained in the text message when prompted.
- **Mobile App**   The user installs a mobile authentication app that generates a periodically changing series of numbers and is configured using a QR (Quick Response) code

associated with their account. The user inputs the current string of numbers when authenticating.

MORE INFO **MULTI-FACTOR ACCESS CONTROL**

To learn more about multi-factor access control, visit *http://technet.microsoft.com/en-us/ library/dn280937.aspx*

MORE INFO **WINDOWS AZURE MULTI-FACTOR AUTHENTICATION**

To learn more about Windows Azure multi-factor authentication, visit *http://technet.micro-soft.com/en-us/library/dn249471.aspx*

Thought experiment
Deploying AD FS at Tailspin Toys

In the following thought experiment, apply what you've learned about this objective to predict what steps you need to take. You can find answers to these questions in the "Answers" section at the end of this chapter.

You are the systems administrator at Tailspin Toys. You are in the process of deploying AD FS and have two forests. You have one AD FS server that will function as the claims-provider federation server in the first forest and one AD FS server that will function as the relying-party federation server. You also want to require two-factor authentication, including phone, SMS, and authenticator app support when users are accessing a claims-aware application.

You have the following objectives:

- Configure a relying-party trust
- Configure a claims-provider trust
- Configure multi-factor authentication

With the preceding information in mind, answer the following questions.

1. On which server should you configure the relying-party trust?
2. On which server should you configure the claims-provider trust?
3. Which Microsoft service can you use to support two-factor authentication using SMS messages or an authenticator app?

Objective summary

- A federation server must be installed on a domain member

- Web application proxy server relays AD FS traffic to a federation server and should be deployed on a perimeter network. This role was performed by the federation proxy server in the Windows Server 2012 implementation of AD FS.

- Relying-party servers are located in the forest that has the resources that will be accessed.

- Claims-provider servers are located in the forest that hosts the user accounts that need to access those resources.

- You configure relying-party trusts on the claims-provider server.

- You configure claims-provider trusts on the relying-party server.

- Workplace Join allows non-domain joined clients to access resources and claims-aware applications on protected networks.

- Multi-factor access control allows you to require two forms of authentication when users authenticate against AD FS.

Objective review

Answer the following questions to test your knowledge of the information in this objective. You can find the answers to these questions and explanations of why each answer choice is correct or incorrect in the "Answers" section at the end of the chapter.

1. You are configuring AD FS. Which server should you deploy on your organization's perimeter network?

   A. Web appplication proxy

   B. Relying-party server

   C. Federation server

   D. Claims-provider server

2. The Wingtip Toys forest hosts a web application that users in the Tailspin Toys forest need to access. You are the system administrator at Tailspin Toys. A single federation server is present in each forest and you are configuring a federated trust. Which of the following statements are true about the deployment solution? (Choose all that apply.)

   A. The AD FS server in the Wingtip Toys forest will function as the claims-provider server.

   B. The AD FS server in the Wingtip Toys forest will function as the relying-party server.

   C. You need to configure a relying-party trust on the AD FS server in the Tailspin Toys forest.

   D. You need to configure a claims-provider trust on the AD FS server in the Tailspin Toys forest.

3. The Wingtip Toys forest hosts a web application that users in the Tailspin Toys forest need to access. You are the system administrator at Wingtip Toys. A single federation server is present in each forest and you are configuring a federated trust. Which of the following statements are true about the deployment solution? (Choose all that apply.)

   A. The AD FS server in the Tailspin Toys forest will function as the claims-provider server.

   B. The AD FS server in the Tailspin Toys forest will function as the relying-party server.

   C. Configure a relying-party trust on the Wingtip Toys AD FS server.

   D. Configure a claims-provider trust on the Wingtip Toys AD FS server.

4. Which of the following authentication types must you enable to support Workplace Join?

   A. Forms

   B. Windows

   C. Certificate

   D. Device

Objective 6.2: Install and configure Active Directory Certificate Services (AD CS)

Active Directory Certificate Services (AD CS) is as much a part of a modern network infrastructure as DNS and DHCP. For the 70-412 exam, you need to understand the critical components of an AD CS deployment and how they fit together so that certificates can be used seamlessly in your organization's environment. This means understanding the different certificate authority types, how to put in place an effective revocation infrastructure, and how to ensure that AD CS is administered in a secure manner.

> **This objective covers how to:**
> - Install an Enterprise Certificate Authority (CA)
> - Configure CRL Distribution Points (CDP)
> - Install and configure online responders
> - Implement administrative role separation
> - Configure CA backup and recovery

Installing an Enterprise Certificate Authority (CA)

The Active Directory Certificate Services (AD CS) role allows a computer running Windows Server 2012 or Windows Server 2012 R2 to function as a Certificate Authority (CA). When you install the AD CS role, you can choose between deploying an enterprise root, enterprise subordinate, standalone root, or standalone subordinate CA. Figure 6-6 shows the installation of an enterprise root CA.

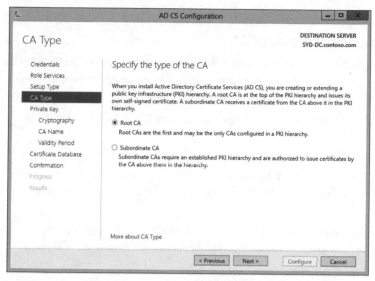

FIGURE 6-6 Specifying the CA type

Deploying an enterprise root CA

Root CAs are certificate servers that sign their own certificate. An *enterprise root CA* is a root certificate server that is a member of an Active Directory Domain Services (AD DS) domain that can issue certificates based on templates that you can configure. These templates are stored within Active Directory. All computer that are members of the same Active Directory forest will automatically trust certificates issued by an enterprise CA and can use Active Directory to perform certificate revocation checks. Enterprise CAs allow you to configure certificate auto-enrollment, which reduces the administrative overhead of managing certificates.

When considering whether to deploy an enterprise root CA, take into account the following:

- Because of the Active Directory dependencies, enterprise root CAs must remain online. This does not include maintenance downtime.

- Enterprise root CAs are often the only CA deployed in organizations that have less than 300 users. In organizations with large numbers of users, it is prudent to deploy an offline standalone root CA and then use enterprise subordinate CAs for the certificate deployment and management.

- Enterprise root CAs can issue certificates automatically to devices and users that are members of the same Active Directory environment. They can also issue certificates to devices and users that are not members of the Active Directory environment, but this process is not automatic.

- Enterprise root CAs can provide signing certificates to both enterprise subordinate and standalone subordinate CAs.

- Must be deployed on a server that is a member of an Active Directory forest.
- Avoid deploying more than one enterprise root CA in a forest. Although it is possible, it is not recommended.

Deploying an enterprise subordinate CA

Like enterprise root CAs, enterprise subordinate CAs are fully integrated into Active Directory and allow certificates to be issued based upon configurable certificate templates. Enterprise subordinate CAs allow you to implement certificate autoenrollment.

When considering whether to deploy an enterprise subordinate CA, take into account the following:

- Enterprise subordinate CAs obtain their signing certificate from an enterprise root or standalone root CA. In three or more tiered CA hierarchies, enterprise subordinate CAs can also obtain their signing certificates from enterprise subordinate or standalone subordinate CAs.
- Enterprise subordinate CAs can be used with offline root CAs to increase security. The offline root CA is only brought online to issue or revoke subordinate CA signing certificates.
- You can deploy multiple enterprise subordinate CAs in a forest. You can configure each enterprise subordinate CA to issue certificates based on different templates.
- Enterprise subordinate CAs can issue signing certificates to enterprise or standalone subordinate CAs.
- Enterprise subordinate CAs must be deployed on a server that is a member of an Active Directory forest.
- Because of Active Directory dependencies, enterprise subordinate CAs must remain online.

Deploying a standalone root CA

Standalone root CAs are root CAs that can be installed on computers irrespective of the computer's domain membership. As they are not integrated directly into Active Directory in the way that enterprise CAs are, you need to take special steps to ensure that clients in a forest trust certificates issued by a standalone root CA. Standalone root CAs can issue signing certificates to standalone subordinate CAs as well as enterprise subordinate CAs.

In large environments, standalone root CAs can be configured to function as offline root CAs. An *offline root CA* is one that is only brought online when a subordinate CA's signing certificate needs to be issued, renewed, or revoked. The advantage of an offline root CA is that because it is offline most of the time, it is difficult for an attacker to compromise. Because they are switched off most of the time, offline root CAs should be installed on standalone computers. If a subordinate CA is compromised, the offline root CA can be brought online to revoke the compromised CA's signing certificate. When configuring an offline root CA, you need to configure CRL (Certificate Revocation List) and AIA (Authority Information Access) distribution points as well as a copy of the CA certificate that will be hosted in locations that remain online.

When considering whether to deploy a standalone root CA, take into account the following:

- A standalone root CA can be installed on computers that are not members of an Active Directory domain.
- A standalone root CA can only issue certificates based on a limited set of templates. These templates cannot be modified and standalone CAs cannot issue certificates based on certificate templates stored in Active Directory.
- A standalone root CA does not directly support certificate autoenrollment and renewal.
- A standalone root CA can issue signing certificates to subordinate CAs.
- A standalone root CA does not need to remain online, but requires CRL, AIA distribution points, and a copy of the CA certificate be available to clients that consume certificates issued by the CA.
- Certificate request and issuance must be performed manually.

Deploying a standalone subordinate CA

Like standalone root CAs, standalone subordinate CAs are not integrated into Active Directory and can only issue certificates from a limited number of certificate templates that cannot be modified. Standalone subordinate CAs are often deployed on perimeter networks, allowing for the issuance of certificates to clients from outside the organization. You can configure Active Directory clients to trust certificates issued by a standalone subordinate CA by importing the CA's certificate into a GPO.

When considering whether to deploy a standalone subordinate CA, take into account the following:

- A standalone subordinate CA can be installed on computers that are not members of an Active Directory domain.
- A standalone subordinate CA can only issue certificates based on a limited number of non-editable templates.
- A standalone subordinate CA does not directly support certificate autoenrollment and renewal.
- A standalone subordinate CA can issue signing certificates to subordinate CAs.
- A standalone subordinate CA does not need to remain online, but requires CRL, AIA distribution points, and a copy of the CA certificate be available to clients that consume certificates issued by the CA.
- Certificate request and issuance must be performed manually.

> **MORE INFO**   **TYPES OF CERTIFICATION AUTHORITIES**
>
> To learn more about the different types of certification authorities, visit *http://technet.microsoft.com/en-us/library/cc732368.aspx*.

Configuring CRL Distribution Points (CDP)

Certificate Revocation Lists (CRLs) are lists of certificates that have been revoked by the administrator of an issuing CA. A CRL Distribution Point (CDP) is the location that hosts this list. When a client device encounters a new certificate, it checks the CDP to determine if the certificate has been revoked. CDPs host the following files:

- **CRL** A list of all certificates revoked on a CA at the time of publication. CAs installed on Windows Server 2012 and Windows Server 2012 R2 publish CRLs every seven days by default.

- **Delta CRL** A list of all certificates revoked since the publication of the last CRL. These are published every 24 hours.

A CA can have multiple CDPs. Enterprise CAs also publish CRL information to Active Directory. You configure CDP information on the Extensions tab of a CA's Properties dialog box, as shown in Figure 6-7. When you publish a CRL, the CA will write the CRL to these locations. When you add additional locations, you need to ensure that the computer account of the CA has permission to write information to those locations.

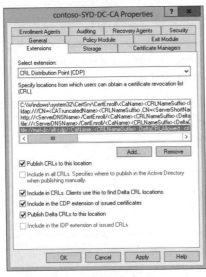

FIGURE 6-7 Configuring a CDP

The default locations for an Enterprise CA are as follows:

- C:\Windows\system32\CertSrv\CertEnroll\<CaName><CRLNameSuffix><DeltaCRLAllowed>.crl

- Ldap:///CN=<CATruncadedName><CRLNameSuffix>,CN=<ServerShortName>,CN=CDP, CN=Public Key Services,CN=Services,<ConfigurationContainer> <CDPObjectClass>

- http://<ServerDNSName>/CertEnroll<CaName><CRLNameSuffix><DeltaCRLAllowed>.crl

- File://<ServerDNSName>/CertEnroll<CaName><CRLNameSuffix> <DeltaCRLAllowed>.crl

If you need to make the CRLs available to external clients, you'll need to publish the CRL to a location that is accessible to those clients. Many organizations publish CRLs to web servers located on perimeter networks. You'll also need to configure an alternative AIA point if you implement an online responder. Online responders are covered later in this chapter.

EXAM TIP

If you don't want to wait for a CRL or delta CRL to be published according to the default schedule, you can trigger CRL publication. It is important to note that in most cases a client will check a certificate's validity only periodically; a client will not check a certificate's validity each time the certificate is used. This period is based on the CRL publication interval.

MORE INFO   CRL DISTRIBUTION POINTS (CDPS)

To learn more about CRL Distribution Points, visit *http://technet.microsoft.com/en-us/library/cc753296.aspx*.

Installing and configuring online responders

Online responders provide a streamlined way for clients to perform certificate revocation checks. Instead of downloading the entire CRL and delta CRL and checking the resultant list against the certificate identifier, the client queries the online responder using the certificate identifier to determine if the certificate is valid. The advantage to this approach is that it reduces the amount of traffic to the client and reduces the load on CDPs. The drawback is that online responders are supported only by client computers running Windows Vista and later and servers running Windows Server 2008 or later. Additionally, some third-party and mobile device operating systems don't support online responders, meaning you will still need to deploy CDPs when supporting some heterogeneous environments.

MORE INFO   ONLINE RESPONDERS

To learn more about online responders, visit *http://technet.microsoft.com/en-us/library/cc770413%28v=ws.10%29.aspx*.

Implementing administrative role separation

Delegating tasks related to certificate management is as important to an organization's security process as delegating tasks related to user account password management. Members of the following groups can manage a CA by default:

- Domain Admins group
- Enterprise Admins group
- Local Administrators group

You can configure a CA so that only specific users are able to approve the issuance of certificates. This allows you to delegate CA management tasks to users without needing to add them to any of these sensitive groups. You do this on the Security tab of the CA's properties, as shown in Figure 6-8.

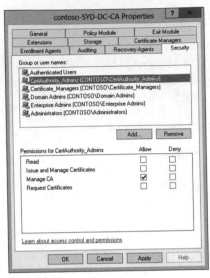

FIGURE 6-8 Configuring a CA

Assigning these permissions grants the following abilities:

- **Read** Allows the user to view CA configuration including CA settings, a list of issued and revoked certificates, and a list of CA templates the CA is configured to issue.

- **Issue And Manage Certificates** Allows the user to approve certificate requests, revoke certificates, and publish CRLs.

- **Manage CA** Allows the user to manage the CA. Includes the ability to change security settings, alter recovery agents, and modify certificate server extensions.

- **Request Certificates** Allows the user to request certificates from the CA. You might wish to restrict which users can request certificates in highly secure environments. Members of the authenticated users group have this permission by default.

You can use the Certificate Managers tab of the CA properties dialog box, shown in Figure 6-9, to limit groups assigned the Issue And Manage Certificates permission to the management of specific templates. For example, you might create a security group named WebServerCertificates and use this functionality so that members of this group are only able to manage certificates issued from the Web Server Certificate template.

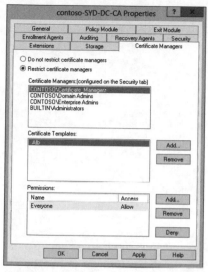

FIGURE 6-9 Configuring certificate managers

MORE INFO **ADMINISTRATIVE ROLE SEPARATION**

To learn more about configuring role-based administration for AD CS, visit *http://technet. microsoft.com/en-us/library/cc732590.aspx*.

Configuring CA backup and recovery

A CA's database and settings are automatically backed up whenever you perform a full server backup or a system state backup. A user can also perform a backup directly from the Certification Authority console if he has been assigned the Manage CA permission. When using the backup wizard available from the console, you can choose to back up the following (as shown in Figure 6-10):

- **Private Key And CA Certificate** Backs up the CA's public and private keys. This allows you to restore the CA on a new computer should the original host fail.

- **Certificate Database And Certificate Database Log** Allows you to recover certificates that have been issued. If you enable key archiving, you can recover private keys associated with the certificates. You'll learn more about key archiving later in this chapter.

MORE INFO **CA BACKUP AND RECOVERY**

To learn more about backing up and restoring a CA, visit *http://technet.microsoft.com/ en-us/library/dn486797.aspx*.

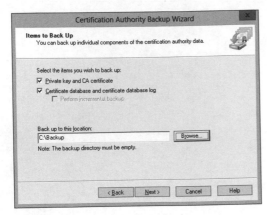

FIGURE 6-10 Selecting items to back up

You can perform a backup of the CA using the certutil command. Windows Server 2012 R2 supports two new Windows PowerShell cmdlets for backing up and restoring a certification authority database:

- **Backup-CARoleService** Allows you to back up the CA database
- **Restore-CARoleService** Allows you to restore the CA database

Thought experiment

Deploying CA at Adatum

In the following thought experiment, apply what you've learned about this objective to predict what steps you need to take. You can find answers to these questions in the "Answers" section at the end of this chapter.

You are the systems administrator at Adatum, which has a single location with an internal and perimeter network. Clients on the Internet can access hosts on the perimeter network. You are planning a certificate server deployment and you have the following objectives:

- Deploy an offline root CA
- Deploy a CA on the perimeter network to allow partner clients to obtain certificates
- Ensure that clients on the Internet can perform certificate revocation checks

With the preceding information in mind, answer the following questions.

1. What type of CA should you deploy as a root CA?
2. What type of CA should you deploy on the perimeter network?
3. How can you ensure that clients on the Internet can perform certificate revocation checks?

Objective summary

- Enterprise CAs can deploy certificates based on customizable templates that are stored within Active Directory. Active Directory clients automatically trust these certificates. Enterprise CAs must be deployed on domain members.

- Standalone CAs deploy certificates based on a limited number of templates. Standalone CAs can be deployed on domain members and computers that are not domain-joined.

- CRL Distribution Points (CDPs) host certificate revocation lists.

- Online responders allow clients to perform CRL checks without having to download CRLs and delta-CRLs.

- Administrative role separation allows you to separate people who manage the CA from people who have permission to issue and revoke certificates based on specific templates.

- You can use the Certification Authority console, the certutil command, or Windows PowerShell cmdlets to back up and restore a CA.

Objective review

Answer the following questions to test your knowledge of the information in this objective. You can find the answers to these questions and explanations of why each answer choice is correct or incorrect in the "Answers" section at the end of the chapter.

1. Which of the following CA types would you deploy if you wanted to deploy a CA at the top of a hierarchy that could issue signing certificates to other CAs and which would be taken offline if not issuing, renewing, or revoking signing certificates?

    A. Enterprise root

    B. Enterprise subordinate

    C. Standalone root

    D. Standalone subordinate

2. Which of the following CA types must be deployed on domain-joined computers?

    A. Enterprise root

    B. Enterprise subordinate

    C. Standalone root

    D. Standalone subordinate

3. Which permission should you assign on a CA to a group of users that you want to be able to respond to certificate requests but you do *not* want to provide them with the ability to change CA security settings?

    A. Read

    B. Issue And Manage Certificates

    C. Manage CA

    D. Request Certificates

4. Which permission should you assign on a CA to a group of users that you want to allow to alter the list of recovery agents?

    A. Read

    B. Issue And Manage Certificates

    C. Manage CA

    D. Request Certificates.

Objective 6.3: Manage certificates

Once you have certificate services servers in place, you need to ensure that you have an effective strategy for deploying and managing certificates. The big advantage of using enterprise CAs over standalone CAs is the degree to which you can automate this process, allowing automatic certificate enrollment and renewal without requiring users to interact directly with your organization's CAs.

> **This objective covers how to:**
> - Manage certificate templates
> - Implement and manage certificate validation and revocation
> - Manage certificate enrollment
> - Manage certificate renewal
> - Configure and manage key archival and recovery
> - Implement and manage certificate deployment

Managing certificate templates

You use Certificate Templates to manage the properties of certificates issued by enterprise root and enterprise subordinate CAs. Certificate templates are stored in Active Directory and are available to any enterprise CA in the forest. This means that if you edit the properties of a certificate template, any CA that issues certificates based on that template will issue certificates based on those updated properties.

Newly installed enterprise CAs will only issue certificates based on a small number of templates. A larger number of templates are stored within Active Directory, but you have to configure each CA to issue certificates based on those templates by enabling the templates. You do this from the Templates node of Certification Authority console by selecting the certificate template you want to enable, as shown in Figure 6-11.

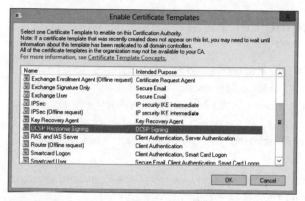

FIGURE 6-11 Enabling certificate templates

You can create new certificate templates by creating a duplicate of an existing template. When you create a new certificate template, you need to choose the compatibility settings of the new template. These settings are shown in Figure 6-12 and determine the minimum CA level and the minimum client level required to issue and use the certificate. If your organization has CAs running previous versions of the Windows Server operating system or you need to support previous versions of the Windows client, you'll need to ensure that you configure the compatibility settings appropriately.

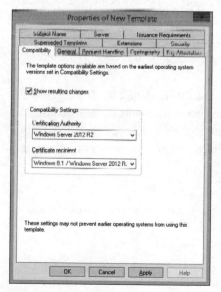

FIGURE 6-12 Configuring compatibility settings

MORE INFO OVERVIEW OF CERTIFICATE TEMPLATES

To learn more about certificate templates, visit *http://technet.microsoft.com/en-us/library/ cc730826.*

Implementing and managing certificate validation and revocation

You revoke a certificate when you don't want it to be treated as valid anymore. To revoke a certificate, you need to locate it on the list of issued certificates on the CA and then use the Revoke Certificate item on the All Tasks submenu of the Action menu. When revoking a certificate, you specify a revocation reason as well as the date and time. The revocation reason allows you to record why the certificate was revoked. You can select one of the following reasons to revoke a certificate:

- **Unspecified** No revocation code is specified. Don't use this code if your organization has strict policies about why certificates are revoked.
- **Key Compromise** Use this code when you believe a certificate might have been misappropriated, such as when a user loses his smart card.
- **CA Compromise** Use this code when you believe the CA's key is compromised.
- **Change of Affiliation** Use this code when a user leaves the organization and you need to revoke the certificates associated with the user.
- **Superseded** Use this code when you've issued an updated certificate and want to invalidate any prior versions of the certificate.
- **Cease of Operation** Use this code when the device that the certificate was issued to is no longer in use.
- **Certificate Hold** Use this code when you need to only temporarily revoke the certificate. Other codes cannot be changed, but you can undo this code to make the certificate valid should circumstances change.

When you revoke a certificate, you should publish a new CRL or delta CRL. The certificate will be not recognized as invalid by all clients immediately because clients cache revocation checks for a length of time based on the CRL or delta CRL publication period. In highly secure environments, you can configure a delta CRL publication period at a frequency of 30 minutes.

MORE INFO CERTIFICATE REVOCATION

To learn more about certificate revocation, visit *http://technet.microsoft.com/en-us/library/ cc771079.aspx.*

Managing certificate enrollment

Certificate enrollment involves performing a certificate request, which is then processed by the CA depending on the properties of the certificate template. You can use the Certificates snap-in of a Microsoft Management console to request a certificate or you can use a web browser interface if the CA is configured for web-based enrollment. The drawback of these two methods is that the process is manual and thus time-consuming. This is not viable when you need to deploy certificates to several thousand computers or users.

Autoenrollment allows you to automatically deploy certificates to users, services, and computers from an enterprise CA as long as those users, service accounts, and computers are members of an Active Directory domain. To support autoenrollment, you need to configure certificate templates with the Autoenroll permission, as shown in Figure 6-13, and you need to configure the Certificate Services Client – Auto-Enrollment group policy item in a policy that applies to the security principal that will be automatically enrolled.

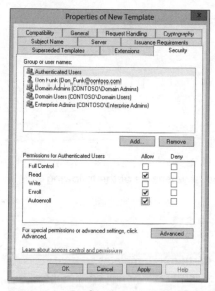

FIGURE 6-13 Configuring certificate templates with the Autoenroll permission

> **MORE INFO** **AUTOENROLLMENT**
>
> To learn more about autoenrollment, visit *http://technet.microsoft.com/en-us/library/cc731522.aspx.*

Managing certificate renewal

You can configure automatic certificate renewal so that a client will contact the issuing CA to be reissued with a certificate that has an updated expiry date. You configure automatic renewal through the Certificate Services Client – Auto-Enrollment group policy item. This is the same policy, but you need to enable the Renew Expired Certificates option, as shown in Figure 6-14.

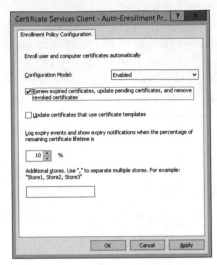

FIGURE 6-14 Renewing expired certificates

When this policy is enabled, automatic renewal will occur when one of the following conditions has been exceeded:

- 80 percent of the certificate's lifespan
- The template configured renewal period

You can also manually trigger reenrollment from the Certificate Templates console by selecting the Reenroll All Certificate Holders action for certificates deployed through autoenrollment from an enterprise CA. Performing this action will not reenroll certificate holders whose certificates have been revoked.

EXAM TIP

Remember the two conditions that can be used to configure automatic renewal and the policy that you need to configure to enable each condition.

Configuring and managing key archival and recovery

When you configure key archiving, a CA will store both the public and private keys associated with a certificate. This allows you to recover the private key in the event that it's lost. Key archiving is not enabled by default. To enable it, you need to enroll at least one user with a certificate issued off a Key Recovery Agent (KRA) certificate template. This template is stored in Active Directory, but is not one that enterprise CAs are configured to issue by default. Once a user has a certificate issued off the KRA certificate template, you can enable the Archive The Key option on the Recovery Agents tab of the CA properties, as shown in Figure 6-15.

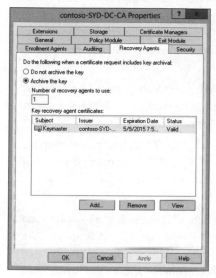

FIGURE 6-15 Configuring recovery agents

Once you enable key archiving, you'll also need to configure each certificate template with the Archive Subject's Encryption Private Key option. Once you've enabled archiving on the CA and you've enabled this option on the certificate template, future certificates issued from that template will have the keys archived. Any certificate issued from the template prior to these steps taken will not have the key archived.

The user that holds the private key associated with the KRA certificate can recover certificate private keys using the certutil command with the getkey option and the certificate serial number. Figure 6-16 shows this process. Running this command will extract a blob. You extract the key from this blob using the certutil command with the recoverkey option. This will output the key in .pfx format, which can then be imported as needed.

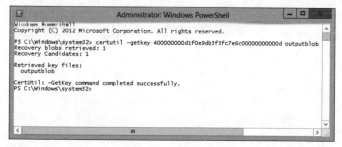

FIGURE 6-16 Extracting a key using the certutil command

Implementing and managing certificate deployment

When implementing and managing certificate deployment, consider the following:

- You can deploy certificate servers in a hierarchy. A single root CA issues the signing certificate for subordinate CAs. You configure the root CA so that it only issues signing certificates. You configure day-to-day certificate issuance tasks to be performed by subordinate CAs. This way, should a subordinate CA become compromised, you can revoke its signing certificate. Where practical, you should use an offline root stand-alone CA.

- Certificates (and private keys, if archiving is enabled) are stored in each CA's database. If you deploy a large number of CAs and you need to recover a certificate or a private key, you'll need to figure out which CA originally issued the certificate.

- If you deploy a large number of CAs, each will have its own CRLs. You can publish the CRLs from different CAs to shared locations. Use multiple CDPs, including one on your organization's perimeter network, to ensure that CRL checks can occur in the event that one or more CDPs become unavailable.

- A CA cannot issue a certificate with an expiration date that exceeds the expiration data of the CA's signing certificate. You need to ensure that the signing certificates of CAs that issue certificates either are configured with a long validity period or are updated on a periodic basis. If you don't do this, the signing certificate and all the certificates issued from the CA will expire at the same time.

- Create a duplicate template each time you want to make changes to an existing template. You can configure template supersedence within the template's properties. Update the compatibility settings to meet the minimum CA server and client operating system level where possible. This allows you to implement more advanced features.

- Use autoenrollment and automatic certificate renewal as much as possible to minimize the amount of administrative effort required around certificate issuance.

- Use the certificate hold status as the primary reason to revoke certificates. This allows you to reverse the revocation should circumstances change.

- Publish a new CRL after performing a certificate revocation. This minimizes the amount of time that the revoked certificate is accepted as valid.

Thought experiment
Managing certificate templates at Contoso

In the following thought experiment, apply what you've learned about this objective to predict what steps you need to take. You can find answers to these questions in the "Answers" section at the end of this chapter.

You are the systems administrator at Contoso.

You have the following objectives:

- Enable private key recovery for all templates
- Enable autoenrollment for user and computer certificates
- Enable automatic renewal for all certificates deployed through autoenrollment

With the preceding information in mind, answer the following questions.

1. What steps do you need to take to enable private key recovery for all templates in use?

2. What steps do you need to take to configure autoenrollment?

3. What steps do you need to take to configure automatic renewal?

Objective summary

- Certificate templates allow you to configure the properties of certificates that are issued from enterprise CAs.
- When revoking a certificate, specify a reason for revocation. You should publish a CRL after performing a revocation.
- You can configure certificate autoenrollment by configuring Group Policy and by enabling the autoenrollment permission on certificate templates.
- You can configure automatic certificate renewal by configuring group policy and by configuring the renewal period on the certificate template.
- You can enable key archiving on a CA if a user has been issued a certificate from a KRA template. You also need to enable key archiving on each certificate template where you want private keys to be archived.

Objective review

Answer the following questions to test your knowledge of the information in this objective. You can find the answers to these questions and explanations of why each answer choice is correct or incorrect in the "Answers" section at the end of the chapter.

1. You want to enable key archiving on a CA. You need to issue a certificate from a specific template to the user who will recover private keys. Which certificate template will you use as the basis for this certificate?

   A. Kerberos authentication

   B. Code signing

   C. OCSP response signing

   D. Key recovery agent

2. Which group policy item should you configure to enable automatic reenrollment of certificates?

   A. Certificate Path Validation Settings

   B. Certificate Services Client – Certificate Enrollment Policy

   C. Certificate Services Client – Auto-Enrollment

   D. Trusted Root Certification Authorities

3. You need to ensure that clients will check at least every 30 minutes as to whether a certificate has been revoked. Which of the following should you configure to accomplish this goal?

   A. Key recovery agent

   B. CRL publication interval

   C. Delta CRL publication interval

   D. Certificate templates.

4. Which of the following revocation statuses can you change to alter the status of a certificate from revoked to valid?

   A. Certificate Hold

   B. CA Compromise

   C. Key Compromise

   D. Change Of Affiliation

Objective 6.4: Install and configure Active Directory Rights Management Services (AD RMS)

Active Directory Rights Management Services (AD RMS) allows you to control who is able to access and distribute documents without worrying about correctly applied file and folder permissions. You can use AD RMS to restrict users from successfully emailing documents as attachments to unauthorized third parties, from copying or changing important documents, or from accessing documents from insecure devices.

> **This objective covers how to:**
> - Install a licensing or certificate AD RMS server
> - Manage AD RMS Service Connection Point (SCP)
> - Manage RMS templates
> - Configure exclusion policies
> - Back up and restore AD RMS

Installing a licensing or certificate AD RMS server

An AD RMS deployment is termed a cluster. This can be confusing because this term applies even though the deployment might not be highly available. When reading AD RMS documentation, remind yourself that in this specific sense, cluster isn't related to failover or load balancing. An AD RMS root cluster manages all of the AD RMS licensing and all of the AD RMS certificate traffic for an Active Directory forest. There is one AD RMS root cluster per forest. Organizations that have multiple Active Directory forests often deploy AD RMS root clusters in each forest. Additional licensing-only clusters distribute the licenses that AD RMS clients require to publish and consume AD RMS protected content.

When deploying the AD RMS role service, you do the following:

1. Select the database that will store AD RMS configuration information. In small deployments, you can use the Windows Internal Database. You should use SQL Server 2008 or later to support large AD RMS deployments.

2. Select a service account. AD RMS requires a domain account. You should use a group-managed service account, supported in Windows Server 2012 R2, because this allows the service account password to be managed by Active Directory.

3. Select a cryptographic mode. Choose between Mode 2 and Mode 1. Mode 2 uses RSA 2048-bit keys and SHA-256 hashes and is the most secure. Mode 1 uses weaker, 1024-bit keys and SHA-1 hashes.

4. Choose a cluster key storage location. The cluster key can be stored in AD RMS or within a special cryptographic service provider (CSP)—if you have one available. The drawback of using a CSP is that you will need to manually distribute the cluster key when adding additional AD RMS servers to your deployment.

5. Input a cluster key password. This allows you to protect the cluster key. You'll need this password when you're adding additional AD RMS servers to a cluster or when you're recovering a cluster from backup.

6. Specify the cluster address. Provide the website address in FQDN (fully qualified domain name) format. You should have installed a web server certificate with the FQDN of the host server, which is usually located on the first AD RMS server. A web server certificate is required if you want to use AD RMS with identity federation.

7. Choose a licensor certificate name. Choose a name used with the licensor certificate that represents the certificate's functionality.

8. Choose whether to register the Service Connection Point (SCP) in Active Directory. The SCP allows clients to locate the AD RMS cluster.

> **MORE INFO INSTALLING AD RMS**
>
> To learn more about installing AD RMS, visit *http://technet.microsoft.com/en-us/library/cc770957.aspx*

Managing AD RMS Service Connection Point (SCP)

The AD RMS SCP allows AD RMS enabled clients to retrieve the connection URL for AD RMS from Active Directory. The AD RMS SCP is registered during AD RMS deployment if you install AD RMS with an account that is a member of the Enterprise Admins group. If the account used to deploy AD RMS is not a member of the Enterprise Admins group, a user that is a member of this group can register or change the SCP by editing the cluster Properties through the AD RMS console, as shown in Figure 6-17. You can only modify the SCP properties after installation if the user account used to perform the procedure is a member of the AD RMS Enterprise Administrators group and the Enterprise Admins group.

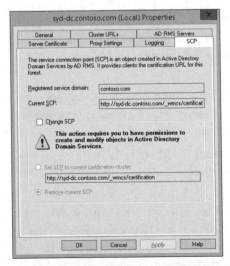

FIGURE 6-17 Modifying SCP properties

Managing RMS templates

Rights policy templates allow users to apply rights policies to templates. Templates can also be applied automatically by Exchange Server transport rules or through File Server Resource Manager. You use the AD RMS Management Console to create rights policy templates. When creating templates, you enable rights on a per-group or per-user basis. AD RMS requires that each security principal has an associated email address. Any right that you don't specifically grant will not be assigned to the user. You can distribute rights policy templates manually or by using group policy. A rights policy template must be distributed to a client before a user can apply the template to protect content. A user can consume rights-protected content even if she doesn't have a copy of the rights policy template. The rights that you can configure are as follows:

- **Full Control**   User has full control over the AD RMS protected content
- **View**   User has the ability to view the AD RMS protected content
- **Edit**   User can modify the AD RMS protected content
- **Save**   User can save AD RMS protected content
- **Export**   User can use the save as function with AD RMS-protected content to save as a different file
- **Print**   User can print the AD RMS protected content
- **Forward**   User can forward protected email messages
- **Reply**   User can reply to protected email messages
- **Reply All**   User can use the reply-all option with a protected email message
- **Extract**   User can copy data from an AD RMS-protected document or email message
- **Allow Macros**   User can use macros with an AD RMS-protected document
- **View Rights**   User can view the rights assigned to the protected content
- **Edit Rights**   User can modify the rights assigned to the protected content

When configuring a template, you can assign different rights to different users or groups. When a user is a member of multiple groups, rights are cumulative.

EXAM TIP

Remember that rights are cumulative.

Content expiration settings allow you to have protected content expire either after a certain number of days have elapsed or after a certain date. As Figure 6-18 shows, you can also configure license expiration. License expiration means that the AD RMS client must make a connection back to the AD RMS server to obtain a new license even though the content has not expired.

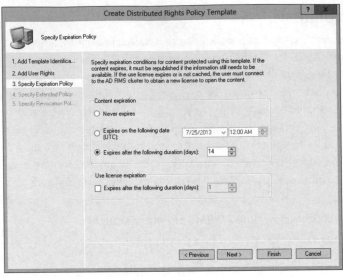

FIGURE 6-18 Specifying an expiration policy

MORE INFO   **RIGHTS POLICY TEMPLATES**

To learn more about rights policy templates, view *http://technet.microsoft.com/en-us/library/cc731599.aspx*.

Configuring exclusion policies

You use exclusion policies to block specific entities (such as applications, users, and lockbox versions) from interacting with AD RMS. You can configure the following types of exclusion:

- **User Exclusion**   Allows you to block a user based on email address or the public key assigned to the user's Rights Account Certificate
- **Lockbox Exclusion**   Allows you to block specific versions of the AD RMS client
- **Application Exclusion**   Allows you to block specific applications based on application name and version, from interacting with AD RMS.

Exclusions apply only to new certificate or licensing requests. If you remove an exclusion, the exclusion still applies to certificates or licensing requests that were generated while the exclusion was active.

Backing up and restoring AD RMS

Being able to backup and recover an AD RMS deployment involves ensuring that you've done the following:

- You have a copy of the cluster key password. If you don't know the cluster key password, you can change it using the AD RMS console.
- You have exported the Export Trusted Publishing Domain. You can perform this step from the AD RMS console.
- You have backed up the AD RMS databases.

AD RMS uses three databases, each of which must be backed up. If you are using SQL Server to host the AD RMS databases, you can use SQL Server backup tools to ensure that these are backed up on a regular basis. If you are using the Windows Internal Database, you can use SQL Server Management Studio to perform a backup (although this involves determining the appropriate connection settings) or you can perform a full server backup. The complicated nature of backing up and restoring AD RMS when you are using the Windows Internal Database presents an excellent argument in favor or using a SQL Server instance to host this information. There are three AD RMS databases:

- **Configuration database**   This database stores all the configuration information that the service requires to manage account certification, licensing, and publishing for the AD RMS cluster.
- **Directory services database**   This database stores identifier information about security principals. This database hosts cached information extracted from Active Directory.
- **Logging database**   This database hosts logs related to license acquisition and client activity.

When performing a restoration, first ensure that the databases are restored. Once the databases are restored on the SQL instance, reinstall the AD RMS role service and choose the Join An Existing Cluster option. You'll be prompted to provide the location of the AD RMS database and the cluster key password. You can then import the trusted publishing domain.

Thought experiment

Deploying AD RMS at Wingtip Toys

In the following thought experiment, apply what you've learned about this objective to predict what steps you need to take. You can find answers to these questions in the "Answers" section at the end of this chapter.

You are the systems administrator at Wingtip Toys. You are planning an immediate trial deployment of AD RMS by deploying a single server. In six months time, when the trial nears completion, you will add more servers to the AD RMS cluster and then modify the SCP.

You have the following objectives:

- Register the SCP during AD RMS deployment
- Add additional AD RMS servers in six months
- Modify the SCP in six months

With the preceding information in mind, answer the following questions.

1. Which groups must the user account be a member of to deploy AD RMS and to be a member of in order to register the SCP during deployment?

2. Which groups must the user account be a member of to modify the SCP in six months be a member of?

3. Which password must be known in order to add additional AD RMS servers in six months?

Objective summary

- An AD RMS deployment is termed a cluster, even though it doesn't imply that the deployment is highly available.
- The AD RMS Service Connection Point (SCP) allows AD RMS clients to locate the AD RMS cluster.
- AD RMS templates control which actions an AD RMS client can perform with AD RMS-protected content.
- Exclusion policies allow you to exclude users, AD RMS clients, and applications from consuming AD RMS-protected content
- When backing up the AD RMS cluster, ensure you have a copy of the cluster key password, export the trusted publishing domain, and back up the AD RMS databases.

Objective review

Answer the following questions to test your knowledge of the information in this objective. You can find the answers to these questions and explanations of why each answer choice is correct or incorrect in the "Answers" section at the end of the chapter.

1. Which security groups must a user account be a member of to modify the AD RMS SCP? (Choose two answers. Each answer forms part of a complete solution.)

   A. Domain Admins

   B. AD RMS Enterprise Administrators

   C. Enterprise Admins

   D. Cryptographic Operators.

2. Which of the following would you configure if you wanted to block computers running Windows 7 and earlier operating systems from consuming AD RMS-protected content?

   A. Trusted publishing domain

   B. Trusted user domain

   C. Exclusion policies

   D. Super Users

3. Which of the following must you back up or have a copy of to be able to ensure that you can restore an AD RMS cluster in the event that a single server hosting all AD RMS components suffers complete data loss? (Choose three answers.)

   A. Cluster key password

   B. Trusted publishing domain

   C. Trusted user domain

   D. AD RMS databases

Answers

This section contains the solutions to the "Thought experiments" and the "Objective review" questions in this chapter.

Objective 6.1: Thought experiment

1. You should configure the relying-party trust on the claims-provider federation server.

2. You should configure the claims-provider trust on the relying-party federation server.

3. You can use Windows Azure multi-factor authentication to support two-factor authentication using SMS messages or an authenticator app.

Objective 6.1: Review

1. **Correct Answer:** A

    A. **Correct:** You deploy a web application proxy on a perimeter network.

    B. **Incorrect:** The relying-party server is a federation server on a protected network.

    C. **Incorrect:** The federation server should be deployed on a protected network.

    D. **Incorrect:** The claims-provider server is a federation server on a protected network.

2. **Correct Answers:** B, C

    A. **Incorrect:** The server in the forest that hosts the resources to be accessed functions as the relying-party server.

    B. **Correct:** The server in the forest that hosts the resources to be accessed functions as the relying-party server.

    C. **Correct:** You configure a relying-party trust on the claims-provider server. Because the users are in the Tailspin Toys forest, you configure a relying-party trust on this server.

    D. **Incorrect:** You configure a relying-party trust on the claims-provider server. Because the users are in the Tailspin Toys forest, you configure a relying-party trust on this server.

3. **Correct Answers:** A, D

    A. **Correct:** The claims-provider server is located in the forest that hosts the user accounts.

    B. **Incorrect:** The claims-provider server is located in the forest that hosts the user accounts.

    C. **Incorrect:** You configure the claims-provider trust on the relying-party server, which is located in the forest that hosts the resources.

    D. **Correct:** You configure the claims-provider trust on the relying-party server, which is located in the forest that hosts the resources.

4. **Correct Answer:** D

  A. **Incorrect:** Workplace Join uses device authentication.

  B. **Incorrect:** Workplace Join uses device authentication.

  C. **Incorrect:** Workplace Join uses device authentication.

  D. **Correct:** Workplace Join uses device authentication.

Objective 6.2: Thought experiment

1. You should deploy a standalone root CA because you can take this CA offline. An enterprise root CA must remain online.

2. You should deploy a standalone subordinate CA on the perimeter network. This type of CA can be deployed on a non-domain joined server.

3. You need to configure a CDP in a location that is accessible to clients on the Internet, such as stored on a host on the perimeter network.

Objective 6.2: Review

1. **Correct Answer:** C

  A. **Incorrect:** Because enterprise CAs are integrated into Active Directory, they should not be taken offline.

  B. **Incorrect:** Because enterprise CAs are integrated into Active Directory, they should not be taken offline. Additionally, subordinate CAs are not at the top of a CA hierarchy.

  C. **Correct:** You can take a standalone root CA offline and it functions as the top of a CA hierarchy.

  D. **Incorrect:** Subordinate CAs are not at the top of a CA hierarchy.

2. **Correct Answers:** A, B

  A. **Correct:** Enterprise CAs must be deployed on domain-joined computers.

  B. **Correct:** Enterprise CAs must be deployed on domain-joined computers.

  C. **Incorrect:** Standalone CAs can be deployed on non-domain-joined computers.

  D. **Incorrect:** Standalone CAs can be deployed on non-domain-joined computers.

3. **Correct Answer:** B

  A. **Incorrect:** The Issue And Manage Certificates permission allows a security principal to respond to certificate requests.

  B. **Correct:** The Issue And Manage Certificates permission allows a security principal to respond to certificate requests.

  C. **Incorrect:** The Issue And Manage Certificates permission allows a security principal to respond to certificate requests.

  D. **Incorrect:** The Issue And Manage Certificates permission allows a security principal to respond to certificate requests.

4. **Correct Answer:** C

   A. **Incorrect:** The Manage CA permission allows users to alter the list of recovery agents.

   B. **Incorrect:** The Manage CA permission allows users to alter the list of recovery agents.

   C. **Correct:** The Manage CA permission allows users to alter the list of recovery agents.

   D. **Incorrect:** The Manage CA permission allows users to alter the list of recovery agents.

Objective 6.3: Thought experiment

1. You need to configure the CA to issue a certificate based of a KRA template, enable key recovery on the CA, and enable key archiving on all certificate templates in use.

2. You need to grant the enroll, read, and autoenroll permissions on the user and computer certificate templates. You also need to configure the Certificate Services Client – Auto-Enrollment group policy item.

3. You need to configure the renewal period on the user and computer certificate templates. You also need to configure the Certificate Services Client – Auto-Enrollment group policy item and ensure you enable the Renew Expired Certificates option.

Objective 6.3: Review

1. **Correct Answer:** D

   A. **Incorrect:** You need to issue a certificate from the key recovery agent template to a user before you can enable key archiving on a CA.

   B. **Incorrect:** You need to issue a certificate from the key recovery agent template to a user before you can enable key archiving on a CA.

   C. **Incorrect:** You need to issue a certificate from the key recovery agent template to a user before you can enable key archiving on a CA.

   D. **Correct:** You need to issue a certificate from the key recovery agent template to a user before you can enable key archiving on a CA.

2. **Correct Answer:** C

   A. **Incorrect:** This policy allows you to configure which root CAs clients trust.

   B. **Incorrect:** This policy allows you to modify the default certificate enrollment policy.

   C. **Correct:** You configure automatic reenrollment by configuring the Certificate Services Client – Auto-Enrollment policy.

   D. **Incorrect:** This policy allows you to configure trusted root CAs.

3. **Correct Answer:** C

   A. **Incorrect:** You can't configure revocation check frequency using key recovery agents.

   B. **Incorrect:** The minimum period for automatic CRL publication is daily. More frequent publication requires the use of delta CRLs.

   C. **Correct:** A delta CRL can be published as frequently as every 30 minutes, meaning clients will check at least this often to determine if a certificate has been revoked.

   D. **Incorrect:** You can't configure revocation check frequency using certificate templates.

4. **Correct Answer:** A

   A. **Correct:** You can remove a Certificate Hold status, which means that the certificate will be recognized as valid.

   B. **Incorrect:** This status cannot be modified once set.

   C. **Incorrect:** This status cannot be modified once set.

   D. **Incorrect:** This status cannot be modified once set.

Objective 6.4: Thought experiment

1. A user must be a member of the Enterprise Admins group to register the SCP during deployment.

2. The user account used to modify the SCP must be a member of the AD RMS Enterprise Administrators and the Enterprise Admins group.

3. The cluster key password must be known to add additional AD RMS servers in six months.

Objective 6.4: Review

1. **Correct Answers:** B, C

   A. **Incorrect:**. The user account used to modify the SCP must be a member of the AD RMS Enterprise Administrators group and the Enterprise Admins group.

   B. **Correct:** The user account used to modify the SCP must be a member of the AD RMS Enterprise Administrators group and the Enterprise Admins group.

   C. **Correct:** The user account used to modify the SCP must be a member of the AD RMS Enterprise Administrators group and the Enterprise Admins group.

   D. **Incorrect:** The user account used to modify the SCP must be a member of the AD RMS Enterprise Administrators group and the Enterprise Admins group.

2. **Correct Answer:** C

   A. **Incorrect:** You configure an exclusion policy based on the lockbox to block AD RMS clients running particular operating systems.

   B. **Incorrect:** You configure an exclusion policy based on the lockbox to block AD RMS clients running particular operating systems.

   C. **Correct:** You configure an exclusion policy based on the lockbox to block AD RMS clients running particular operating systems (such as Windows 7).

   D. **Incorrect:** You configure an exclusion policy based on the lockbox to block AD RMS clients running particular operating systems.

3. **Correct Answers:** A, B, D

   A. **Correct:** You need to have access to the cluster key password, the backed up trusted publishing domain, and the AD RMS databases to restore an AD RMS cluster in the event that a single server hosting all AD RMS components suffers complete data loss.

   B. **Correct:** You need to have access to the cluster key password, the backed up trusted publishing domain, and the AD RMS databases to restore an AD RMS cluster in the event that a single server hosting all AD RMS components suffers complete data loss.

   C. **Incorrect:** You need to have access to the cluster key password, the backed up trusted publishing domain, and the AD RMS databases to restore an AD RMS cluster in the event that a single server hosting all AD RMS components suffers complete data loss.

   D. **Correct:** You need to have access to the cluster key password, the backed up trusted publishing domain, and the AD RMS databases to restore an AD RMS cluster in the event that a single server hosting all AD RMS components suffers complete data loss.

Index

A

access-denied assistance, classifying files and folders, 117
Access-Denied Assistance tab (FSRM Options dialog box), 117
access policies, DAC, 118–122
    creating a central access poilicy that includes claims, 118–121
    deploying central access policy to the servers, 122
access protection
    AD CS, 318–326
        administrative role separation, 323–324
        CA backup and recovery, 325
        CRL Distribution Points, 322–323
        installing an enterprise CA, 318–322
        online responders, 323–324
    AD FS, 309–316
        authentication policies, 312–313
        claims-based authentication, 310–313
        installation, 310
        multi-factor authentication, 315–316
        Workplace Join, 313–314
    AD RMS, 337–342
        backing up and restoring, 341–342
        exclusion policies, 340
        installing a licensing or certificate AD RMS server, 337–330
        SCP (Service Connection Point), 338–339
        templates, 339–340
    certificate management, 328–334
        certificate deployment, 334
        Certificate Templates, 328–329
        enrollment, 331–332
        key archival and recovery, 332–333
        renewal, 332–333
        validation and revocation, 330–331

access rules, 101
accounts
    Windows Azure Backup feature, 163
Active Directory
    configuring infrastructure
        forests/domains, 267–273
        sites, 284–292
        trusts, 276–281
    replication
        RODCs, 294–297
        SYSVOL, 300
Active Directory Certificate Services. *See* AD CS (Active Directory Certificate Services)
Active Directory Detached Clusters, 24–25
Active Directory Domain Services (AD DS)
    updating with classifiable properties, 109–110
Active Directory Federation Services. *See* AD FS (Active Directory Federation Services)
Active Directory Rights Management Services. *See* AD RMS (Active Directory Rights Management Services)
active screening, 93
AD CS (Active Directory Certificate Services), 318–326
    administrative role separation, 323–324
    CA backup and recovery, 325
    CRL Distribution Points, 322–323
    installing an enterprise CA, 318–322
    online responders, 323–324
Add Claims Provider Trust Wizard, 312
Add-ClusterDisk cmdlet, 26–27
Add/Edit Port Rule dialog box, 8–9, 10–11
Add Host To Cluster Wizard, 12
Add Initiator ID dialog box, 132
Add Items option (Select Items For Backup page), 155–157
Additional Recovery Points option, 192
Add-NlbClusterNode cmdlet, 12

Add-NlbClusterNodeDip cmdlet, 12
Add-NlbClusterPortRule cmdlet, 12
Add-NlbClusterVip cmdlet, 12
Add Or Edit Server dialog box, 246–247
Add Relying Party Trust Wizard, 311
address space, IPAM, 250–258
Add Roles and Features Wizard, 3
    installing Windows Server Backup feature, 152
AD DS (Active Directory Domain Services)
    updating with classifiable properties, 109–110
Add-WindowsFeature cmdlet, 3
Add-WindowsFeature FS-iSCSTarget-Server cmdlet, 127
AD FS (Active Directory Federation Services), 309–316
    authentication policies, 312–313
    claims-based authentication, 310–313
    installation, 310
    multi-factor authentication, 315–316
    Workplace Join, 313–314
administrative role separation, AD CS, 323–324
AD RMS (Active Directory Rights Management
        Services), 337–342
    backing up and restoring, 341–342
    exclusion policies, 340
    installing a licensing or certificate AD RMS
        server, 337–338
    SCP (Service Connection Point), 338–339
    templates, 339–340
Advanced Boot Option menu, server recovery, 174–176
advanced DHCP solutions, 215–225
    configuring DNS registration, 223–224
    DHCPv6, 218–221
    high availability, 222–224
    multicast scopes, 218
    Name Protection, 224–225
    superscopes, 216–217
advanced DNS solutions, 228–236
    analyzing zone-level statistics, 235–236
    configuring cache locking, 230–231
    configuring logging, 231–232
    delegated administration, 232–233
    DNSSEC, 229–230
    DNS Socket Pool, 230
    GlobalNames zones, 235
    netmask ordering, 234–235
    recursion, 233–234
advanced file services, configuring, 83–97
    BranchCache, 84–92
        clients for Distributed Cache mode, 90–91

clients for Hosted Cache mode, 91–92
content servers, 87–89
Distributed Cache mode, 86
Hosted Cache mode, 85
hosted cache servers, 89–90
    file access auditing, 95–96
    FSRM (File Server Resource Manager), 92–95
        file management tasks, 95
        file screens, 93
        quotas, 94
        storage reports, 94–95
    installation of Server for NFS, 96–97
Advanced Options screen (Windows RE), 180
Advanced Password Replication Policy dialog box, 297
Advanced Security Settings For Permissions dialog
        box, 120
Advanced Settings dialog box
    Exclusions tab, 156
    VSS Settings tab, 157–158
Advanced Settings (Select Items For Backup
        page), 156–157
Advanced tab, DNS server properties, 233
Affinity settings, Multiple Host filtering mode, 9–10
Allow Macros rights, 339
Allow Replication From Any Authenticated Server
        option, 189
Allow Replication From The Specified Servers
        option, 189
Alternate Shell, 178
analyzing zone-level statistics, DNS, 235–236
Application Exclusions, 340
Applications And Services Logs folder, DNS server
        logs, 231
Archive Subject's Encryption Private Key option, 333
Assign iSCSI Target page (New iSCSI Virtual Disk
        Wizard), 132
attributes
    users, devices, and files, 101–102
attribute store, 311
auditing file access, 118
Authentication And Ports area (Hyper-V Settings dialog
        box), 187–188
authentication, configuring trusts, 280–281
authentication policies
    AD FS, 312–313
Authentication Policies, 271
Authentication Policy Silos, 271
authentication scopes, configuring forest trusts, 278

Authorization And Storage area (Hyper-V Settings dialog box), 189–190
autoenrollment, certificates, 331
automatic classification, classifying files and folders, 111–116

B

backing up AD RMS, 341–342
Backup Agent, Windows Azure, 164
Backup-CARoleService cmdlet, 326
backup exclusions, 156
Back Up Now option (Windows Azure Backup feature), 167–168
Backup Once Wizard, 152
Backup Operators group, 160
Backup Options page (Windows Server Backup feature), 153–154
backups, 151–170
    Backup Operators, 160
    command-line tools, 159
    Performance settings, 158–159
    selecting destination, 157–158
    Shadow Copies feature, 160–162
    Windows Azure Backup feature, 162–170
        Backup Agent, 164
        Back Up Now option, 167–168
        creating an account, 163
        creating a recovery vault, 163
        enabling bandwidth throttling, 169–170
        Recover Data option, 168–169
        registering servers, 164–165
        Schedule Backup Wizard, 165–167
    Windows Server Backup feature, 152–159
        Backup Options page, 153–154
        Select Backup Configuration page, 153
        Select Items For Backup page, 154–157
backups, CAs, 325
Backup Schedule Wizard, 152
Back Up To A Dedicated Hard Disk option (backup destination), 157
Back Up To A Volume option (backup destination), 158
bandwidth throttling, Windows Azure Backup feature, 169–170
Bare Metal Recovery option (Select Items dialog box), 155
Bcdboot command-line recovery tool, 183

BCD (Boot Configuration Data) store, 182
Bcdedit command
    booting into Safe Mode, 177–178
    recovery tool, 183
bidirectional trusts, 276
Boot Configuration Data (BCD) store, 182
booting into Safe Mode, server recovery, 177–178
BOOTREC command-line recovery tool, 182
Bootrec /FixBoot option (Bootrec.exe utility), 182
Bootrec /FixMbr option (Bootrec.exe utility), 183
Bootrec /RebuildBcd option (Bootrec.exe utility), 183
Bootrec /ScanOs option (Bootrec.exe utility), 183
BranchCache, 84–92
    configuring
        clients for Distributed Cache mode, 90–91
        clients for Hosted Cache mode, 91–92
        content servers, 87–89
        hosted cache servers, 89–90
        Distributed Cache mode, 86
        Hosted Cache mode, 85
BranchCache For Network Files component, installation, 88
business continuity
    backups, 151–170
        Backup Operators, 160
        Shadow Copies feature, 160–162
        Windows Azure Backup feature, 162–170
        Windows Server Backup feature, 152–159
    configuring site-level fault tolerance, 186–207
        Global Update Manager, 205
        Hyper-V physical host servers, 186–190
        Hyper-V Replica Extended Replication, 204–205
        Hyper-V Replica failover options, 197–201
        Hyper-V Replica in a failover cluster, 201–205
        recovering multi-site failover clusters, 206
        VMs (virtual machines), 190–197
    server recovery, 174–183
        Advanced Boot Option menu, 174–176
        booting into Safe Mode, 177–178
        installation media, 178–183

C

cache locking, DNS, 230–231
CA Compromise, revoking certificates, 330
Cancel Failover option, 200
CAP (client access point), 202

CAs (Certificate Authorities)
  backup and recovery, 325
  certificate management, 328–334
    certificate deployment, 334
    Certificate Templates, 328–329
    enrollment, 331–332
    key archival and recovery, 332–333
    renewal, 332–333
    validation and revocation, 330–331
  installing enterprise CAs, 318–322
CAU (Cluster Aware Updating), 34–38
CDPs (CRL Distribution Points), 322–323
Cease of Operation, revoking certificates, 330
Central Access Policies Configuration dialog box, 122
central access policies, DAC
  configuring, 118–121
  deploying to servers, 122
Central Access Rule dialog box, 119–120
Certificate Authentication, 313
Certificate Authorities. See CAs (Certificate Authorities)
certificate-based authentication, 188
Certificate-Based Authentication (HTTPS), 188
Certificate Hold, revoking certificates, 330
certificate management, 328–334
  certificate deployment, 334
  Certificate Templates, 328–329
  enrollment, 331–332
  key archival and recovery, 332–333
  renewal, 332–333
  validation and revocation, 330–331
Certificate Revocation Lists (CRLs), 322
Certificate Services Client-Auto-Enrollment group
    policy, 331
Certificate Templates, 328–329
certutil command, 326, 333
Change of Affiliation, revoking certificates, 330
Choose An Option screen (Windows RE), 179
Choose Initial Replication Method page (Enable
    Replication wizard), 194
Choose Move Type page (Move Wizard), 70
Choose Replication VHDs page (Enable Replication
    wizard), 192
claim rules, 311
claims, 310
  defined, 100–101
  user and device claim types, 104–105
claims-based authentication
  AD FS, 310–313

claims-based authentication, DAC, 103–106
  defining user and device claims types, 104–105
  enabling Kerberos support, 106
claims-provider trusts, configuring, 312–313
classification methods, 113–114
Classification Parameters dialog box, 114–115
classification rules
  creating, 111–112
  schedule, 116
  scope, 112–113
classifications (resource properties). See resource
    properties
Classification tab (Create Classification Rule dialog
    box), 113–114
client access point (CAP), 202
clients
  configuring BranchCache
    Distributed Cache mode, 90–91
    Hosted Cache mode, 91–92
Cluster Aware Updating (CAU), 34–38
Cluster-Aware Updating dialog box, 35–36
cluster.exe command, 206
Cluster IP Addresses page (New Cluster Wizard), 6
Cluster IP Address option, Add/Edit Port Rule page, 9
Cluster IP Configuration settings, New Cluster: Cluster
    Parameters page, 7
Cluster Operation Mode, New Cluster: Cluster
    Parameters page, 7
Cluster Parameters page (New Cluster Wizard), 7
clusters
  failover clustering, 20–23
    Active Directory Detached Clusters, 24–25
    configuring cluster networking settings, 23–24
    configuring storage, 25–32
    migration, 38–39
  NLB
    creating and configuring, 3–7
    upgrading, 14
Cluster Shared Volume File System (CSVFS), 29
cluster-shared volumes (CSVs), 29–31
  moving VM storage to, 60–63
cmdlets
  Add-ClusterDisk, 26–27
  Add-ClusterSharedVolume, 30
  Add-WindowsFeature, 3
  Add-WindowsFeature FS-iSCSTarget-Server, 127
  Backup-CARoleService, 326
  Enable-ADFSDeviceRegistration, 314

Enable-BCDistributed, 90
Enable-BCHostedClient, 91
Enable-BCHostedServer, 89
Export-BCCachePackage, 89
Get-BCStatus, 89
Get-DnsServerStatistics, 235
Get-WindowsFeature, 137
Import-BCCachePackage, 90
Initialize-ADFSDeviceRegistration, 314
Install-WindowsFeature, 3, 137
Install-WindowsFeature BranchCache, 87
Install-WindowsFeature FS-BranchCache, 88
Install-WindowsFeature FS-NFS-Services, 96
Install-WindowsFeature IPAM, 240
Install-WindowsFeature Windows-Server-
    Backup, 152
Invoke-Gpupdate, 247
Invoke-IpamGpoProvisioning, 246
New-IscsiServerTarget, 131
NLB, 12–13
Publish-BCFileContent, 89
Publish-BCWebContent, 89
Remove-WindowsFeature, 3
Restore-CARoleService, 326
Set-DNSServerCache, 231
Set-FileStorageTier, 142
Set-NetIPInterface, 219
Set-NetRoute, 219
Set-Service msiscsi, 128
Set-VMProcessor VMname, 67
Start-Service msiscsi, 128
Suspend-ClusterNode, 49
Test Cluster, 21
Uninstall-WindowsFeature, 3, 137
Update-FSRMClassificationPropertyDefinition, 109
command-line tools
    backups, 159
    recovery, 182–183
commands
    Bcdedit, booting into Safe Mode, 177–178
    certutil, 326, 333
    cluster.exe, 206
    Netsh, 219
    Net Use, 179
    Shutdown /r /o, 175
components
    iSCSI storage, 128–129
Configuration database (AD RMS), 341

Configure Access and Information Protection Solutions
    domain
    AD CS, 318–326
        administrative role separation, 323–324
        CA backup and recovery, 325
        CRL Distribution Points, 322–323
        installing an enterprise CA, 318–322
        online responders, 323–324
    AD FS, 309–316
        authentication policies, 312–313
        claims-based authentication, 310–313
        installation, 310
        multi-factor authentication, 315–316
        Workplace Join, 313–314
    AD RMS, 337–342
        backing up and restoring, 341–342
        exclusion policies, 340
        installing a licensing or certificate AD RMS
            server, 337–338
        SCP (Service Connection Point), 338–339
        templates, 339–340
    certificate management, 328–334
        certificate deployment, 334
        Certificate Templates, 328–329
        enrollment, 331–332
        key archival and recovery, 332–333
        renewal, 332–333
        validation and revocation, 330–331
Configure Cluster Quorum Settings, 32–33
Configure Custom Fields dialog box, 253
Configure Discovery Settings dialog box, 244
Configure Hosted Cache Servers policy setting, 92
Configure IP Address Utilization Threshold dialog
    box, 257
Configure Recovery History page (Enable Replication
    wizard), 192–195
Configure Self-Updating Options Wizard, 36
Configure Utilization Threshold option, IPAM
    Settings, 257
configuring
    Active Directory infrastructure
        forests/domains, 267–273
        sites, 284–292
        trusts, 276–281
    AD CS, 318–326
        administrative role separation, 323–324
        CA backup and recovery, 325
        CRL Distribution Points, 322–323

installing an enterprise CA, 318–322

online responders, 323–324

AD FS, 309–316

  authentication policies, 312–313

  claims-based authentication, 310–313

  multi-factor authentication, 315–316

  Workplace Join, 313–314

AD RMS, 337–342

  backing up and restoring, 341–342

  exclusion policies, 340

  installing a licensing or certificate AD RMS server, 337–338

  SCP (Service Connection Point), 338–339

  templates, 339–340

advanced file services, 83–97

  BranchCache, 84–92

  file access auditing, 95–96

  FSRM (File Service Resource Manager), 92–95

  installation of Server for NFS, 96–97

backups, 151–170

  Backup Operators, 160

  Shadow Copies feature, 160–162

  Windows Azure Backup feature, 162–170

  Windows Server Backup feature, 152–159

certificate management, 328–334

  certificate deployment, 334

  Certificate Templates, 328–329

  enrollment, 331–332

  key archival and recovery, 332–333

  renewal, 332–333

  validation and revocation, 330–331

cluster storage pools, 28

constrained delegation, 59

DAC

  access policies, 118–122

  claims-based authentication, 103–106

  file classification, 107–118

DHCPv6, 221–222

failover clustering, 17–39

  Active Directory Detached Clusters, 24–25

  CAU (Cluster Aware Updating), 34–38

  cluster networking settings, 23–24

  cluster storage, 25–32

  creating clusters, 20–23

  fundamentals, 18–20

  migration, 38–39

  Quorum, 32–33

  roles, 42–53

network services

  advanced DHCP solutions, 215–225

  advanced DNS solutions, 228–236

  IPAM, 239–258

NLB, 1–14

  fundamentals, 2–3

  NLB clusters, 3–7

  port rules, 8–13

  upgrading clusters, 14

replication

  RODCs, 294–297

  SYSVOL, 300

site-level fault tolerance, 186–207

  Global Update Manager, 205

  Hyper-V physical host servers, 186–190

  Hyper-V Replica Extended Replication, 204–205

  Hyper-V Replica failover options, 197–201

  Hyper-V Replica in a failover cluster, 201–205

  recovering multi-site failover clusters, 206

  VMs (virtual machines), 190–197

storage services, 126–143

  Data Deduplication, 139–142

  Features on Demand, 136–139

  iSCSI storage, 126–142

  storage tiers, 142

Connect page (New Cluster Wizard), 4–5

constrained delegation, configuring, 59

Content Classifier option (classification methods), 114

content servers, configuring BranchCache, 87–89

Create Central Access Rule page, 118–119

Create Claim Type page, 105–106

Create Classification Rule dialog box, 112–113

Create Cluster Wizard, 21

creating

  certificate templates, 329

  classification rules, 111–112

  custom fields, IPAM, 252–254

  DHCP split scopes, 222–223

  DHCP superscopes, 217

  failover clusters, 20–23

  IP address range groups, 254–255

  selected resource properties, 107–108

  site links, 287–289

  Windows Azure Backup accounts, 163

Credential Security Support Provider (CredSSP), 58

CredSSP (Credential Security Support Provider), 58

CRL Distribution Points (CDPs), 322–323

CRLs (Certificate Revocation Lists), 322

cryptographic keys, DNSSEC, 229
cryptographic service provider (CSP), 337
CSP (cryptographic service provider), 337
CSVFS (Cluster Shared Volume File System), 29
CSVs (cluster-shared volumes), 29–31
  moving VM storage to, 60–63
custom fields, creating in IPAM, 252–254
Customize Message For Access Denied Errors policy
    setting, 117

D

DAC (Dynamic Access Control), 100–122
  access policies, 118–122
      creating a central access poilicy that includes
          claims, 118–121
      deploying central access policy to the
          servers, 122
  claims-based authentication, 103–106
      defining user and device claims types, 104–105
      enabling Kerberos support, 106
  file classification, 107–118
      adding resource properties to resource
          properties list, 108
      classifying files and folders, 110–118
      enabling/creating selected resource
          properties, 107–108
      updating Active Directory file and folder
          objects, 109–110
  introduction, 101–103
database storage, IPAM, 258
Data Deduplication, 139–142
DDPEval.exe (Deduplication Data Evaluation Tool), 141
Debugging Mode option (Advanced Boot Options
    menu), 176
Debug Logging tab, DNS server proeprties, 232
Dedicated IP Addresses setting, New Cluster: Host
    Parameters page, 6
Deduplication Data Evaluation Tool (DDPEval.exe), 141
Default-First-Site-Name, 284
default locations, Enterprise CAs, 322
delegated administration, DNS, 232–233
Delta CRLs, 322
deployment
  certificate management, 334
  enterprise root CAs, 319–320
  enterprise subordinate CAs, 320

Federation Server role, 310
IPAM, 239–258
  database storage, 258
  installation and configuration, 240–249
  managing address space, 250–258
  purpose and functionality, 239–240
standalone subordinate CAs, 321
stnadalone root CAs, 320–321
destination, backups, 157–158
device claims types, DAC, 104–105
DFSR (Distributed File System Replication), upgrading
    SYSVOL replication to, 300
DHCID (Dynamic Host Configuration Identifier), 225
DHCP solutions, 215–225
  configuring DNS registration, 223–224
  DHCPv6, 218–221
  high availability, 222–224
  multicast scopes, 218
  Name Protection, 224–225
  superscopes, 216–217
DHCPv6, 218–221
dialog boxes
  Add/Edit Port Rule, 8–9, 10–11
  Add Initiator ID, 132
  Add Or Edit Server, 246–247
  Advanced Password Replication Policy, 297
  Advanced Security Settings For Permissions, 120
  Advanced Settings
      Exclusions tab, 156
      VSS Settings tab, 157–158
  Central Access Policies Configuration, 122
  Central Access Rule, 119–120
  Classification Parameters, 114–115
  Cluster-Aware Updating, 35–36
  Configure Custom Fields, 253
  Configure Discovery Settings, 244
  Configure IP Address Utilization Threshold, 257
  Create Classification Rule, 112–113
  File Properties, 161–162
  Hyper-V Settings, 58, 186–187
  IPAM Settings, 252–253
  Move Server, 291–292
  Move Virtual Machine Storage, 60–61
  Name Protection, 225
  Optimize Backup Performance, 158
  Permission Entry For Permissions, 120
  Select Items, 155–156
  Select Resource Properties, 108

Select Services, 51

Digest authentication, 280

digital certificates, DNSSEC, 229

direction of trust, specifying, 276–277

Directory services database (AD RMS), 341

Disable Automatic Restart on System Failure option
(Advanced Boot Options menu), 176

Disable Driver Signature Enforcement option (Advanced
Boot Options menu), 177

Disable Dynamic Updates for DNS PTR Records option,
configuring DNS registration, 224

Disable Early Launch Anti-Malware Driver option
(Advanced Boot Options menu), 177

Disable-NlbClusterPortRule cmdlet, 12

disaster recovery

    backups, 151–170

        Backup Operators, 160

        Shadow Copies feature, 160–162

        Windows Azure Backup feature, 162–170

        Windows Server Backup feature, 152–159

    configuring site-level fault tolerance, 186–207

        Global Update Manager, 205

        Hyper-V physical host servers, 186–190

        Hyper-V Replica Extended Replication, 204–205

        Hyper-V Replica failover options, 197–201

        Hyper-V Replica in a failover cluster, 201–205

        recovering multi-site failover clusters, 206

        VMs (virtual machines), 190–197

    server recovery, 174–183

        Advanced Boot Option menu, 174–176

        booting into Safe Mode, 177–178

        installation media, 178–183

Discard A And PTR Records When Lease Is Deleted
option, configuring DNS registration, 224

Distributed Cache mode, BranchCache, 86, 90–91

Distributed File System Replication (DFSR), upgrading
SYSVOL replication to, 300

DNS

    configuring registration, 223–224

DnsAdmins domain local group, 233

DNSKEY records, 230

DNSSEC, 229–230

DNS Socket Pool, 230

DNS solutions, 228–236

    analyzing zone-level statistics, 235–236

    configuring cache locking, 230–231

    configuring logging, 231–232

    delegated administration, 232–233

    DNSSEC, 229–230

    DNS Socket Pool, 230

    GlobalNames zones, 235

    netmask ordering, 234–235

    recursion, 233–234

Domain Admins group, 233

domain controllers

    moving between sites, 291–292

    RODCs. *See* RODCs (Read Only Domain Controllers)

domains, configuring

    interoperability with previous versions of AD, 270–
271

    multi-domain AD environments, 268–269

    multi-forest AD environments, 269–270

    multiple UPN siffixes, 272–273

    upgrading existing forests and domains, 271–272

downloading

    Windows Azure Backup Agent, 164

drain on shutdown, VM migration, 73

Drainstop function, 14

Duplicate Files reports, 94

Dynamic Access Control. *See* DAC (Dynamic Access
Control)

Dynamically Update DNS Records For DHCP Clients
That Do Not Request Updates option,
configuring DNS registration, 224

Dynamic Host Configuration Identifier (DHCID), 225

E

Edit rights, 339

Edit Rights rights, 339

Enable Access-Denied Assistance On Client For All File
Types policy setting, 117

Enable-ADFSDeviceRegistration cmdlet, 314

Enable Automatic Hosted Cache Discovery By Service
Connection Point policy setting, 92

Enable-BCDistributed cmdlet, 90

Enable-BCHostedClient cmdlet, 91

Enable-BCHostedServer cmdlet, 89

Enable Boot Logging option (Advanced Boot Options
menu), 176

Enable DNS Dynamic Updates According To The
Settings Below option, configuring DNS
registration, 224

Enable Low-Resolution Video option (Advanced Boot
Options menu), 176

Enable-NlbClusterPortRule cmdlet, 12
Enable Replication wizard, 191
enabling
    bandwidth throttling, Windows Azure Backup
        feature, 169–170
    certificate templates, 329
    device authentication, 314–315
    DHCP Name Protection, 224–225
    hash publication, 88–89
    iSCSI Initiator, 128
    Kerberos (HTTP), 187
    Kerberos support for claims-based access
        control, 106–107
    selected resource properties, 107–108
    Workplace Join, 314
enabling firewall rules, VM monitoring, 50
enrollment, certificate management, 331–332
Enterprise Admins group, 233
enterprise CAs, installation, 318–322
Evaluation Type tab (Create Classification Rule dialog
    box), 116
Event Logging tab, DNS server properties, 231
exclusion policies, AD RMS, 340
exclusions, backups, 156
Exclusions tab (Advanced Settings dialog box), 156
expiration policy, 340
Export-BCCachePackage cmdlet, 89
Export rights, 339
Extended Replication, Hyper-V Replica, 204–205
external trusts, configuring, 277–278
Extract rights, 339

F

failback settings, failover clustering, 47
failed migrations, VMs, 66
failover
    Hyper-V Replica options, 197–201
    TCP/IP settings, 195–196
failover clustering, 17–39
    Active Directory Detached Clusters, 24–25
    CAU (Cluster Aware Updating), 34–38
    cluster networking settings, 23–24
    cluster storage, 25–32
    creating clusters, 20–23
    fundamentals, 18–20
    installation, 20

migration, 38–39
Quorum, 32–33
roles, 42–53
    assigning startup priorities, 48–49
    configuring, 42–48
    monitoring services on clustered virtual
        machines, 50–53
    node drain, 49
Failover Cluster Manager, 201
failover settings, failover clustering, 47
Faster Backup Performance, 159
fault tolerance, 186–207
    configuring Hyper-V physical host servers, 186–190
    configuring VMs (virtual machines), 190–197
        failover TCP/IP settings, 195–196
        resynchronizing primary and replica VMs, 196–
            197
    Hyper-V Replica Extended Replication, 204–205
    Hyper-V Replica failover options, 197–201
    Hyper-V Replica in a failover cluster, 201–205
    recovering multi-site failover clusters, 206
feature files, removing (Feature on Demand), 137
Features on Demand, 136–139
federated relationships. See AD FS
Federation Server Proxy role, 310
Federation Server role, deployment, 310
file access auditing, 95–96, 118
File And Storage Services role
    Data Deduplication, 139–142
    iSCSI Target Server component, 127–128
file classification, DAC, 107–118
    adding resource properties to resource properties
        list, 108
    classifying files and folders, 110–118
    enabling/creating selected resource
        properties, 107–108
    updating Active Directory file and folder
        objects, 109–110
file management tasks, FSRM, 95
file objects, classifying, 110–118
    access-denied assistance, 117
    automatic classification, 111–116
    manual classification, 110–111
File Properties dialog box, 161–162
Files by File Group reports, 94
Files By Owner reports, 94
Files By Property reports, 94
File Screening Audit reports, 94

file screens, FSRM, 93
File Server For General Use (file server type), 44
File Server role types, configuring failover clustering roles, 44–45
File Service Resource Manager. *See* FSRM
file services, configuring, 83–97
  BranchCache, 84–92
    clients for Distributed Cache mode, 90–91
    clients for Hosted Cache mode, 91–92
    content servers, 87–89
    Distributed Cache mode, 86
    Hosted Cache mode, 85
    hosted cache servers, 89–90
  DAC
    access policies, 118–122
    claims-based authentication, 103–106
    file classification, 107–118
  file access auditing, 95–96
  FSRM (File Server Resource Manager), 92–95
    file management tasks, 95
    file screens, 93
    quotas, 94
    storage reports, 94–95
  installation of Server for NFS, 96–97
Filtering Mode option, Add/Edit Port Rule page, 9
firewall rules, VM monitoring, 50
Flexible Single Master Operations (FSMO) roles, 271
Folder Classifier option (classification methods), 114
folder objects, classifying, 110–118
  access-denied assistance, 117
  automatic classification, 111–116
  manual classification, 110–111
Folders By Property reports, 94
Forefront Threat Management Gateway (TMG), 2
forests, configuring
  interoperability with previous versions of AD, 270–271
  multi-domain AD environments, 268–269
  multi-forest AD environments, 269–270
  multiple UPN siffixes, 272–273
  upgrading existing forests and domains, 271–272
forest trusts, configuring, 278–279
forest-wide authentication, 278
Forms Authentication, 313
Forward rights, 339
FSMO (Flexible Single Master Operations) roles, 271
FSRM (File Server Resource Manager), 92–95
  file management tasks, 95

  file screens, 93
  quotas, 94
  storage reports, 94–95
Full Backup, 159
Full Control rights, 339
fundamentals
  failover clustering, 18–20
  NLB, 2–3

G

General tab (Create Classification Rule dialog box), 112
Generate Passphrase option, 165
Generic Application role, 44
Get-BCStatus cmdlet, 89
Get-Command -Module WindowsServerBackup command-line tool, 160
Get-DnsServerStatistics cmdlet, 235
Get-NlbCluster cmdlet, 12
Get-NlbClusterNode cmdlet, 13
Get-NlbClusterNodeDip cmdlet, 13
Get-NlbClusterNodeNetworkInterface cmdlet, 13
Get-NlbClusterPortRule cmdlet, 13
Get-NlbClusterVip cmdlet, 13
Get-WindowsFeature cmdlet, 137
global authentication policy, configuring, 312
GlobalNames zones, 235
Global Resource Property List, 108
Global Update Manager, 205
GPOs (Group Policy Objects)
  IPAM, 246
GPT (GUID Partition Table) partition style, 26
Group Managed Service Accounts, 270
Group Policy
  configuring access-denied assistance, 117
  deploying central access policies to servers, 122
  enabling Kerberos support for claims, 106
  provisioning the IPAM Server, 242–243
  User Rights Assignment, 160
Group Policy Objects (GPOs)
  IPAM, 246
GUID Partition Table (GPT) partition style, 26

H

Handling Priority setting, editing port rules, 10–11

hard quotas, 94
hardware requirements
    failover clustering, 19–20
hash publication, enabling, 88–89
heartbeat setting thresholds, 48
high availability
    failover clustering, 17–39
        Active Directory Detached Clusters, 24–25
        CAU (Cluster Aware Updating), 34–38
        cluster networking settings, 23–24
        cluster storage, 25–32
        configuring roles, 42–53
        creating clusters, 20–23
        fundamentals, 18–20
        migration, 38–39
        Quorum, 32–33
    NLB, 1–14
        fundamentals, 2–3
        NLB clusters, 3–7
        port rules, 8–13
        upgrading clusters, 14
    VM migration, 56–73
        drain on shutdown feature, 73
        enabling processor compatability, 66–68
        live migrations, 57–66
        matching names of virtual switches, 68–70
        network health protection, 72–73
        storage migration, 70–72
high availability, DHCP, 222–224
High Availability Wizard, 42–43, 201
historical naming structure, domains, 268
Hosted Cache mode, BranchCache, 85, 91–92
hosted cache servers, configuring BranchCache, 89–90
Host Parameters page (New Cluster Wizard), 5
Hot Standby Mode, configuring DHCP failover, 222
Hyper-V Replica
    configuring site-level fault tolerance, 186–207
        Extended Replication, 204–205
        failover cluster, 201–205
        failover options, 197–201
        Global Update Manager, 205
        physical host servers, 186–190
        VMs (virtual machines), 190–197
Hyper-V Replica Broker role, 201
Hyper-V Replica HTTP Listener (TCP-In), 187
Hyper-V Settings, configuring, 57
Hyper-V Settings dialog box, 58, 186–187

I

IGMP Multicast mode, NLB cluster operation, 7
implementation
    AD CS, 318–326
        administrative role separation, 323–324
        CA backup and recovery, 325
        CRL Distribution Points, 322–323
        installing an enterprise CA, 318–322
        online responders, 323–324
    AD FS, 309–316
        authentication policies, 312–313
        claims-based authentication, 310–313
        installation, 310
        multi-factor authentication, 315–316
        Workplace Join, 313–314
    advanced DHCP solutions, 215–225
        configuring DNS registration, 223–224
        DHCPv6, 218–221
        high availability, 222–224
        multicast scopes, 218
        Name Protection, 224–225
        superscopes, 216–217
    advanced DNS solutions, 228–236
        analyzing zone-level statistics, 235–236
        configuring cache locking, 230–231
        configuring logging, 231–232
        delegated administration, 232–233
        DNSSEC, 229–230
        DNS Socket Pool, 230
        GlobalNames zones, 235
        netmask ordering, 234–235
        recursion, 233–234
    DAC, 100–122
        access policies, 118–122
        claims-based authentication, 103–106
        file classification, 107–118
        introduction, 101–103
    file access auditing, 95–96
Import-BCCachePackage cmdlet, 90
Incremental Backup, 159
information security
    AD CS, 318–326
        administrative role separation, 323–324
        CA backup and recovery, 325
        CRL Distribution Points, 322–323
        installing an enterprise CA, 318–322
        online responders, 323–324

AD FS, 309–316
    authentication policies, 312–313
    claims-based authentication, 310–313
    installation, 310
    multi-factor authentication, 315–316
    Workplace Join, 313–314
AD RMS, 337–342
    backing up and restoring, 341–342
    exclusion policies, 340
    installing a licensing or certificate AD RMS
        server, 337–338
    SCP (Service Connection Point), 338–339
    templates, 339–340
certificate management, 328–334
    certificate deployment, 334
    Certificate Templates, 328–329
    enrollment, 331–332
    key archival and recovery, 332–333
    renewal, 332–333
    validation and revocation, 330–331
Initial Host State setting, New Cluster: Host Parameters
    page, 6
Initialize-ADFSDeviceRegistration cmdlet, 314
installation
    AD FS, 310
    AD RMS
        installing a licensing or certificate AD RMS
            server, 337–338
    BranchCache For Network Files component, 88
    enterprise CAs, 318–322
    Failover Clustering, 20
    IPAM, 240–249
    iSCSI Target Server, 127–128
    NLB (Network Load Balancing), 3
    online responders, 323–324
    Server for NFS, 96–97
    Windows Azure Backup Agent, 164
    Windows Server Backup feature, 152
installation media, server recovery, 178–183
    command-line recovery tools, 182–183
    System Image Recovery, 181–182
Install-WindowsFeature BranchCache cmdlet, 87
Install-WindowsFeature cmdlet, 3, 137
Install-WindowsFeature FS-BranchCache cmdlet, 88
Install-WindowsFeature FS-NFS-Services cmdlet, 96
Install-WindowsFeature IPAM cmdlet, 240
Install-WindowsFeature Windows-Server-Backup
    cmdlet, 152

Internet iStorage Name Service (iSNS Server), 136
interoperability, configuring with previous versions of
    AD, 270–271
Invoke-Gpupdate cmdlet, 247
Invoke-IpamGpoProvisioning cmdlet, 246
IP addresses
    applying custom fields to, 254
    creating custom fields, 252–254
    creating range groups, 254–255
    delegating IPAM administration, 258
    finding and allocating from a range, 255–256
    viewing and configuring utilization thresholds, 256–
        257
IP Address Management. *See* IPAM
IPAM, 239–258
    database storage, 258
    installation and configuration, 240–249
    managing address space, 250–258
    purpose and functionality, 239–240
IPAM Settings dialog box, 252–253
IPv6 protocol flags, 220
IQN (iSCSI qualified name), 129
iSCSI Initiator
    configuring, 133
    enabling, 128
iSCSI qualified name (IQN), 129
iSCSI storage, 126–142
    components, 128–129
    configuring iSCSI Initiator, 133
    configuring new disks on remote servers, 134
    enabling iSCSI Initiator, 128
    installing iSCSI Target Server, 127
    iSNS Server, 136
    local storage servers, 129–132
    managing virtual disks and targets, 135–136
iSCSI Target Server, installation, 127–128
iSNS Server (Internet iStorage Name Service), 136
Issue And Manage Certificates permission, 324

K

/kcc switch, repadmin command-line tool, 299–300
KCC (Knowledge Consistency Checker), 299
KDC (Key Distribution Center), support for claims, 270
Kerberos, 58–59
    support for claims-based access control, 106–107
Kerberos (HTTP), enabling, 187

Kerberos tokens, DAC, 103
Kerberos V5 authentication protocol, 280
key archival, certificate management, 332–333
Key Compromise, revoking certificates, 330
Key Distribution Center (KDC), support for claims, 270
Key Recovery Agent (KRA) certificate template, 333
Key Signing Key (KSK), 229
Knowledge Consistency Checker (KCC), 299
KRA (Key Recovery Agent) certificate template, 333
KSK (Key Signing Key), 229

L

Large Files reports, 94
Last Known Good Configuration option (Advanced Boot
    Options menu), 176
Least Recently Accessed Files reports, 95
license expiration, configuring, 340
limitations, IPAM, 240
live migrations
    virtual machines, 57–66
        moving VM storage to a CSV, 60–63
        nonclustered live migration, 63–66
        preparations, 58–60
Load Sharing Mode, configuring DHCP failover, 222
Load Weight setting, editing port rules, 10–11
Local Computer Policy
    User Rights Assignment, 160
Local Drives option (backup destination), 158
local security groups, IPAM server, 258
local storage servers, configuring iSCSI storage, 129–
    132
Locator Records, 290–291
Lockbox Exclusions, 340
Logging database (AD RMS), 341
logging, DNS, 231–232
logical unit number (LUN) 18, 128
LUN (logical unit number) 18, 128

M

MADCAP (Multicast Address Dynamic Client Allocation
    Protocol), 218
Makecert.exe command-line utility, 163
Manage CA permission, 324
managed address configuration flag (M-flag), 220

management
    AD replication, 298–300
    backups, 151–170
        Backup Operators, 160
        Shadow Copies feature, 160–162
        Windows Azure Backup feature, 162–170
        Windows Server Backup feature, 152–159
    high availability
        failover clustering, 17–39, 42–53
        NLB, 1–14
        virtual machine migration, 56–73
    IPAM, 239–258
        database storage, 258
        installation and configuration, 240–249
        managing address space, 250–258
        purpose and functionality, 239–240
    iSCSI virtual disk options, 135
    registration of SRV records, 290–291
management certificates, 163
manual classification, classifying files and folders, 110–
    111
manual configuration, IPAM servers, 248–249
Master Boot Record (MBR), 182
Master Boot Record (MBR) partition style, 26
matching names of virtual switches, VM migration, 68–
    70
MBR (Master Boot Record), 182
MBR (Master Boot Record) partition style, 26
M flag (managed address configuration flag), 220
Microsoft's Windows Azure Multi-Factor Authentication
    service, 315
Migrate a Cluster Wizard, 38–39
migrating clients, DHCP superscopes, 217
migration
    failover clusters, 38–39
    virtual machines, 56–73
        drain on shutdown, 73
        enabling processor compatability, 66–68
        live migrations, 57–66
        matching names of virtual switches, 68–70
        network health protection, 72–73
        storage migration, 70–72
Mobile App multi-factor authentication, 315
monitoring
    AD replication, 298–300
Most Recently Accessed Files reports, 95
Move Server dialog box, 291–292
Move Virtual Machine Storage dialog box, 60–62

Move Wizard, 70
moving domain controllers between sites, 291–292
Msconfig (System Configuration Utility), booting into
    Safe Mode, 177–178
Multicast Address Dynamic Client Allocation Protocol
    (MADCAP), 218
Multicast mode, NLB cluster operation, 7
multicast scopes, DHCP, 218
multi-domain AD environments, configuring, 268–269
multi-factor authentication, AD FS, 315–316
Multi-Factor Authentication service, 315
multi-forest AD environments, configuring, 269–270
Multiple Host filtering mode, Add/Edit Port Rule
    page, 9
multi-site failover clusters, 206

N

Name Protection, DHCP, 224–225
Name Protection dialog box, 225
Name Resolution Policy Table (NRPT), 230
name suffix routing, configuring, 281–282
netmask ordering, DNS, 234–235
Netsh command, 219
Net Use command, 179
Network File System (NFS)
    Server for NFS component, 96–97
network health protection, VM migration, 72–73
Network Load Balancing. *See* NLB (Network Load
    Balancing)
network services
    advanced DHCP solutions, 215–225
        configuring DNS registration, 223–224
        high availability, 222–224
        implementing DHCPv6, 218–221
        multicast scopes, 218
        Name Protection, 224–225
        superscopes, 216–217
    advanced DNS solutions, 228–236
        analyzing zone-level statistics, 235–236
        configuring cache locking, 230–231
        configuring logging, 231–232
        delegated administration, 232–233
        DNSSEC, 229–230
        DNS Socket Pool, 230

GlobalNames zones, 235
    netmask ordering, 234–235
    recursion, 233–234
IPAM, 239–258
    database storage, 258
    installation and configuration, 240–249
    managing address space, 250–258
    purpose and functionality, 239–240
New Cluster Wizard, 4
New-IscsiServerTarget cmdlet, 131
New iSCSI Virtual Disk Wizard, 129–132
New-NlbCluster cmdlet, 13
New Storage Pool Wizard, 28
Next Secure (NSEC/NSEC3) records, 230
NFS (Network File System)
    Server for NFS component, 96–97
NLB (Network Load Balancing), 1–14
    creating and configuring clusters, 3–7
    fundamentals, 2–3
    installation, 3
    port rules, 8–13
        adding hosts in an NLB cluster, 12
        cmdlets for Windows PowerShell, 12–13
    upgrading clusters, 14
node drain, failover clustering roles, 49
Node Majority configuration (Quorum), 32
nodes, failover clusters, 18
nonclustered live migration, VMs, 63–66
Normal Backup Performance, 159
NRPT (Name Resolution Policy Table), 230
NSEC/NSEC3 (Next Secure) records, 230

O

O-flag (other address configuration flag), 220
one-way incoming trusts, 276
one-way outgoing trusts, 276
online responders, installation, 323–324
optimal utilization, IP addresses, 256
Optimize Backup Performance dialog box, 158
other address configuration flag (O-flag), 220
overutilization thresholds, IP addresses, 256–257
Overview page, Server Manager, 241–249

P

partitioned clusters, 206
passive screening, 93
Password Replication Policies (PRPs), 295
performance settings, backup operations, 158–159
Permission Entry For Permissions dialog box, 120
permissions, configuring CAs, 324–325
Phone Call multi-factor authentication, 315
physical host servers, Hyper-V, 186–190
planned failovers, Hyper-V Replica, 197–198
Port Range and Protocols option, Add/Edit Port Rule
      page, 9
port rules, NLB, 8–13
    adding hosts in an NLB cluster, 12
    cmdlets for Windows PowerShell, 12–13
ports, configuring trusts, 280
PowerShell, Windows
    Add-WindowsFeature FS-iSCSTarget-Server
        cmdlet, 127
    Backup-CARoleService cmdlet, 326
    Enable-ADFSDeviceRegistration cmdlet, 314
    Enable-BCDistributed cmdlet, 90
    Enable-BCHostedClient cmdlet, 91
    Enable-BCHostedServer cmdlet, 89
    Export-BCCachePackage cmdlet, 89
    Get-BCStatus cmdlet, 89
    Get-DnsServerStatistics cmdlet, 235
    Get-WindowsFeature cmdlet, 137
    Import-BCCachePackage cmdlet, 90
    Initialize-ADFSDeviceRegistration cmdlet, 314
    Install-WindowsFeature BranchCache cmdlet, 87
    Install-WindowsFeature cmdlet, 137
    Install-WindowsFeature FS-BranchCache cmdlet, 88
    Install-WindowsFeature FS-NFS-Services cmdlet, 96
    Install-WindowsFeature IPAM cmdlet, 240
    Install-WindowsFeature Windows-Server-Backup
        cmdlet, 152
    Invoke-Gpupdate cmdlet, 247
    Invoke-IpamGpoProvisioning cmdlet, 246
    New IscsiServerTarget cmdlet, 131
    NLB cmdlets, 12–13
    Publish-BCFileContent cmdlet, 89
    Publish-BCWebContent cmdlet, 89
    Restore-CARoleService cmdlet, 326
    Set-DNSServerCache cmdlet, 231
    Set-FileStorageTier cmdlet, 142
    Set-NetIPInterface cmdlet, 219
    Set-NetRoute cmdlet, 219
    Uninstall-WindowsFeature cmdlet, 137

/pq switch (cluster.exe command), 206
predefined resource properties, 108–109
preferred owners settings, failover clustering, 45–46
Prepopulate Passwords button, 297
Previous Versions feature, 160
Previous Versions tab (File Properties dialog box), 161–
      162
principal, defined, 120
Print rights, 339
Priority (Unique Host Identifier) setting, New Cluster:
      Host Parameters page, 6
processor compatability
    VM migration, 66–68
properties
    configuring failover clustering roles, 45–48
Protected Users, 270
provisioning IPAM Server, 242–243
proxy server/firewall farms, 2
/prp switch, repadmin command-line tool, 300
PRPs (Password Replication Policies), 295
Publish-BCFileContent cmdlet, 89
Publish-BCWebContent cmdlet, 89

Q

/queue switch, repadmin command-line tool, 300
Quorum, 32–33
quotas, FSRM, 94
Quota Usage reports, 95

R

Read-Only Domain Controllers. See RODCs (Read Only
      Domain Controllers)
Read permission, 324
Recover Data option (Windows Azure Backup
      feature), 168–169
recovering servers, 174–183
    Advanced Boot Options menu, 174–176
    booting into Safe Mode, 177–178
    installation media, 178–183
        command-line recovery tools, 182–183
        System Image Recovery, 181–182
recovery
    CAs (Certificate Authorities), 325
    certificate management, 332–333

recovery vault, Windows Azure Backup feature, 163
recursion, DNS, 233–234
regex (regular expressions), 115
registering servers, Windows Azure Backup feature, 164–165
Register Server Wizard, 164–165
registration
   SRV records, 290–291
registration, DNS, 223–224
regular expressions (regex), 115
reinstalling feature files, 138
relative identifiers (RIDs), 268
relying party trusts, configuring, 311–312
Remote Access role, 310
Remote Desktop Server farms, 2
Remote Shared Folder option (backup destination), 158
Remove-NlbCluster cmdlet, 13
Remove-NlbClusterNode cmdlet, 13
Remove-NlbClusterNodeDip cmdlet, 13
Remove-NlbClusterPortRule cmdlet, 13
Remove-NlbClusterVip cmdlet, 13
Remove-WindowsFeature cmdlet, 3
removing
   feature files (Feature on Demand), 137
renewal, certificate management, 332–333
Renew Expired Certificates option, 332
repadmin command-line tool, 298–299
Repair Your Computer option (Advanced Boot Options menu), 176
/replicate switch, repadmin command-line tool, 300
replicate-single-object (RSO) operations, 295
replication, configuring
   RODCs, 294–297
   SYSVOL, 300
replication settings, Hyper-V hosts, 186–190
/replsingleobj switch, repadmin command-line tool, 300
replsummary option, repadmin command-line tool, 298–299
Reply All rights, 339
Reply rights, 339
Request Certificates permission, 324
resource properties
   defined, 101
resource properties, domain controllers, 107–108
Resource Record Signature (RRSIG) records, 229
resource records, implementing DNSSEC, 229–230
Restore-CARoleService cmdlet, 326

restoring AD RMS, 341–342
Resume-NlbCluster cmdlet, 13
Resume-NlbClusterNode cmdlet, 13
Resume Replication option, 200
retention range, 166
retention settings, 166
Reverse Replication Wizard, 199–200
revocation, certificate management, 330–331
RIDs (relative identifiers), 268
RMS encryption, 117
RODCs (Read Only Domain Controllers), configuring replication, 294–297
roles
   failover clustering, 42–53
      assigning startup priorities, 48–49
      configuring, 42–48
      monitoring services on clustered virtual machines, 50–53
      node drain, 49
rolling upgrades, NLB clusters, 14
Root CAs, 319–320
RRSIG (Resource Record Signature) records, 229
RSO (replicate-single-object) operations, 295

S

Safe Mode option (Advanced Boot Options menu), 176
Safe Modes, server recovery, 177–178
Safe Mode With Command Prompt option (Advanced Boot Options menu), 176
Safe Mode With Networking option (Advanced Boot Options menu), 176
Save rights, 339
Scale-Out File Server For Application Data (file server type), 44
Scale-Out File Server role, 31
Scale-Out File Servers (SoFS), 44
Schannel authentication, 280
Schedule Backup Wizard, 165–167
schedule, classification rules, 116
scheduling backups, 165–167
sConfigure Hosted Cache Servers policy setting, 92
scope, classification rules, 112–113
Scope tab (Create Classification Rule dialog box), 112–113
SCP (Service Connection Point), 338–339
Secure Boot feature, 177

security
    AD CS, 318–326
        administrative role separation, 323–324
        CA backup and recovery, 325
        CRL Distribution Points, 322–323
        installing an enterprise CA, 318–322
        online responders, 323–324
    AD FS, 309–316
        authentication policies, 312–313
        claims-based authentication, 310–313
        installation, 310
        multi-factor authentication, 315–316
        Workplace Join, 313–314
    AD RMS, 337–342
        backing up and restoring, 341–342
        exclusion policies, 340
        installing a licensing or certificate AD RMS
            server, 337–338
        SCP (Service Connection Point), 338–339
        templates, 339–340
    certificate management, 328–334
        certificate deployment, 334
        Certificate Templates, 328–329
        enrollment, 331–332
        key archival and recovery, 332–333
        renewal, 332–333
        validation and revocation, 330–331
security groups, IPAM server, 258
Security IDentifier (SID) filtering, configuring, 280
Security tab, DNS server properties, 233
Select Backup Configuration page (Windows Server
        Backup feature), 153
selected resource properties, domain controllers, 107–
        108
Select iSCSI Virtual Disk Location page (New iSCSI
        Virtual Disk Wizard), 131
Select Items dialog box, 155–156
Select Items For Backup page (Windows Server Backup
        feature), 154–157
selective authentication, 278
Select Resource Properties dialog box, 108
Select Services dialog box, 51
self-signed client certificates, 163
self-updating mode, Cluster-Aware Updating, 36–37
Server for NFS, installation, 96–97
SERVER INVENTORY page, IPAM client of Server
        Manager, 245
Server Message Block (SMB) protocol, 96

servers
    recovery, 174–183
        Advanced Boot Option menu, 174–176
        booting into Safe Mode, 177–178
        installation media, 178–183
    registering, Windows Azure Backup feature, 164–
        165
Service Connection Point (SCP), 338–339
Set BranchCache Hosted Cache mode policy setting, 92
Set-DNSServerCache cmdlet, 231
Set-FileStorageTier cmdlet, 142
Set-NetIPInterface cmdlet, 219
Set-NetRoute cmdlet, 219
Set-NlbCluster cmdlet, 13
Set-NlbClusterNode cmdlet, 13
Set-NlbClusterNodeDip cmdlet, 13
Set-NlbClusterPortRule cmdlet, 13
Set-NlbClusterPortRuleNodeHandlingPriority
        cmdlet, 13
Set-NlbClusterPortRuleNodeWeight cmdlet, 13
Set-NlbClusterVip cmdlet, 13
Set-Service msiscsi cmdlet, 128
Set-VMProcessor VMname cmdlet, 67
Shadow Copies feature, 160–162
shared virtual hard disks, failover cluster storage, 31–32
shortcut trusts, configuring, 279
/showrepl option, repadmin command-line tool, 299
Shutdown /r /o command, 175
side-by-side store, 136
SID (Security IDentifier) filtering, configuring, 280
Single Host filtering mode, Add/Edit Port Rule page, 10
single-label name resolution, 235
single sign-on (SSO), Workplace Join, 314
site-level fault tolerance, 186–207
    configuring Hyper-V physical host servers, 186–190
    configuring VMs (virtual machines), 190–197
        failover TCP/IP settings, 195–196
        resynchronizing primary and replica VMs, 196–
        197
    Global Update Manager, 205
    Hyper-V Replica Extended Replication, 204–205
    Hyper-V Replica failover options, 197–201
    Hyper-V Replica in a failover cluster, 201–205
    recovering multi-site failover clusters, 206
site links (AD), creating and configuring, 287–289
sites (AD), configuring, 284–292
    moving domain controllers between sites, 291–292
    registration of SRV records, 290–291

site links, 287–289

sites and subnets, 284–286

Sites And Services console, Active Directory, 284–285

SLAAC (stateless address autoconfiguration), 219

SMB (Server Message Block) protocol, 96

Socket Pool, DNS, 230

SoFS (Scale-Out File Servers), 44

soft quotas, 94

software requirements, failover clustering, 20

Specify Connection Parameters page (Enable Replication wizard), 191–192

Specify Replica Server page (Enable Replication wizard), 191

Specify Retention Setting page (Schedule Backup Wizard), 166

split brain clusters, 206

split clusters, 206

Split-Scope Configuration Wizard (DHCP), 223–224

SRV records, registration, 290–291

SSO (single sign-on), Workplace Join, 314

standalone root CAs, 320–321

standalone subordinate CAs, 321–322

Start-NlbCluster cmdlet, 13

Start-NlbClusterNode cmdlet, 13

Startrep command-line recovery tool, 182

Start-Service msiscsi cmdlet, 128

startup priority settings, failover clustering roles, 48–49

stateful addressing, DHCPv6 and, 220

stateless address autoconfiguration (SLAAC), 219

statistics, DNS servers, 235–236

Stop-NlbCluster cmdlet, 13

Stop-NlbClusterNode cmdlet, 13

storage

    failover clusters, 25–32

        adding new disks to a cluster, 25–27

        creating storage pools, 28–29

        CSVs (cluster-shared volumes), 29–31

        shared virtual hard disks, 31–32

    IPAM databases, 258

storage migration, VMs, 70–72

storage reports, FSRM, 94–95

storage requirements, failover clustering, 19

storage services, configuring, 126–143

    Data Deduplication, 139–142

    Features on Demand, 136–139

    iSCSI storage, 126–142

        components, 128–129

        configuring iSCSI Initiator, 133

        configuring new disks on remote servers, 134

        enabling iSCSI Initiator, 128

        installing iSCSI Target Server, 127–128

        iSNS Server, 136

        local storage servers, 129–132

        managing virtual disks and targets, 135–136

    storage tiers, 142

Storage Spaces feature, 28

storage tiers, 142

subnets, configuring, 284–286

subordinate CAs, 320

superscopes, DHCP, 216–217

Superseded, revoking certificates, 330

Suspend-ClusterNode cmdlet, 49

Suspend-NlbCluster cmdlet, 13

Suspend-NlbClusterNode cmdlet, 13

System Center 2012 R2 Data Protection Manager, 164

System Configuration Utility (Msconfig), booting into Safe Mode, 177–178

System Image Recovery, configuring, 181–182

System State option (Select Items dialog box), 155

SYSVOL replication

    upgrading to DFSR, 300

T

targets, ISCSI, 128

TCP/IP settings, configuring VMs, 195–196

templates

    AD RMS, 339–340

Test-Cluster cmdlet, 21

test failovers, Hyper-V Replica, 200–201

Text Message multi-factor authentication, 315

Timeout setting, 10

trust anchor key, DNSSEC, 229

trust authentication, configuring, 280–281

trusted domains, defined, 276

trust groups, 189

trusting domains, defined, 276

trusts

    claims-provider, configuring, 312–313

    relying party, configuring, 311–312

trusts, configuring, 276–281

    external trusts, 277–278

    forest trusts, 278–279

    name suffix routing, 281–282

    shortcut trusts, 279

SID filtering, 280
trust authentication, 280–281
trust concepts, 276–277
trust transitivity, defined, 276
two-way trusts, 276

U

underutilization thresholds, IP addresses, 256–257
Unicast mode, NLB cluster operation, 7
Uninstall-WindowsFeature cmdlet, 3, 137
unplanned failovers, Hyper-V Replica, 198–200
Unspecified reason, revoking certificates, 330
Update-FSRMClassificationPropertyDefinition
      cmdlet, 109
upgrading
    existing forests and domains, 271–272
    NLB clusters, 14
    SYSVOL replication to DFSR, 300
UPN (user principal name) suffixes, configuring, 272–
    273
user claims types, DAC, 104–105
User Exclusions, 340
user principal name (UPN) suffixes, configuring, 272–
    273
User Rights Assignment, 160

V

Validate A Configuration Wizard, 21
validation, certificate management, 330–331
View rights, 339
View Rights rights, 339
virtual disks, iSCSI, 128
virtual machines. *See* VMs
VMs
    migration, 56–73
        drain on shutdown, 73
        enabling processor compatability, 66–68
        live migrations, 57–66
        matching names of virtual switches, 68–70
        network health protection, 72–73
        storage migration, 70–72
    monitoring services on clustered machines, 50–53
VMs (virtual machines)
    site-level fault tolerance, 190–197

failover TCP/IP settings, 195–196
resynchronizing primary and replica VMs, 196–
    197
Volume Shadow Copy Service (VSS), 157
VPN server farms, 2
VSSAdmin /?, 162
VSSAdmin command-line utility, 162
VSSAdmin Create Shadow, 162
VSSAdmin Delete Shadow, 162
VSSAdmin List Shadows, 162
VSSAdmin Revert Shadow, 162
VSS Copy Backup, 157
VSS Full Backup, 157
VSS Settings tab (Advanced Settings dialog box), 157–
    158
VSS (Volume Shadow Copy Service), 157

W

Wbadmin.exe utility, 159
WDS (Windows Deployment Services), 218
Web Application Proxy role, 310
web farms, 2
Web Server Certificate template, 324
Windows Authentication, 313
Windows Azure Backup feature, 162–170
    Backup Agent, 164
    Back Up Now option, 167–168
    creating an account, 163
    creating a recovery vault, 163
    enabling bandwidth throttling, 169–170
    Recover Data option, 168–169
    registering servers, 164–165
    Schedule Backup Wizard, 165–167
Windows Azure Multi-Factor Authentication
    service, 315
Windows clients, DHCPv6 and, 220
Windows Deployment Services (WDS), 218
Windows PowerShell
    Add-WindowsFeature FS-iSCSTarget-Server
      cmdlet, 127
    Backup-CARoleService cmdlet, 326
    Enable-ADFSDeviceRegistration cmdlet, 314
    Enable-BCDistributed cmdlet, 90
    Enable-BCHostedClient cmdlet, 91
    Enable-BCHostedServer cmdlet, 89
    Export-BCCachePackage cmdlet, 89

Get-BCStatus cmdlet, 89
Get-DnsServerStatistics cmdlet, 235
Get-WindowsFeature cmdlet, 137
Import-BCCachePackage cmdlet, 90
Initialize-ADFSDeviceRegistration cmdlet, 314
Install-WindowsFeature BranchCache cmdlet, 87
Install-WindowsFeature cmdlet, 137
Install-WindowsFeature FS-BranchCache cmdlet, 88
Install-WindowsFeature FS-NFS-Services cmdlet, 96
Install-WindowsFeature IPAM cmdlet, 240
Install-WindowsFeature Windows-Server-Backup cmdlet, 152
Invoke-Gpupdate cmdlet, 247
Invoke-IpamGpoProvisioning cmdlet, 246
New-IscsiServerTarget cmdlet, 131
NLB cmdlets, 12–13
Publish-BCFileContent cmdlet, 89
Publish-BCWebContent cmdlet, 89
Restore-CARoleService cmdlet, 326
Set-DNSServerCache cmdlet, 231
Set-FileStorageTier cmdlet, 142
Set-NetIPInterface cmdlet, 219
Set-NetRoute cmdlet, 219
Uninstall-WindowsFeature cmdlet, 137
Windows PowerShell Classifier option (classification method), 114
Windows Recovery Environment, 178
Windows Server Backup feature, 152–159
Backup Options page, 153–154
Select Backup Configuration page, 153
Select Items For Backup page, 154–157
witness, 32
wizards
Add Claims Provider Trust, 312
Add Host To Cluster, 12

Add Relying Party Trust, 311
Add Roles and Features, 3
istalling Windows Server Backup feature, 152
Backup Once, 152
Backup Schedule, 152
Configure Self-Updating Options, 36
Create Cluster, 21
Enable Replication, 191
High Availability, 42–43, 201
Migrate a Cluster, 38–39
Move, 70
New Cluster, 4
New iSCSI Virtual Disk, 129–132
New Storage Pool, 28
Register Server, 164–165
Reverse Replication, 199–200
Schedule Backup, 165–167
Split-Scope Configuration (DHCP), 223–224
Validate A Configuration, 21
Workplace Join, 313–314

Z

zone-level statistics, DNS, 235–236
-ZoneName parameter, Get-DnsServerStatistics cmdlet, 236
Zone Signing Key (ZSK), 229
ZSK (Zone Signing Key), 229

About the authors

ORIN THOMAS is an MVP, an MCT, and has a string of Microsoft MCSE and MCITP certifications. He has written more than 25 books for Microsoft Press and is a contributing editor at Windows IT Pro magazine. He has been working in IT since the early 1990s. He regularly speaks on Windows Server, Windows Client, System Center and security topics at events like TechED in Australia and around the world. Orin founded and runs the Melbourne System Center, Security, and Infrastructure Group. You can follow him on twitter at @orinthomas.

J.C. MACKIN (MCSA, MCSE, MCT) is a writer, analyst, and trainer who has specialized in Windows networks since Windows NT 4.0. He has written or co-authored more than 10 books about Windows Server administration and certification. You can follow him on Twitter at @jcmackin.

Now that you've read the book...

Tell us what you think!

Was it useful?
Did it teach you what you wanted to learn?
Was there room for improvement?

Let us know at http://aka.ms/tellpress

Your feedback goes directly to the staff at Microsoft Press,
and we read every one of your responses. Thanks in advance!